Modèle

N? 3969 bis

Paris. Boulevart des Italiens.

A French Fashion Doll's Wardrobe

Patterns: 1864-1874

A French Fashion Doll's Wardrobe

Patterns: 1864-1874

Louise Hedrick

Reverie

PUBLISHING COMPANY

DEDICATION

To Bob, whose incredible talent in making the patterns and photos look so beautiful made this book possible. I will always be grateful for your enthusiastic support and patient encouragement during these many years.

ACKNOWLEDGMENTS

This book has been a remarkable journey over the past fifteen years: first to find the dolls, fabrics and trims, then to stitch and photograph them and, finally, to write the book. I want to thank the individuals who did so much to make this possible: Krystyna Poray Goddu for bringing order, beauty and sensibility to my rambling text; Lynn Amos for her amazing creativity in the design of the book; Tammy Blank for her expert correction of every pattern detail; Michael Canadas and David Robinson of the Carmel Doll Shop for finding Linette, Lily's trunk and wonderful accessories; Alice Leverett, whose beautiful Ultimate Fashions brought popularity to the French fashion dolls; Janice Naibert who never hesitated to have produced the reproduction French fashion fabrics and trims that we all needed; Marion Nuernberg, who is always here to help keep LH Studio running; Sylvia Mac Neil, whose knowledge of French fashions has always been a continual inspiration, and who supplied me with many of the gorgeous fabrics and trims of this period; Karen Rockwell, both for her on-going support and for sharing her knowlege of these early dolls; Florence Theriault of Theriault's for permission to use Blondinette's dress and for insight into the student album and convent collection; lastly, but most appreciatively, Rob Wynne, who for the entire time has seen that my fashions have beautiful accessories and fabrics.

First edition/First printing

To purchase additional copies of this book, please contact: Reverie Publishing Company, 130 South Wineow Street, Cumberland, Maryland 21502. 888-721-4999. www.reveriepublishing.com

Library of Congress Control Number: 201095228
ISBN: 978-1-932485-57-8

Project Editor: Krystyna Poray Goddu
Design: Lynn Amos
Patterns Production and Proofreading: Tammy S. Blank
Interior Photography: Louise and Robert Hedrick

On the cover: The antique 18-inch Lily is dressed in a red wool winter ensemble, embellished with ivory soutache; her accessories are lamb fur. (Photo: Robert Hedrick)

On page 2: Lily presents a regal look in her flowered tulle-over-taffeta ballgown, accessorized with an antique gilded tiara.

Printed and bound in Korea

TABLE OF CONTENTS

Let me tell you about a doll named Lily...

I n France during the 1850s dolls dressed in fashions of the times were the most popular among girls who could afford costly playthings. Many entrepreneurs addressed the desires of the young ladies of Paris by creating splendid dolls with couture clothes and a multitude of accessories. Certainly Adelaide Huret dominated this field with her 45-centimeter (17-5/8-inch) young lady fashion doll, which had a porcelain or bisque shoulder head and gutta percha body. By the beginning of the 1860s, however, another young woman, Jeanne Leoncie Péronne, entered this glamorous world and made an impression that would dominate the doll world for years to come.

Mlle Péronne was a doll seamstress in Paris who worked for a dollmaker, Mme Machett. In 1863 Mlle Péronne had the opportunity to take over this business. Investing part of the inheritance she received from her father's estate, she became the proprietress of the shop at 21 rue de Choiseul known as A La Poupée de Nuremberg. Her shop featured the popular *poupée* that bore her label (see photo on opposite page). Note that this label carries her married name, Lavallée-Péronne; she became known as Madame de Lavallée-Péronne after her marriage in 1865 to François Charles Jean Gustave Lavallée. She had admired the 45-centimeter poupees of Mlle Huret, and sold only dolls of that size, also known as #4, in her shop. The most popular fashion dolls of that period were designated by size as #1 (13-1/2 inches/35 centimeters) through #6 (20-7/8 inches/53 centimeters). More #4 dolls were made than any other size, and most of the accessories produced were in scale for dolls of this size.

Mlle Péronne ordered the dolls made to her specifications from other dollmakers, in assorted prices and styles, and attached her label to them. Some were bisque shoulder heads, some had a swivel head; bodies were kid, kid

Lily's pose in this ornate antique salesman's sample wicker chair shows off her fully articulated wooden body, which is known to have been made according to the Anqueulles' 1865 patent. The crocheted shawl was made by Alice Leverett Senior.

Below: This canvas-covered trunk, home to both Lily and her extensive wardrobe, bears the label from Mlle Péronne's shop, A La Poupée de Nuremberg.

Right: The Lavallée-Péronne label affixed to Lily's upper torso is the only way to identify a true Lily.

over wood, partially and fully articulated wood. Some had bisque arms. The label is how we identify a true Lily today.

The same year that Mlle Péronne bought A La Poupée de Nuremberg, 1863, the publishers of *Journal des Demoiselles*, a magazine marketed to teenagers, launched a new monthly publication, *La Poupée Modèle,* aimed at girls aged six to twelve. While *La Poupée Modèle* was truly a magazine for little girls, it was presented in the same style and format of magazines geared to their mothers. It contained beautiful colored drawings of girls wearing the latest fashions, advice on proper behavior for young ladies, stories, music, poetry, games, paper dolls and, most importantly, patterns for their beloved *poupées.* Each issue brought new patterns for their dolls, including embroidery lessons. At first the patterns appeared on pale-yellow thin tissue-type paper; later this paper was replaced by the now-well-known pink. Minimal directions were given for techniques to assemble the clothing and bonnets.

Mlle Péronne, who had worked on *Journal des Demoiselles,* became the driving force behind *La Poupée Modèle.* From the first issue, Mlle Péronne referred to the doll that the patterns would fit as "Lily," and even though she was referring to the Lily sold by her shop, the

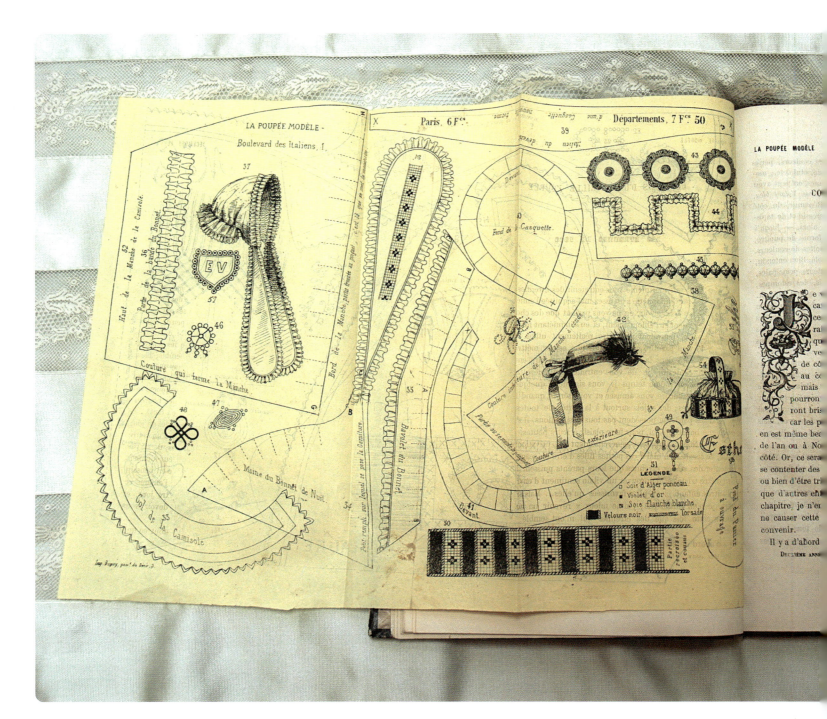

young ladies of Paris began to call their dolls, regardless of size, "Lily." Lily's popularity (and Mlle Péronne's) was unprecedented. The magazine and shop were an immediate success that lasted for many years.

A La Poupée de Nuremberg was a popular destination for all the young ladies who already owned dolls. It was often the custom in France for a child to have but one doll, and gifts to celebrate holidays frequently included a visit to the store for this plaything to be properly outfitted with all manner of necessities and luxuries. She occasionally had a trunk that was large enough to hold not only her wardrobe, but the doll as well. Shown on page 7 is a trunk bearing the original shop label, 19-5/8 inches (50 centimeters) wide, 11 inches (28 centimeters) deep and 9 inches (22 centimeters) high. The outer covering is painted canvas with black metal straps and brass studs. There are metal handles on the sides and a working lock with a key in the front. Inside, the lining is an ivory paper with small blue print. The interior lid has crossed pink ribbons meant for holding bonnets. The bottom interior has a partition to hold Lily, as well as a bonnet stand and another small partition for accessories. There are two trays at the top, each with crossed pieces of twill tape that fit perfectly, one on top of the other.

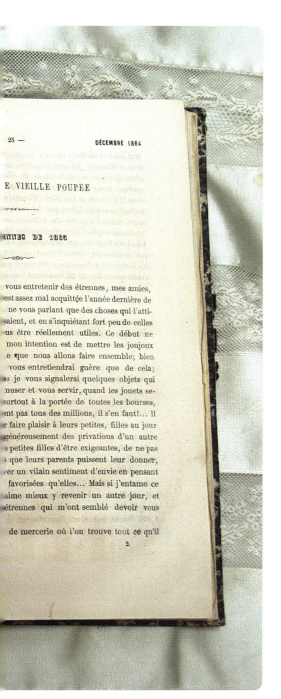

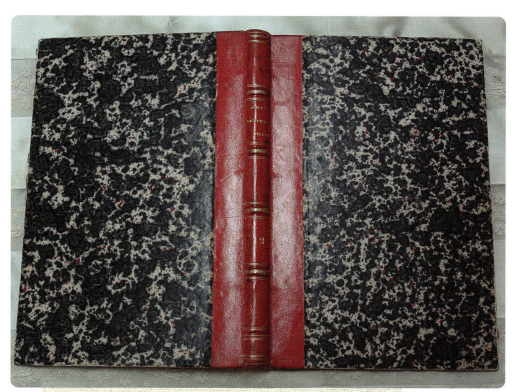

Above: This original bound volume of La Poupée Modèle holds issues dating from December 1864 to November 1865, the magazine's second year of publication.

Left: The yellow tissue-thin pattern is bound into the book. Note the sketch at far left for the Night Bonnet shown on page 78 of this book.

The shop also carried many beautiful completed garments for #4 fashion dolls. This was a period when seamstresses possessed great skills. The sewing machine had been invented and patented by Elias Howe in 1845, but did not come into general use in France until after the Franco-Prussian war in the early 1870s. During the middle of the nineteenth century there were few occupations acceptable for women. One was fine sewing, and young ladies, often convent trained, became highly skilled. Some used this skill to remain in the convents, some married and used it in homemaking and others sought employment in European cities. Many of the items that Mlle Péronne sold in her shop were pieces she purchased from skilled seamstresses who stitched them at home.

The green moiré paper-backed sample cards shown on pages 12 and 13 were discovered in a convent in northern France, and date from the mid-nineteenth century. They were probably made by the nuns themselves, to serve as examples for the students to aspire to. The many stitches are presented on fine mousseline, which was then stitched onto the silk-like paper and bordered in gilt. This particular collection included twenty-five samples, and I consider myself fortunate to have obtained these two. They represent the finest and most detailed embroidery.

When young ladies attended sewing instruction in the convents, they were often required to put together a sample book of lessons. Photographs of some of the pages of such a book are shown on pages 14 and 15. This sample book, dating from the mid-nineteenth century, was the work of the Mlles Cousabant d'Alkemade, students at the

Below: The sewing tools in m'lady's sewing basket are as ornate and beautiful as the laces and embroideries she used. This woven basket holds antique tools of sterling silver, mother-of-pearl and bone.

Opposite page: The top color plate of girls playing dress-up is from the August 1864 issue of La Poupée Modèle; *the bottom plate is from the November 1875 issue. Note the similarity of the doll's and young ladies' dresses.*

La Poupée Modèle.
Journal des petites filles.

Journal des petites filles. La Poupée Modèle Nº 3969 bis
Paris. Boulevard des Italiens. 1

Maison Lacroix Rotonde Colbert spécialité pour Costumes de petits garçons Foulards de la Malle des Indes.
Passage Verdeau Toilettes des Magasins du Petit St Thomas, Rue du Bac. 27-35.
Machines à Coudre de Weeler et Wilson. Boulevard Sebastopol. 70.

convent of the Dames Ursulines de Atournai. Each of the twenty-nine pages shows all manner of hand sewing, embroidery, tatting, lace making, repairs, knitting and crocheting, all of them absolutely perfect. Each sample has been stitched by hand onto a page. The title page, which the student hand inked, has the word "Album" artistically illuminated, and includes the name of the convent. It's interesting to reflect on the size of the stitches in this album, in comparison to what we see today. In the samples shown on page 14, top right and bottom left, the stitches count an average of 40 stitches per inch. In the sample shown on page 15, bottom right, the satin stitches are so small and perfect that, even with a needle, I cannot separate and count them. In the sample shown on pages 14 and 15, bottom center, the lace-making lesson, the stitches and spacing are so faultless the lace appears as though it had been machine made.

If children wished to make their own clothes for Lily, or if they prevailed upon mothers and aunts, they would turn to the pattern pages of *La Poupée Modèle*. The objective of all the patterns in the magazine was to provide for Lily a wardrobe with accessories that could outfit the most stylish young ladies of the period. In the early years of the magazine, the dresses were short, typically miniaturizations of the styles worn by adults, using the same ornamentation and fabrics. The length

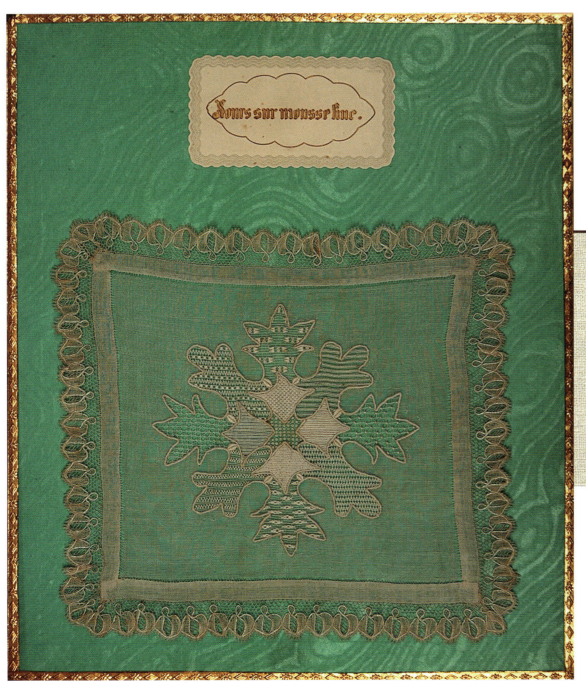

The sample cards at left and on the opposite page were discovered in a convent in northern France, and date from the mid-nineteenth century. This embroidered piece is labeled Jours sur mousse-line, *and features thirteen different types of pulled thread, cutwork and satin embroidered leaves on a square piece of cotton mousseline, finished with hem stitching and hand-made lace.*

stopped at mid-calf, but otherwise the young lady dolls wore many of the same silhouettes as their owners and their mothers did. Stylish bonnets of straw and fabrics, trimmed in elegant feathers and flowers, completed the look. Undergarments were also much like those worn by women, including corsets and wire cage hoops. As time went on, patterns were introduced for the most elegant attire, including a ball gown, trained walking dresses and dressing gowns. From month to month, and year to year, Mlle Péronne presented all manner of garments to create the finest and most extensive wardrobe and accessories. As styles changed, her patterns changed with them. Eventually the skirts' fullness gravitated toward the back,

creating an entirely different silhouette.

This book, with patterns dating from 1864 to 1874, offers a brief glimpse of the fashions as they changed during this era. The garments and accessories demonstrate most of the shapes that were popular then. Photographs of both the 12-inch and 18-inch dolls illustrate as closely as possible the patterns as presented in *La Poupée Modèle*, with some simplifications made for the 12-inch doll. The collection includes all the basic shapes of sleeves, bodices and skirts. By making slight variations in the patterns, fabrics and trims, a seamstress can enlarge this comprehensive wardrobe even further.

For each pattern, the antique fabrics that were used for

This embroidered piece from the convent is labeled Broderie Appliqué *and features a bouquet of flowers stitched with satin-stitched embroidery and cutwork. The piece is also finished with hem stitching and handmade lace. These cards were probably made by the nuns themselves, to serve as examples for the students to aspire to.*

the 18-inch Lily, as well as those used for the reproduction pieces for the 12-inch Linette, are all listed. All the fabrics, old and new, are natural fibers—silk, cotton, wool and linen. The reproduction silk taffeta has been milled recently, copying antique samples. Many antique Swiss embroideries are used, but the new ones milled in Switzerland today are of the same quality and patterns of the old. The same is true of the fine cottons, cotton soutache, silk fringe and other trims and laces.

The creation of these fashions, and this book, has been a dream of mine for more than twenty years. I have always been drawn to the early French fashion dolls—perhaps to their clothing and accessories even more than to the dolls! For me, this period of lady fashions epitomizes the classic beauty of design, fabric and embellishments. This was the era when hand sewing and creative stitching were at their best. Certainly, this was also the time when the skill of the artisans produced the finest, most intricate

Clockwise from right: This page shows the lesson on variations of the hem stitch, tucks, cording and, at top, the tiniest of ruching of a ruffle finished with hem stitching ■ *note the perfect hem stitching and handmade lace trim on this page of satin stitches, eyelets and shadow stitching of a bird and bouquet of flowers* ■ *this page demonstrates three examples of handmade lace stitched on fine tulle* ■ *the student's skill at cutwork and satin stitching is displayed in this stem of flowers and leaves, uniquely edged with a handmade chain of buttonhole stitched loop* ■ *the title page of the student sample book of lessons is beautifully executed by hand in black ink, with elaborately illustrated letters* ■ *the example of the lesson on ruching and hemmed scallops features hemming on the scallops and backstitching on the gathers that measure 40 stitches per inch.*

accessories. Mlle Péronne's patterns enabled me to re-create the authentic styles of the period and to execute them following the construction techniques used during that era. It is my hope that with time, patience and skill, today's seamstress can enjoy reproducing a complete and varied wardrobe for her French fashion doll.

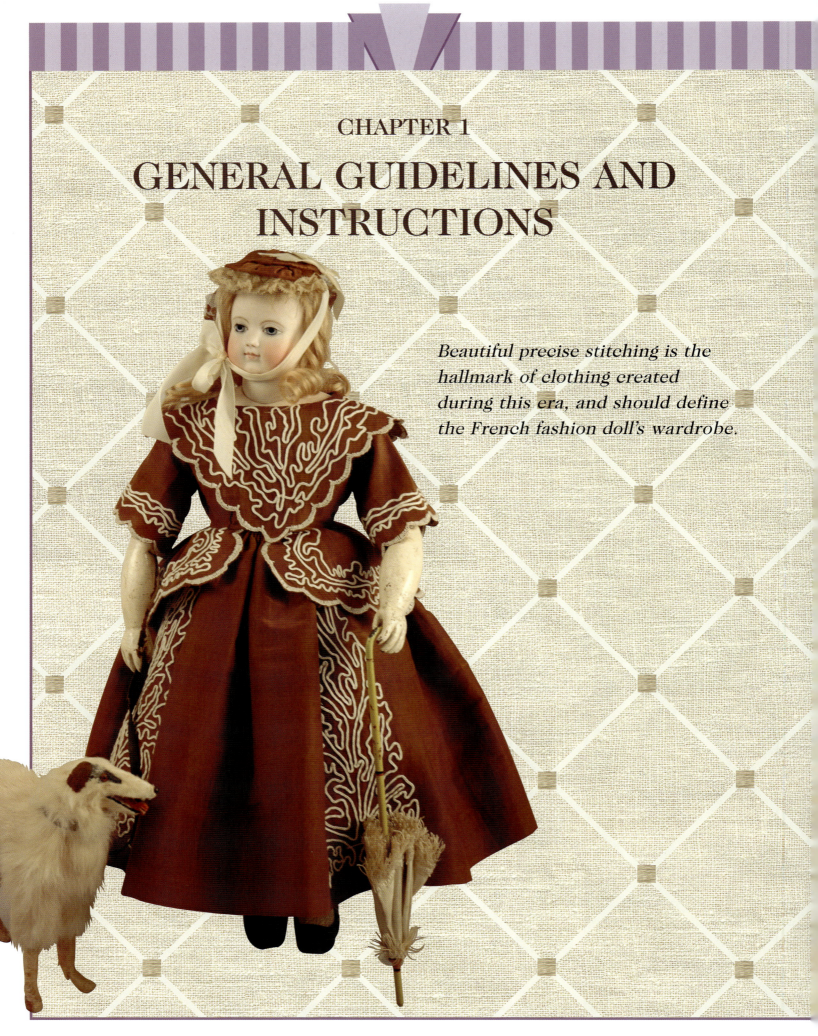

CHAPTER 1
GENERAL GUIDELINES AND INSTRUCTIONS

Beautiful precise stitching is the hallmark of clothing created during this era, and should define the French fashion doll's wardrobe.

Hemming Stitch (Blind Stitch)

Left Pannier
cut 1 dress

The Dolls in This Book

The French fashion dolls wearing the garments portrayed in this book are all antique. Lily, of course, is the star and appears most often. It is interesting to find that no matter which 18-inch dolls of the 1864-1874 period model these clothes, the fit is good. With that in mind, readers will be introduced not only to Lily, but also to a 45-centimeter (17 5/8-inch) painted-eye Huret with a shoulder plate on a blown-kid body and an early 45-centimeter (17 5/8-inch) Rohmer with glass eyes and a shoulder plate on a kid body. This doll's upper arms and upper legs are kid over wood; she is well articulated and has very long, graceful arms. The fourth fashion doll in this size range is a 44-centimeter (17 1/4-inch) unmarked E. Barrois shoulder head known as the Empress Eugenie, with a slight gentle smile. She is on a kid body with above-the-elbow arms and hands that are beautifully shaped.

The antique 30.5-centimeter (12-inch) early china fashion doll, whom I have named Linette, is on an early kid body with long china arms. She has little articulation, but is gusseted at the hips. While her head is unmarked, there is a black stamp on her torso; the only legible letters, however, read "Paris." All early fashions of this period have larger arms, legs and feet than their later sisters, and a somewhat larger waist. By the 1870s they begin to have wide shoulders, a tapered waist and pronounced hips, with slightly thinner and smaller arms and legs.

For those who wish to dress a reproduction 18-inch fashion doll, I have used Leontine, a reproduction of a French Rohmer, as a model. (See Resources, page 256). She is shown below, left, as a china with painted eyes, china arms and a kid body, wearing an ensemble shown on page 108 in Chapter 3. This is Lily's dress; to fit Leontine, the cuff of the sleeve must have a smaller circumference.

The popularity of the 12-inch French fashion doll has grown immensely since the doll artist Alice Leverett began production of her "Ultimate Fashion" in 2004. She began by sculpting a well-articulated resin body after the antique doll known as Phenix, and then sculpted the fully articulated body of Lily. She made molds of the heads of all four of the

This china-glazed reproduction of an 18-inch French fashion doll, Leontine, was made by Mary Raleigh, with a kid body by Create a Doll. Leontine wears the striped silk dress shown on page 108.

Alice Leverett's 12-inch Ultimate Fashion Doll, Isabelle, molded from an original antique Empress Eugenie doll, wears the piqué soutache dress shown on page 84 and the bonnet shown on page 200.

18-inch antique dolls in this book. She then molded them down to achieve the proper size for the 12-inch dolls. Her 12-inch Empress Eugenie is shown on the opposite page, modeling a dress shown on page 84 in Chapter 3. All of the patterns in this book for the 12-inch French fashion doll were drafted to fit Alice Leverett's Ultimate Fashion body. Head sizes, of course, differ with each example. The clothes that are shown on the antique 12-inch fashion doll use these same patterns, but 1/2" has been added to both the back and the front patterns, the waist being 3/4" larger. By adjusting these patterns in advance, it is easy to construct the entire 12-inch wardrobe on an antique doll.

Subsequently, other doll artists and mold companies have come out with their reproductions of the 12-inch French fashion doll. Most notable is the composition body with various head molds from the New York Doll Products Company. (See Resources, page 256). An example of this body, with the Rohmer porcelain head and glass eyes, Mlle Dee, is shown below, wearing the dress shown on page 84 in Chapter 3.

Mlle Dee, a reproduction of an 11 1/2-inch fashion doll by Bob Severns, models the same ensemble as the Ultimate Fashion doll on the opposite page. The doll's composition body and head mold is by the New York Doll Products Company.

Sewing Guidelines

1. In the instructions for the patterns in Chapters 2 through 6, the first number given represents the figure to be used in making the pattern for the 12-inch French fashion doll. The second number, in parentheses, represents the figure to be used in making the pattern for the 18-inch doll.

2. Every doll, whether antique or reproduction, differs somewhat in size. It always helps to make a muslin or paper-toweling sample of the pattern before cutting into the fabric. It is also helpful to place the general measurements of your doll on a piece of paper in the book, as you will refer to them often. The most important ones are shoulder width, waist measurement, length of arm, total height, hand, neck and head circumference.

3. When making any garment, read the entire set of directions for that pattern before you begin.

4. Measurements for the required fabric are given in the following order: height followed by width.

5. In cutting out the final fabric, cut all the pattern pieces at one time. This makes the best use of expensive material.

6. A 1/4" seam allowance is assumed and is included in the pattern pieces, unless noted otherwise in the pattern instructions.

7. When determining the size and fit of outer garments, be sure your doll is dressed in the appropriate undergarments when trying the muslin or paper-towel pieces. If you are stitching a coat or apron, add the dress, as well.

8. Neck facings and waist measurements are approximate. It is important to make note of your doll's neck and waist measurements. Add 1/2" to the neck measurement when making a neck facing and one inch to the waist measurement when making a waistband.

9. During this era, most dresses and skirts were lined. When assembling the pieces of a skirt or bodice, place the wrong side of the lining against the wrong side of the outer fabric and treat as one piece. Some find it easier to temporarily baste these two pieces together before assembling the garment. The linings of the 1860s were often a glazed cotton, sometimes colored, most often in shades of tan to brown. This fabric had a nice sizing, which gave body to the garment. Today, batiste, from sheer to dress weight, is a good choice. Spray starching the lining first, before cutting the fabric, adds to the stability of the piece.

10. When there is a reference to "narrow hem," primarily in lingerie-type clothing, it means to turn up and press 1/8", then 1/8" again. This hem is usually stitched with a running stitch. However, rolling and whipping may be used instead.

11. When stitching a garment such as a coat or outer jacket, stitch the lining separately from the wool or silk, so that no seams show when m'lady removes it.

Sewing Stitches

When first viewing the patterns from *La Poupée Modèle*, the reader is immediately aware that very few instructions for stitching and construction are offered. It is therefore important to understand the method of construction that was used during this early period of French fashion dolls and their wardrobes. Seams of skirts and bodices were stitched with the tiniest of running stitches and finished with overcast stitches. The seams of whitework, both the under-linens and nightwear, were French seamed. On more elaborate pieces, the French seams were pressed to the back of the garment and back stitched or blind stitched down the entire length. There were certain special stitches and techniques that were used to construct and finish the garments.

In order for your wardrobe to truly look as if it belongs to this early period, it is important to take all these notes into consideration. The first issue of *La Poupée Modèle* recommended four of the most basic stitches as the guide for all patterns shown in the magazine: running stitch, hemming (blind) stitch, whip stitch and back stitch. These four, and several other important, stitches of the period are diagramed and explained below. The photographs are enlarged and stitched with black thread to show detail.

Running Stitch: The running stitch is by far the most-used stitch in sewing. It consists of small, very even stitches made with the needle held parallel to the edge of the fabric. It works up very quickly if you use a crewel needle, which enables you to "load" the stitches on the needle. It is used in almost every garment for seams, and also for hemming thin fabrics such as batiste and lightweight silk.

Hemming (Blind) Stitch: To create this stitch, working from right to left, bring the needle up from the wrong side of the folded hem, go down at #1 and up at #2. From #1 to #2, pick up only one or two threads. Slide the needle under the folded edge and come up at #3, slightly forward of #2. Even tension is important. Keep the thread from pulling to assure an invisible look on the right side.

Whip Stitch: The whip stitch is used as an overcast stitch. Come up about 1/16" to 1/8" from the edge of the fabric at #1. Holding the needle at a right angle to the raw edge and a little forward of #1, go from the wrong side, #2, and come up at #3. If these stitches are the same depth and length, the result is a lovely, straight finished edge. This stitch is used to overcast the seams. It can be worked from top to bottom, bottom to top and right to left.

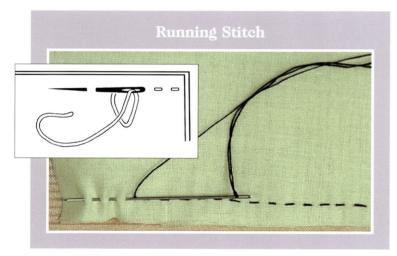

Running Stitch

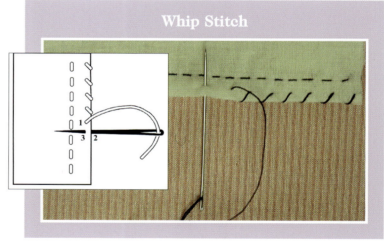

Whip Stitch

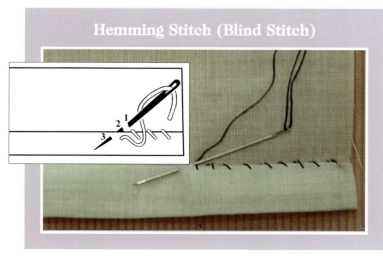

Hemming Stitch (Blind Stitch)

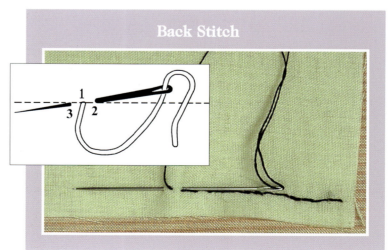

Back Stitch

Back Stitch: Working from right to left, bring the needle up from the wrong side at #1, go down at #2 and up at #3. The distance from #2 and #3 varies from 1/16" to 1/8". This stitch is used as a decorative stitch to stabilize a French seam. It is a good way to accurately stitch a tight curve, such as inserting a sleeve into an armhole. It is also useful in anchoring the thread at the beginning and end of sewing.

French Seam: Place wrong sides together, stitch a 1/8" seam, press to one side and trim as close to the stitching as possible (*Step 1*). Then place right sides together, and stitch another 1/8" seam, making certain you have covered the first seam (*Step 2*).

Rolling and Whipping (Mock): If you are not familiar with the traditional rolled hem method, the following method is easy to learn, and achieves the same result.

1. Working from the wrong side of the fabric, fold the top edge of the fabric toward you 1/16".

2. Work from right to left. Hide the knot of the thread under the fold and take a tiny stitch in the top edge of the fold.

3. Take the next tiny stitch just off the fold into the main piece of the fabric and a little forward of the first stitch. The needle should pierce only the main piece of the fabric, not the folded-over portion.

4. Repeat these stitches to cover about an inch of fabric. The effect will be zig-zag stitches. Draw the thread up and the hem will roll. Repeat to the end of the project. See diagram below.

Herringbone Stitch: This stitch is frequently seen as the hemming of a jacket, or the lining of a jacket, particularly when the jacket is outlined in cording, as this gives weight and substance to the stitching process. It is still very popular in French couture today. The herringbone stitch can also be used in a contrasting embroidery thread, such as DMC, as a decorative stitch.

Diagram A: Imagine two parallel lines about 1/8" to 1/4" wide, as shown by the dotted lines on the diagram. Come up at #1 on the lower line, down at #2, up at #3, about 1/6". This stitch should be about 1/8" in front of #1, and on the upper line. *Diagram B*: Repeat this stitch on the lower line: down at #4, up at #5. *Diagram C* shows the start of a new stitch.

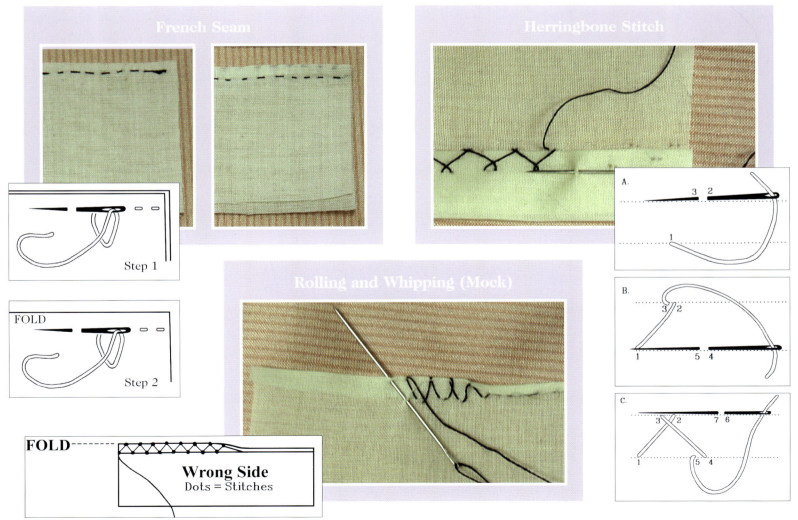

French Seam

Step 1

FOLD

Step 2

Herringbone Stitch

A.

B.

C.

Rolling and Whipping (Mock)

FOLD

Wrong Side
Dots = Stitches

Embroidery Stitches

The following embroidery stitches are used on the patterns in this book. Cotton embroidery thread usually consists of six strands, which can be separated and used one at a time. Silk embroidery thread is similarly constructed, but can consist of five to twelve strands. Most stitching is done with one strand threaded into a fine embroidery needle, but when a more pronounced stitch is called for, two or more threads can be used at a time. The more strands of thread used, the larger the needle must be. It is important that when the thread pierces the fabric, the hole made by the needle is large enough to accommodate the thread. Embroidery threads must always lie smoothly on the surface of the fabric. Practice the stitches on a scrap of material first to ensure even uniform stitches. Embroider the pieces before cutting the fabric. The embroidery pattern can be marked on the fabric with a #1 or #2 pencil, very lightly. Two types of pencils that produce a fine line, the width of one strand of embroidery, are the "Ultimate Marking Pencil" and "Sewline Fabric Pencil." Both of these are readily available in most quilting shops.

It is most helpful to stitch embroidery in a small hoop, 5" to 6" in diameter. After completing the embroidery, remove the piece from the hoop. Steam press well on the wrong side of the fabric, padding the ironing board with a few pieces of terry toweling; this raises the embroidery stitches and allows for the creases between the different parts to disappear. After pressing, cut out the pattern pieces.

French Knot: *Diagram A* shows the position of the needle as held by the right hand. Bring the needle up at #1 and wrap it once around the needle, holding it firmly against the needle with the left hand. *Diagram B*: Go down at #2, going back into the fabric close to, but not into, the same hole as #1. Hold the thread firmly, but not tightly; go slowly so that the knot stays on the surface of the fabric and does not disappear in back. *Diagram C* shows the completed tiny knot enlarged, no more than 1/16". The French knots on the peignoirs shown on pages 57 and 58 in Chapter 2 are stitched with two or three strands of floss in a #9 needle, with only one wrap. The "one-wrap" French knot, using more than one strand, is a rather recent practice. It allows the knot to be perfectly coiled and sit perfectly on the surface of the fabric.

Couching Stitch: The couching stitch is an overhand stitch that allows a heavier thread, narrow trim or ribbon to lie in a predetermined path on your garment. In this case, it is used to outline the heading of the lace on the front and lower edge of the peignoir shown on page 58 in Chapter 2. Lay the narrow ribbon on the line to be followed. These stitches should be parallel to each other and approximately 1/8" apart. Using fine embroidery thread, bring the thread up from the wrong side at #1, slightly under the base of the trim, and go down at #2, slightly under the base cord. #3 is the start of a new stitch.

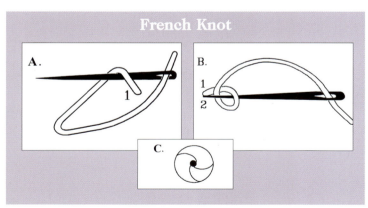

French Knot

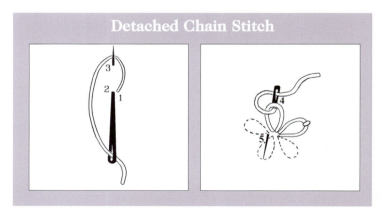

Detached Chain Stitch

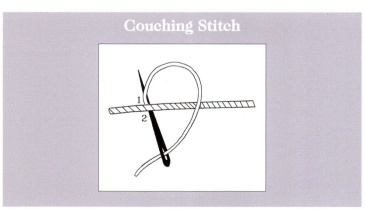

Couching Stitch

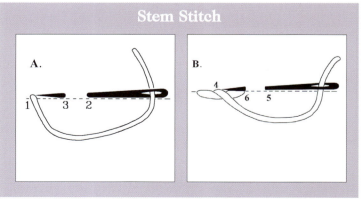

Stem Stitch

Detached Chain Stitch: *Diagram A:* For the basic chain stitch, come up at #1, down at #2, and up at #3. *Diagram B:* To begin the second petal of the flower, follow the design path as shown in the diagram. This flower can have four, five or six petals. Always begin each succeeding petal at the center. This is the flower used on the peignoirs shown on pages 57 and 58 in Chapter 2.

Stem Stitch: In the stem stitch, the thread is held below the line. A similar stitch, the outline, is worked in the same manner, but with the thread always held above the line. You may choose either method, but be sure to consistently hold the thread above or below the line to achieve a smooth stitch. *Diagram A:* Come up at #1, down at #2, up at #3. *Diagram B:* #4 is the same as #3 in diagram A (i.e. the needle goes into the same hole). From this point on, each stitch should be about 1/10" in front of the previous one. Go down at #5 and up at #6. #6 is the same as #2 in diagram A (i.e. the needle goes into the same hole).

Satin Stitch: Always use an embroidery hoop for creating this stitch. Draw the design you wish to create on the fabric first, and use one strand of cotton or silk embroidery thread for a smooth satin result. Come up on the left side of the fabric from the wrong side. Go down at #1 and up at #2, holding your needle almost parallel to your stitch. Come up as close to the previous stitch as possible without going into the same hole. Every "bud" on the 18-inch apron shown on page 219 in Chapter 6 is created using the satin stitch.

Granitos Stitch: The size and depth of this stitch varies with the number of strands of floss used and the number of stitches in each granitos. Thread your needle with one strand of floss. *Diagram A:* Come up at #1 and down at #2. *Diagram B:* Using the same holes, come up at #3 and down at #4, swinging the stitch to the left of the first stitch. Pull the stitch through until it is the same length as the first stitch and lying evenly next to it. Repeat with #5 and #6, using the same holes, positioning this stitch to the right of the first stitch. *Diagram C* shows the completed stitch. Every "bud" on the 12-inch apron shown on page 218 in Chapter 6 is created using the granitos stitch.

Buttonhole Stitch: *Diagram A:* Come up at #1, down at #2, up at #3. *Diagram B:* #1, the first stitch, should be as close to the following stitch as possible. Stitch size may vary from 1/16" to 1/8". *Diagram C:* This same stitch is used to create a scallop border. To create a scallop border, begin by drawing the scallop design on the fabric. Stitch a running stitch along the scallop line. Then stitch a stem stitch on this line. Stitch a buttonhole stitch over this line, keeping stitches as uniform as possible. When you are finished, carefully cut along the scallop edge, taking care not to cut into the stitches. This scallop is used on the several pieces of the soutache-trimmed dresses on pages 129 and 130 in Chapter 3, as well as the traditional method of creating buttonholes. Below is a picture of beautifully stitched buttonholes, three different types, from the student sample book.

Satin Stitch

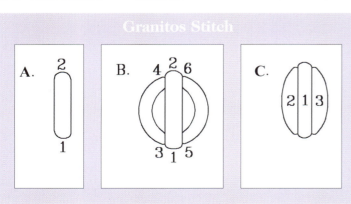

Granitos Stitch

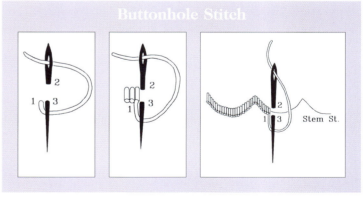

Buttonhole Stitch

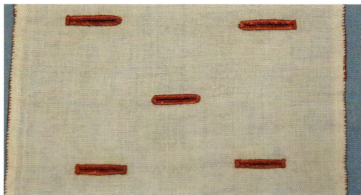

Construction Details

Certain construction practices are used for most of the patterns in this book. The most common ones are described below.

Cutting the Skirt: During the time of the first publication of *La Poupée Modèle*, skirts were bell-shaped with fullness gathered or pleated all around, supported by the cage hoop. As the decade progressed, the fullness started to move toward the back, and the front panel became A-line and smooth. Most of the skirt patterns in the mid 1860s required just the measurement of length and width, and then they were adjusted as shown below.

Diagram A: Fold the fabric rectangle in half and mark the center front fold. Mark half way across from where there would be a "side seam." Draw a line from the side marker to the 1/2" marker and cut along this line. For the 18-inch pattern, measure down 3/4" from center front and follow the directions above. This allows the pattern of the skirt to continue in an unbroken line across the bottom of the skirt. It also allows the skirt to hang properly; otherwise it would appear shorter in the back. *Diagram B* shows the entire skirt unfolded and cut.

Cartridge Pleating: Cartridge pleating is a method of gathering a large amount of fabric into a small space with no bulk, and was widely used for ladies' clothing as well as dolls' clothing in the nineteenth century.

1. Turn the upper edge of the skirt (both the skirt fabric and lining) to the wrong side 1/4" (1/2") and press to a sharp edge. Stitch basting threads 1/4" apart, and 1/16" (1/8") down, going through all four layers with a running stitch. Stitch a second row 1/16" (1/8") below this, matching your stitches from the first row *exactly*. This diagram shows the skirt from the right side.

2. Pull up the threads evenly to fit the waistband or bodice. This will result in perfectly even gathers, beautifully pleated. This diagram shows the skirt from the right side.

3. Attach to the waistband or bodice, working from the *wrong* side. As you stitch, catch the tip of the front of the pleats with the first stitch and attach them to the bottom of the waistband or bodice with the second stitch. This diagram shows the skirt from the wrong side.

Lined Sleeves: Every seamstress seems to have her own method of lining sleeves. There were many different techniques used in the nineteenth century. Following is my favorite, which goes together easily and works well with no bulk, even on the smallest dolls. It leaves a finished edge at the bottom of the sleeve. With right sides together, stitch the long seams of both the dress fabric and the lining fabric of the sleeves. Press seams to one side. Put the right sides of the dress fabric against the right sides of the linings and stitch across the bottom of the sleeve. Open up and press seam allowances toward the linings. Stitch the shorter sleeve seam as shown in the diagram on the opposite page. Turn the sleeve to the right side, and press the short seam and bottom of the sleeve.

Covered Buttons: Many of the bodices and jackets of this period were decorated with fabric buttons that either matched, or contrasted with, the garment. In the nineteenth century they used bone or mother-of-pearl two- or three-hole buttons, and covered them with fabric to make

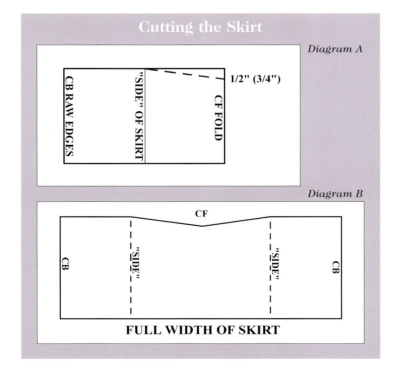

Cutting the Skirt

Diagram A

CB RAW EDGES | "SIDE" OF SKIRT | CF FOLD — 1/2" (3/4")

Diagram B

CF — "SIDE" — "SIDE" — CB — CB

FULL WIDTH OF SKIRT

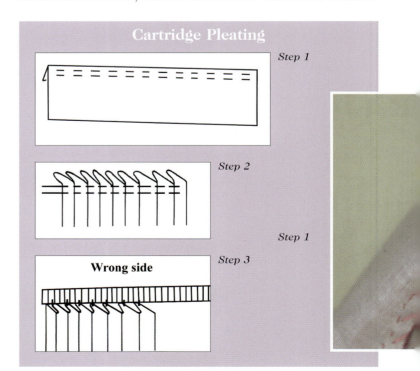

Cartridge Pleating

Step 1

Step 2

Step 1

Step 3 — Wrong side

a flange button. *Diagram A*: Cut a small square of fabric and, with a dot of white glue, fasten to the center of the fabric and let dry completely. *Diagram B*: Stitch very tiny gathering stitches around the button. These stitches should be about 1/2 of the diameter from the outer edge of the button. For example, with a 1/8" button, the stitches should be 1/16" from the outer edge of the button.

Diagram C: Cut out the fabric circle, leaving 1/16" to 1/8" outside the stitching. It is helpful to seal the fabric with a seam sealer before continuing. *Diagram D*: Pull up the gathers as tight as possible. Stitch back and forth around the circle at right angles, drawing in the button as tight as possible. Use the tip of embroidery scissors to make sure there are no loose edges and that you have a perfect circle on the right side. Without cutting the thread, stitch your completed flange button to the garment.

Soutache: Soutache is a very narrow flat braid that is used to stitch all manner of ornamental designs onto clothing. It was used extensively in the nineteenth century on both women's and children's clothing, as well as on dolls' clothing. The indentation in the middle of the braid allows it to be stitched "in the ditch" with matching thread and a running stitch so that the stitching does not show on the right side. There is always a beautiful contrasting pattern on the wrong side because of the stitching. Soutache was originally made of a variety of materials in all colors. Cotton was the most common, but silk, wool and later, rayon, were available. Wool was the rarest; in this book both the red winter skating ensemble shown on page 164 in Chapter 4, and the green shot-taffeta evening cape shown on page 193 in Chapter 4, have the ornamentation of wool soutache in

a slightly wider version. Antique cotton was used for all the other garments. We are fortunate today that narrow 1/16" (1 mm) cotton soutache is again being manufactured in Austria and is readily available (see Resources, page 256).

To apply soutache to the garment, first assemble as directed in the pattern. Draw on the soutache pattern very lightly with a #1 or #2 pencil. Again, you can also use the specialty drawing pencils that are suggested in the embroidery section on page 22. To stitch, use two needles, size #20-22 tapestry for the soutache, and size #10-12 for the thread. Thread the soutache in the tapestry needle. Piercing from the top, bring it to the wrong side at the start of the design. Use the smaller needle, threaded with fine matching embroidery thread, to anchor a 1/8"- 1/4" end on the wrong side of the fabric. Once you have done this, remove the tapestry needle and continue to stitch and swirl the soutache braid along the top design. If you are stitching a skirt, begin and end at center back, and use the very same hole where you began stitching to end it. This technique insures that the beginning and end points will never be seen. This same practice is used if the soutache braid is in more than one piece, and you want to end and begin again. If you are stitching a pattern with continuous loops, such as the demi-trained dressing gown shown on page 240 in Chapter 6, it helps to pull short parts of the soutache, 10 or 12 inches at a time, along the edge of the embroidery scissors, in the same manner as you would curl ribbon when wrapping a gift. This causes the soutache to curl naturally, and allows you to stitch even uniform loops. When you reach the end of the design, end by threading the soutache into the larger needle; then pierce the fabric, taking the soutache to the wrong side and anchoring it.

The underside view of this skirt shows the cartridge pleating and overcast seams.

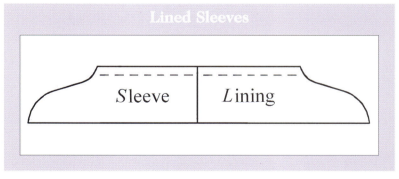

Lined Sleeves

Sleeve   Lining

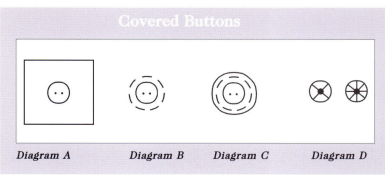

Covered Buttons

| Diagram A | Diagram B | Diagram C | Diagram D |

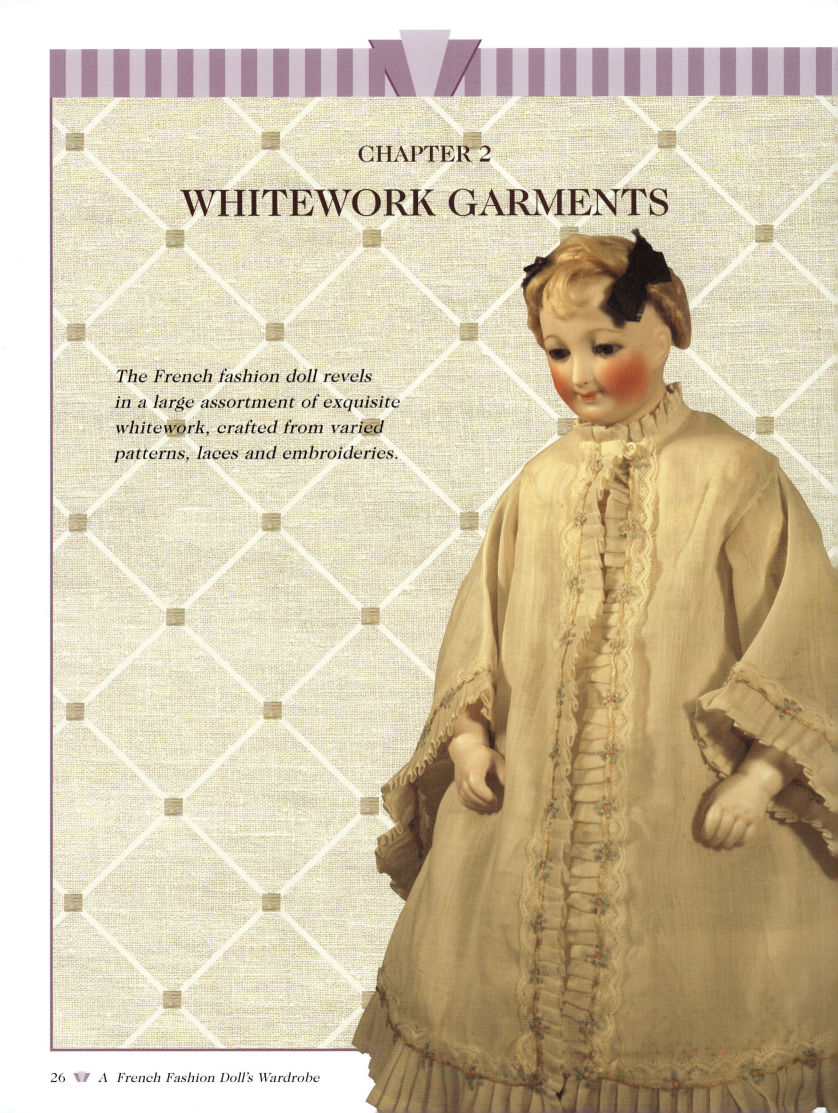

CHAPTER 2
WHITEWORK GARMENTS

The French fashion doll revels in a large assortment of exquisite whitework, crafted from varied patterns, laces and embroideries.

BACK

FRONT

12-inch doll

Peignoir Sleeve

cut 2 back
2 front

LH

18-inch doll

**Combing
Jacket
Collar**

cut 2

FOLD

LH

Basic Chemise, Pantalets and Two Petticoats

Materials

Swiss cotton batiste (shown) or fine Swiss lawn (shown): 9" x 54" (18" x 54")

3/8" Lace edging: 30" (3/4" Swiss embroidery: 32")

1/4" Lace edging: 15" (1/2" Swiss embroidery: 2/3 yard)

1-1/2" Swiss embroidery: 3/4 yard (2-1/2" Swiss embroidery: 42 ")

1/8" Twill tape: 18"

Fine embroidery thread to match

1/8" - 3/16" Mother-of-pearl buttons: 3

#10-#12 Crewel needle

These four basic pieces of underpinnings can be adapted to make several sets of underwear for a lady doll's wardrobe. Embellishments for these were almost always Swiss embroidered edgings or insertions, which are available today, but narrow Valenciennes lace can also be used and is very appropriate. After preparing the folded strip, cut out all the pieces at one time.

Preparation of folded strip: Cut one long edge of fabric 18" (27-1/2") on grain. Fold over 1/4" to the wrong side and press. Trim to 1/8". Fold over again 1/4" and press. Cut fabric 1/8" below the last pressing line. You now have a piece of fabric with no raw edges. These will be stitched over the raw edges of the skirt/embroidered edgings of the second petticoat to create a finished appearance.

Chemise: Note that the picture of the 12-inch fashion shows the opening of the chemise in the back. The pattern allows for this chemise to be worn with either a front or back opening when the opening is unadorned. Cut two of the chemise pattern on the fold. Slash center front 1-1/4" (2-1/2"). Roll and whip this opening. French seam the shoulder seams and press toward the back.

If you use lace: Roll and whip the arm openings. French seam the side seams and press toward the back. Using the 1/4" lace, whip to the edge of the armholes straight. Roll and whip the neckline and stitch on the same lace edging straight. Roll and whip the center front opening on both sides of the opening. *If you use embroidered edging:* Even the Swiss embroidery at the top. With wrong sides together and the edging on top, stitch the embroidered edging to the bottom of the sleeve. Trim the seam to 1/8" or smaller. Turn to the wrong side and stitch again, making certain

that the second row of stitching completely covers the first. This is a French seam using embroidery instead of two pieces of fabric. Repeat this method with both the neckline and front opening, using a regular roll and whip on the left side and the embroidery on the right.

Pantalets (Open Drawers): Each of the legs is constructed separately and put together in the final step. Cut two of the pantalet pattern on the fold. Roll and whip the center front and center back edges of each leg. French seam the leg portion of each leg. *If you use lace:* Roll and whip the leg openings. Stitch 3/8" lace straight to the bottom of each leg. *If you use embroidered edging:* Follow the directions above for the chemise to add embroidered edging to the bottom of the legs.

At the top center front edge only, stitch the two legs together by butting the edges of the rolled hems for one inch only. Make a casing in the top of the pantalets, leaving open at center back as follows. Fold under 1/8" and press. Fold again 1/4" and press. Stitch this casing with a running stitch leaving open at center back. String the 1/8" twill tape through the casing. The pantalets tie at center back on the doll. The finished length of the pantalets measured from center front is 4-7/8" (7-1/8").

Petticoat #1: Cut the skirt 5" x 12" (8" x 19") and the waistband 1" x 5-1/2" (1" x 8-1/2") French seam the center back seam, leaving open 2" (3") at the top. Narrow hem this opening. *If you are using lace:* Gather the remaining 3/8" lace, about 20", by pulling the heavy thread in the heading to fit the bottom edge of the petticoat and stitch on. *If you are using embroidered edging:* Attach the embroidered edging straight just as you did for the chemise arm openings.

Stitch two rows of gathering stitches at the top of the skirt. Pull up the gathers to fit the waistband. Turn under the short ends of the waistband 1/4" to the inside, press and pin to the skirt. With right sides together, stitch the waistband to the skirt. Turn the waistband to the wrong side, turn under the seam allowance and blind stitch. Close the petticoat with a mother-of-pearl button and worked buttonhole. The finished length of the petticoat is 5-1/4" (8").

Linette wears the 12-inch set of basic underpinnings, fashioned from antique cotton batiste, lace and Swiss embroidery. The caged hoop is worn between the two petticoats to create the proper silhouette.

Petticoat #2: Cut the skirt 4-1/2" x 18" (6-1/2" x 27-1/2") and the waistband 1" x 5-1/2" (1" x 8-1/2"). French seam the center back seam, leaving open 2" (3") at the top. Narrow hem this opening. Even the Swiss embroidery at the top. Gather with two rows of gathering stitches the 1-1/2" (2-1/2") edging to fit the bottom of the petticoat, and bind off the threads. With wrong sides together, and the embroidered edging on the top, stitch the edging to the skirt. The raw edges are on the right side. Press the seam up. Trim the seam to 1/8". Stitch the folded strip over the raw edges, stitching two rows at the top and bottom of the strip with tiny stitches. Finish the top of the petticoat in the same manner as petticoat #1. The finished length of this petticoat is 5-1/2" (8-1/4").

This set of basic underwear for the 12-inch doll is fashioned entirely of ivory Swiss cotton batiste. The trim is all batiste with machine-embroidered red scalloped edges.

Basic Chemise, Pantalets and Two Petticoats - 12-inch Doll

Straight Pieces

#1 Petticoat Skirt....................................5" x 12"

#2 Petticoat Skirt ....4-1/2" x 18"

Petticoat Waistband........................2 (1" x 5-1/2")

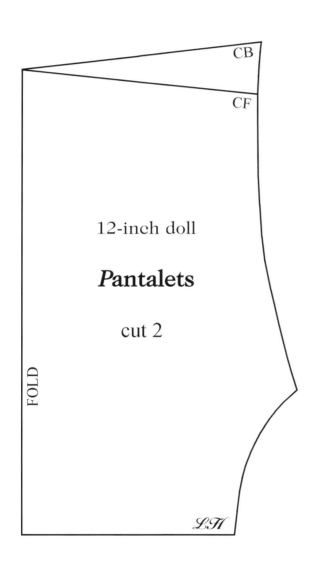

CB

CF

12-inch doll

Pantalets

cut 2

FOLD

LH

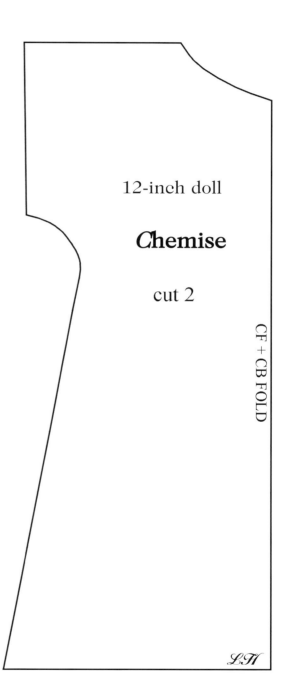

12-inch doll

Chemise

cut 2

CF + CB FOLD

LH

Standing beside an antique nineteenth-century table with pitcher and bowl, 18-inch Lily wears a basic set of underwear made from antique cotton and Swiss embroidery. Note that the opening of the chemise has been changed to the front.

Basic Chemise, Pantalets and Two Petticoats - 18-inch Doll

Straight Pieces

#1 Petticoat Skirt..8" x 19"

#2 Petticoat Skirt ....6-1/2" x 27-1/2"

Petticoat Waistband.........................2 (1" x 8-1/2")

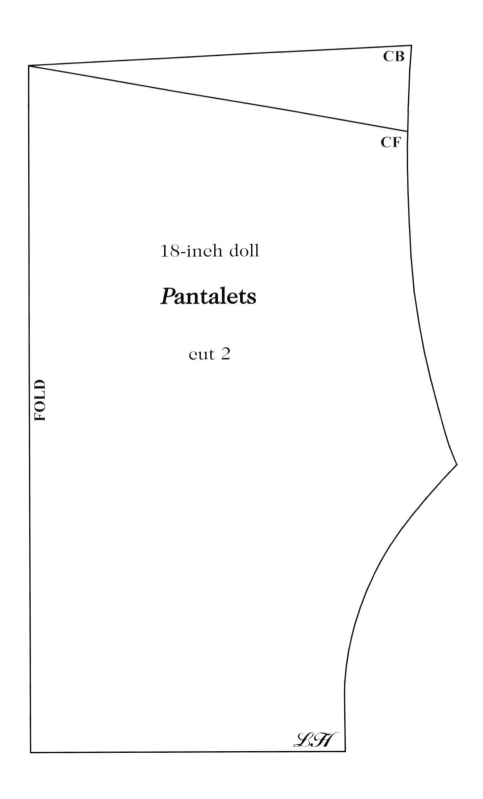

18-inch doll

Pantalets

cut 2

CB

CF

FOLD

LH

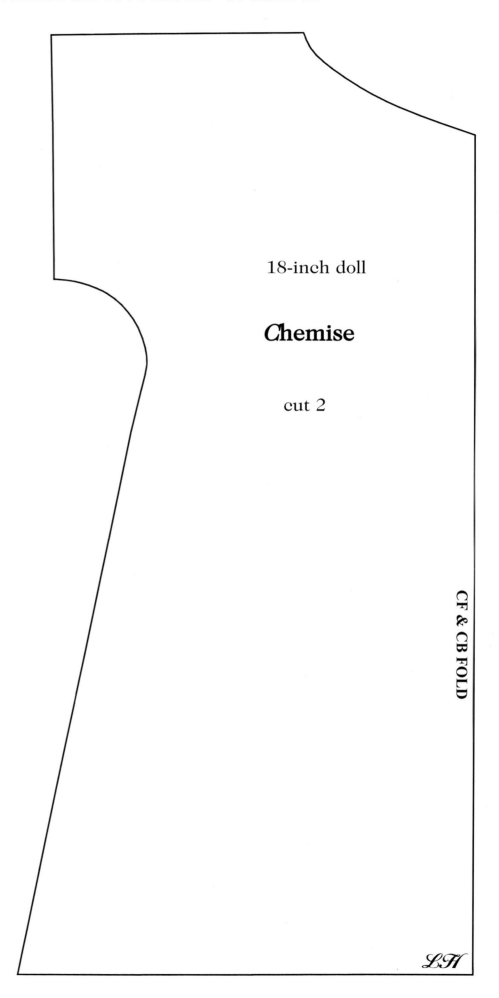

18-inch doll

Chemise

cut 2

CF & CB FOLD

LH

Chemise, Corset Cover, Pantalets and Petticoat

Materials

Swiss batiste (shown on 12-inch doll) or fine Swiss lawn (shown on 18-inch doll): 9" x 45" (21" x 54")
3/8" Lace beading: 3/4 yard (1/2" beading, 40")
3/8" Lace edging: 1-1/3 yards (2 yards)
1/4" Lace edging: 1 yard (1-1/4 yards)
1 mm White cotton cording or string: 1-1/2 yards (2 yards)
1/8" White woven tape: 1/2 yard (32")
3/16" Two-hole mother-of-pearl buttons: 5
Fine embroidery thread to match
#10-#12 Crewel needle

This set of underwear has been adapted from my Lily's antique undergarments, which arrived with her. More elaborate, with beautiful lace and expert stitching, than the basic set, these pieces make an elegant addition to her wardrobe.

Chemise: Cut two sleeves 1" x 3" (1-1/2" x 4-1/2"). Cut a rectangle 14" x 6" (20" x 9"). Fold this piece in half top to bottom, side to side, and cut pattern on double fold.

Roll and whip the bottom of the sleeves, then whip on the 1/4" lace straight. French seam the sleeves to the body of the chemise. Center the sleeves on the fold line at the shoulder, with no gathers. French seam the side seams and press toward the back.

Slash the center front 2-1/2" (3-1/2"). Roll and whip both sides of this opening and press. Roll, whip, and gather the neckline as follows: leave the portion going up and over the shoulder to each side flat. Gather the back to 1-3/4" (2-1/2") and each front to 7/8" (1-1/2"). Stitch on the 1/4" lace flat, using two rows of stitching, so that only the scallop extends above the fabric. Turn up the bottom edge of the chemise 1/4" and press. Turn it up again 3/8" (1/2") and press. Blind stitch this hem. Close center front opening with a 3/16" mother-of-pearl button and thread loop. The finished length of the chemise measuring from the front shoulder fold is 6-1/2" (8-3/4").

Pantalets: The pantalets are constructed of five pieces; the bottoms of the legs are attached to the tops with lace beading. The trim and fabric treatment for the pantalets and the petticoat are the same. Cut two of the pantalets pattern, two lower legs 1-1/2" x 4" (3" x 6-1/4") and one waistband 1" x 5-3/4" (1" x 8").

Bottom edge of the pantalets and petticoat: Begin with the lower leg pieces. Measure up 1/2" (3/4") and fold. Measure up 5/16" (1/2") and fold for a second tuck, measure up 5/16" (1/2") and fold for a third tuck. Press these three fold lines and stitch 1/16" (1/8") tucks. Press the tucks down. Roll and whip (narrow hem) the top and bottom edges. Whip on lace beading to the top of each piece.

Stitch three tucks in the main pantalets piece, measuring the same amounts from the bottom as was measured in the lower leg pieces. Stitch the same three tucks 1/16" (1/8") each. Roll and whip the bottom of each leg piece. Whip the main piece to the beading of the lower leg and press. French seam the leg. Stitch 3/8" lace edging to the bottom of the legs. Roll and whip the center front and center back openings. Butt center fronts together and whip down one inch. Turn the top edge under 3/8", and press.

For the waistband, turn under the short ends 1/4" and press. Fold in half lengthwise. The waistband now measures 1/4" x 5-1/4" (1/4" x 7-1/2"). Cartridge pleat the pantalets. See page 24 in Chapter 1. Close the waistband with a 3/16" mother-of-pearl button and worked buttonhole. The finished length of the pantalets measured from center front is 5-5/8"(8-1/2").

Petticoat: The petticoat has three pieces; cut one body 5" x 18-1/2" (6-7/8" x 27-1/2"), one bottom petticoat 3" x 18-1/2" (4" x 27-1/2") and one ruffle 1-1/2" x 36" (2" x 54"). Measure and stitch for the three 1/16" (1/8") tucks as on the pantalets on the main piece of the petticoat. Roll and whip the lower edge and whip on the 3/8" (1/2") beading.

Turn the top and bottom edges of the lower piece of the petticoat under 1/4". French seam the short ends. Press in half lengthwise so that the piece measures 1-1/4" x 18" (1-3/4" x 27"). Stitch this petticoat bottom to the bottom of the beading so that the folded edge is at the bottom of the petticoat.

Ruffle: French seam the short ends of the ruffle. Roll and whip the lower edge. Whip on the 3/8" lace edging straight. Turn to the wrong side and press the top edge of the ruffle down 1/4". Insert tiny cording in the fold and stitch with a running stitch, enclosing the cord but taking great care not to stitch the cord to the fabric. Because the cording in the antique garment is very tiny, take the 1 mm cord or string, which is usually three strands, and separate it, using only one strand. Pull the cord to gather to fit the bottom of the petticoat. Distribute the gathers evenly. Stitch the ruffle to the petticoat below the beading, even with the petticoat bottom, with the seam at center back. The bottom of the ruffle should be even with the bottom of the petticoat.

Turn the top edge of the petticoat to the wrong side, 1/8"

Lily wears the more elaborate set of antique underwear in which she came to me. Note the slits in the sides of the corset cover that allow it to lie smoothly over the full skirt.

and press. Turn under 1/4" and press again. Make two worked buttonholes 1/8" on either side of center back, in the outside of the casing only. This is where the tape will go in and come out. Stitch with a running stitch to make this casing. Insert 1/8" tape, which will be pulled up to fit the doll's waist. The finished length of the petticoat is 5-1/2" (8-1/4").

Corset Cover: Cut one front, two sides, two backs and two sleeves. Cut two bias strips 1/2" x 3" (1/2" by 4") for the armhole cording. Using the same cording or string used for the petticoat ruffle, cut two pieces 4" (5") each. The cording usually consists of three strands twisted together. Separate it, and use two strands. Stitch the two pieces into the piping, taking care not to catch the cord in the stitching so that it can be pulled and eased into the armhole. The cording should measure 1/4" from the stitching to the raw edge. Trim if necessary.

Stitch the darts into the back pieces. Turn the center back under twice as shown in the pattern and press. Blind stitch. French seam the shoulder seams. French seam the front seams to the side seams and press toward center back. Stitch the side pieces to the back pieces with a French seam, leaving open 1-1/4" (2-1/8") at the bottom.

Narrow hem both sides of this opening. These slits allow the bottom of the corset to rest on the top of the hoop and petticoat, creating a wonderful profile for the complete set of underwear.

Roll and whip the bottom of the sleeves. French seam the sleeve seam. Whip on 1/4" lace edging to the bottom of the sleeves straight covering the hem so that just the bottom of the scallop shows. With right sides together, stitch the cording to the armhole, beginning and ending at the under arm. With right sides together, stitch the sleeves into the armholes. Note the "x" on the pattern pieces and match these. Also note the back and the front to the sleeves, and place properly.

Roll and whip the neck edge. Whip on the 1/4" lace to the neck edge straight as on the sleeves. Close the center back with three 3/16" mother-of-pearl buttons and worked buttonholes: the first is at the neck edge, the second and third are each 3/4" (1") down from the previous one. The bottom button is approximately 1-1/4" (2") above the bottom of the corset cover, which allows the slits to open and spread over the top of the petticoat in the same way as the side slits. The finished length of the corset cover is 3-1/4" (5") as measured from the front shoulder seam.

This is an exact reproduction of the antique underwear worn by Lily, but scaled down to fit the 12-inch fashion doll.

Chemise, Corset Cover, Pantalets and Petticoat - 12-inch Doll

Straight Pieces

Lower Pantalets ....2 (1-1/2" x 4")
Pantalets Waistband ....1-1/4" x 5-3/4"
Petticoat Body ....5" x 18-1/2"
Petticoat Bottom..............................3" x 18-1/2"
Petticoat Ruffle ....1-1/2" x 36"
Chemise Sleeves ....2 (1" x 3")

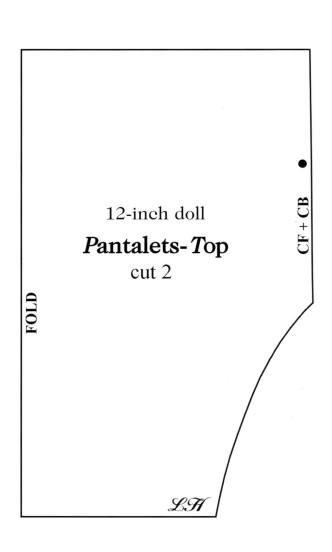

12-inch doll

Pantalets-Top

cut 2

CF + CB

FOLD

LH

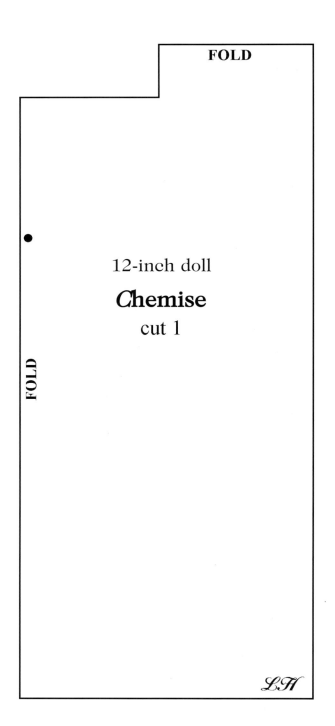

FOLD

12-inch doll

Chemise

cut 1

FOLD

LH

12-inch doll

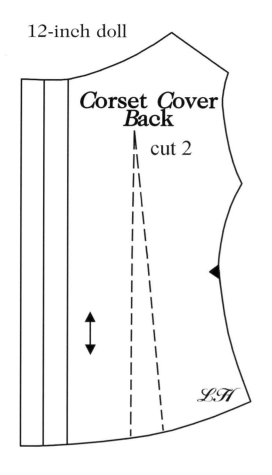

Corset Cover
Back

cut 2

LH

12-inch doll

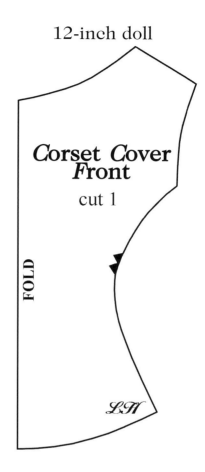

Corset Cover
Front

cut 1

FOLD

LH

12-inch doll

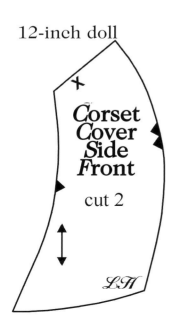

X

Corset
Cover
Side
Front

cut 2

LH

12-inch doll

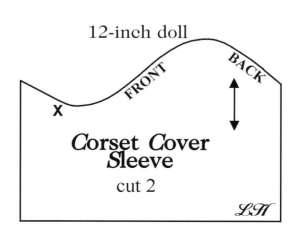

FRONT

BACK

X

Corset Cover
Sleeve

cut 2

LH

Chemise, Corset Cover, Pantalets and Petticoat - 18-inch Doll

Straight Pieces

Lower Pantalets	2 (3" x 6-1/4")
Pantalets Waistband	1-1/2" x 8"
Petticoat Body	6-7/8" x 27-1/2"
Petticoat Bottom	4" x 27-1/2"
Petticoat Ruffle	2" x 54"
Chemise Sleeves	2 (1-1/2" x 4-1/2")

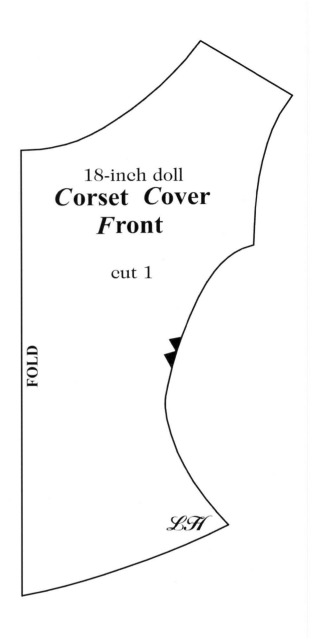

18-inch doll
Corset Cover
Front

cut 1

FOLD

LH

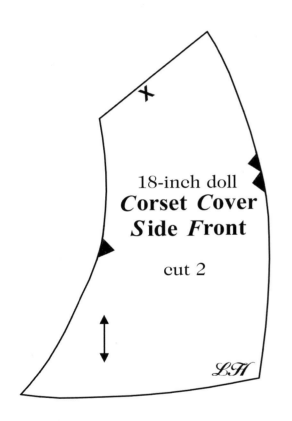

X

18-inch doll
Corset Cover
Side Front

cut 2

LH

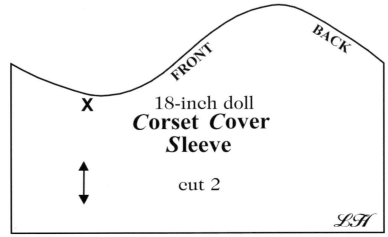

FRONT

BACK

X

18-inch doll
Corset Cover
Sleeve

cut 2

LH

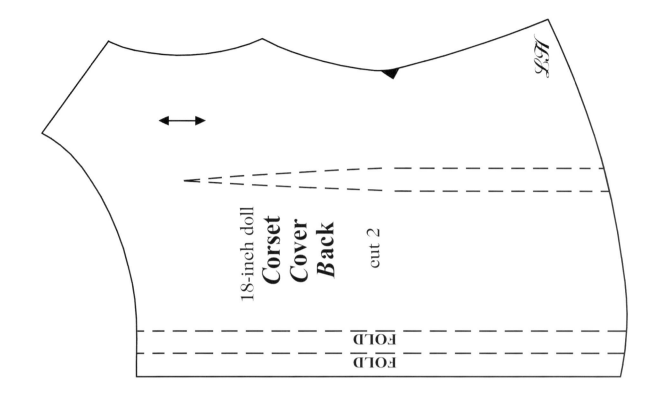

18-inch doll
**Corset
Cover
*Back***

cut 2

FOLD
FOLD

LH

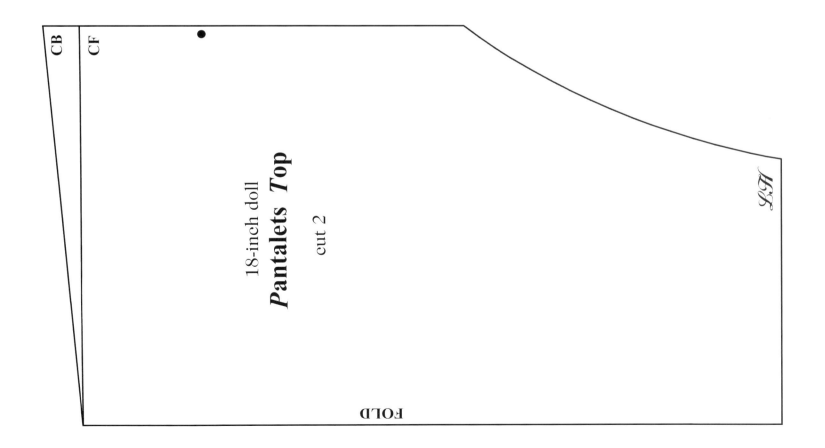

CB
CF

18-inch doll
Pantalets *Top*

cut 2

FOLD

LH

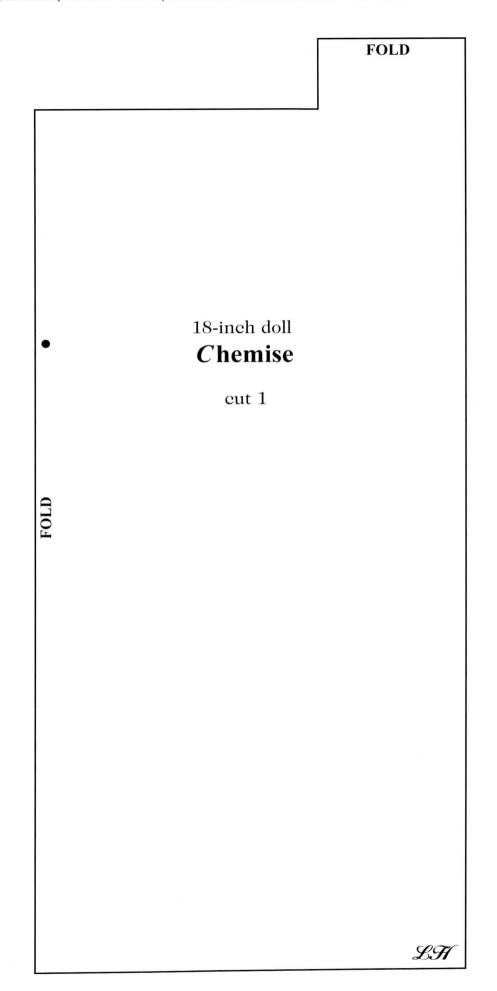

FOLD

18-inch doll

Chemise

cut 1

FOLD

LH

Nightgown from La Poupée Modèle, *June 1869*

Materials

Pima Swiss cotton (shown) or Swiss cotton batiste:
  12" x 45" (16" x 45")
3/8" Cluny type (shown) or Valenciennes lace
  edging: 30" (embroidered edging 1-1/4 yards)
3/8" Embroidered insertion: 8" (5/8" insertion - 10")
3/8" Insertion lace: 9" (1/2" lace - 12")
3/16" Mother-of-pearl buttons: 2
Fine embroidery thread to match
#10-#12 Crewel needle

Nightgown: Cut one front body and one back body on fold, two front yokes, one back yoke and two sleeves on fold. Cut two bias strips to trim the front yoke, 3/4" x 2-1/4" (3/4" x 3"). Take each bias piece and fold both long raw edges under to form two 1/4" x 2-1/4" (1/4" x 3") strips. Trim the raw edges on the wrong side to 1/8".

Only the two front yokes are trimmed in lace. The entredeux, which borders most embroidery insertions today, was not invented until 1910. Therefore, in keeping with the period, if you are using an insertion that has a row of entredeux on either side of the insertion, remove the outer rows of heavy stitching and the bars, leaving the inner heavy rows of stitching to aid in the construction.

Turn under the center front twice as shown on the pattern and blind stitch. Press these seams. Beginning at center front, stitch a row of embroidered insertion on one front. Alternate with the insertion lace and continue until you reach the outer edge. Trim both insertions to match the shape of the front. Repeat with the other side. Join front and back yokes at the shoulder with a French seam.

Slit center front of the body of the nightgown to the dot. Roll and whip the cut edges. Stitch two rows of gathering stitches at the top of the back body. Pull up to fit the back yoke. With right sides together, stitch, trim and overcast. Press up. Repeat with the two fronts. Stitch the bias strips over the front yokes with tiny stitches on both top and bottom.

With right sides together, stitch the sleeves into the armholes. Trim this seam and overcast. There are no gathers on these sleeves. French seam the side seam from the bottom of the nightgown to the bottom of the sleeves. Roll, whip and gather the bottom of the sleeve, making certain you have left enough room to bring the sleeve over the doll's hand, about 2" (3"). Stitch on Cluny lace (embroi-dered edging with evened raw edge) straight.

Narrow hem the bottom of the nightgown. Fold the nightgown body, making a crease at center front, and iron this crease to a sharp edge. Stitch the Cluny lace (embroidered edging with evened raw edge) from the neck edge to the bottom of the skirt twice with the straight edge of the lace or edging butted against the crease.

If you are using lace: roll and whip the neck edge. Whip on the Cluny lace straight. *In you are using an embroidered edging:* with right sides together, stitch the edging to the collar. Cut a piece of nightgown material on the bias, 3/4" x 5-1/2". Stitch this bias over the edging. Trim the seam to 1/8", turn under the raw edge of the bias and blind stitch to the inside of the neck. Close the nightgown with two 3/16" mother-of-pearl buttons on one side, one at the neck, the second at the bottom of the yoke, and thread loops on the other side. The nightgown measures 9-1/2" (14-3/4") from the middle of the shoulder seam.

Standing by a nineteenth-century painted screen, 12-inch Linette prepares to put on her needlepoint slippers. She wears the nightgown of antique broadcloth, lace and Swiss embroidery.

The 18-inch Huret's nightgown is fashioned from antique cotton pereale, trimmed entirely with antique Swiss embroidery.

Nightgown from *La Poupée Modèle*, June 1869
12-inch Doll

Bias Piece
Yoke Trim ....2 (3/4" x 2-1/4")

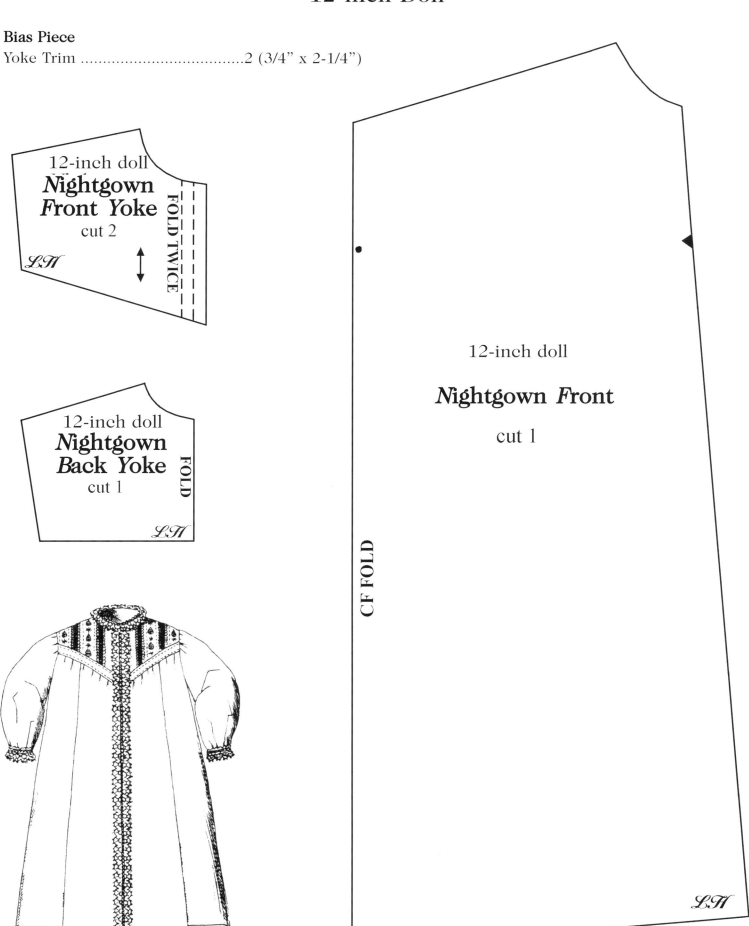

12-inch doll
Nightgown Front Yoke
cut 2

LH

FOLD TWICE

12-inch doll
Nightgown Back Yoke
cut 1

FOLD

LH

12-inch doll
Nightgown Front
cut 1

CF FOLD

LH

12-inch doll
Nightgown *Back*
cut 1

FOLD

TOP

12-inch doll
Nightgown Sleeve
cut 2

FOLD

BOTTOM

LH

LH

Nightgown from *La Poupée Modèle*, June 1869
18-inch Doll

Bias Piece

Front Yoke Trim...................................2 (3/4" x 3")

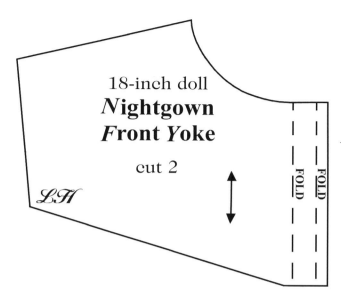

18-inch doll
Nightgown
Front Yoke

cut 2

LH

FOLD
FOLD
FOLD

A

B

18-inch doll
Nightgown
Lower Front

cut 1

CF FOLD

LH

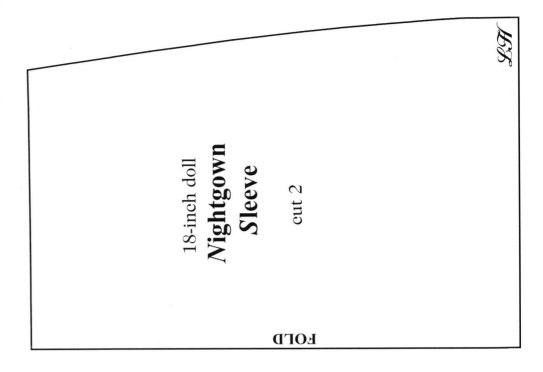

18-inch doll
Nightgown Sleeve

cut 2

FOLD

LH

A   B

18-inch doll

Nightgown Lower Back

cut 1

CB FOLD

LH

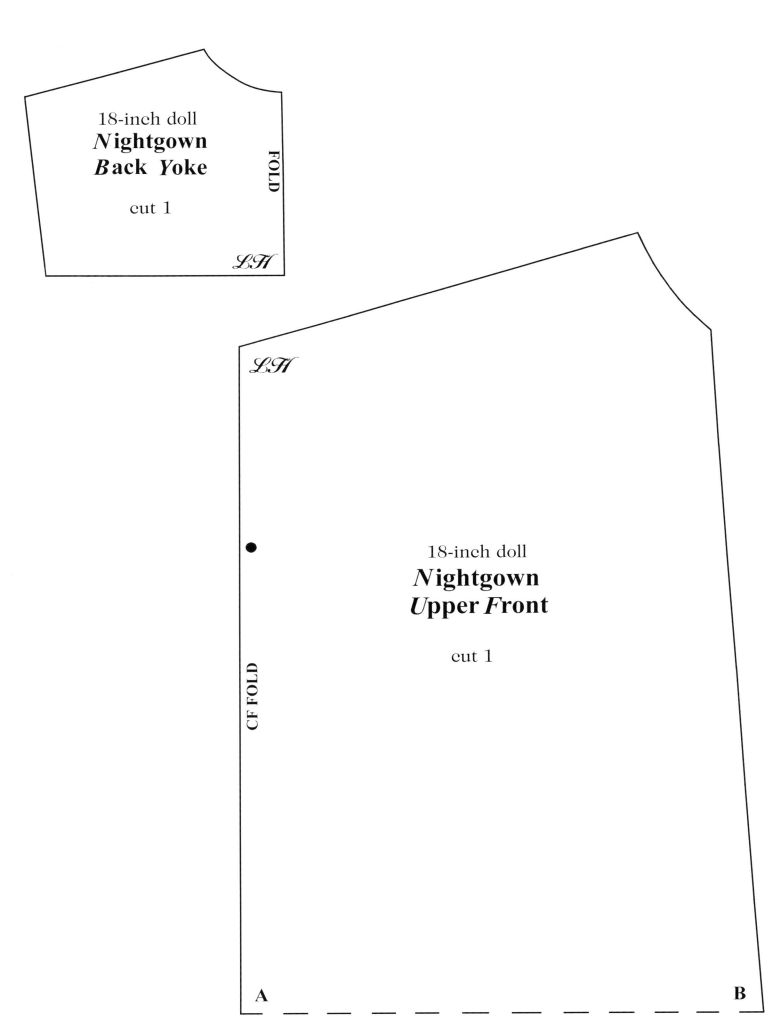

18-inch doll
Nightgown
Back Yoke

cut 1

FOLD

LH

LH

18-inch doll
Nightgown
Upper Front

cut 1

CF FOLD

A

B

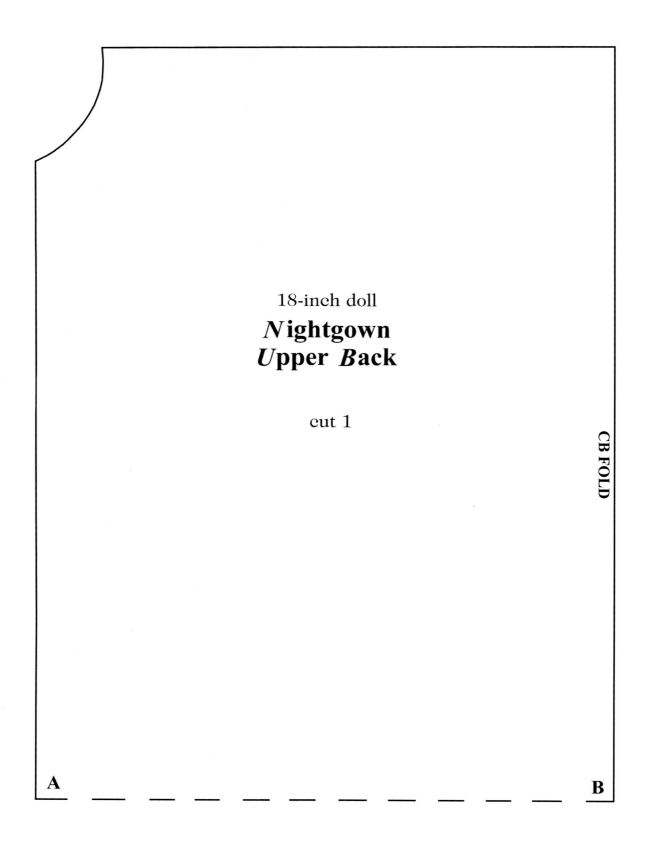

18-inch doll
**Nightgown
Upper Back**

cut 1

CB FOLD

A

B

Combing Jacket
from La Poupée Modèle, November 1864

The A-line cut of this jacket, with its extreme fullness at the bottom, suggests that m'lady wore this just before she put on her gown, with petticoats and hoop already in place. As she sat at her dressing table, her maid would style her hair.

Combing Jacket: Cut one back, two fronts, two revers, two sleeves, two cuffs, two collars and the following bias pieces: neck facing, 3/4" x 4-1/2" (3/4" x 5-3/4") and two cuff bindings, 3/4" x 2-1/4" (3/4" x 4-1/4").

Collar and Cuffs: Even the raw edge of 9" (12") of scalloped edging. With right sides together, baste the raw edges of this edging to one of the collars along the long outer edge and two short edges, easing through the corners. With right sides together, stitch the two collars together on the two short edges and long outer edge with the edging in place. Turn to the right side and press.

Even the raw edge of two 6" (8-1/2") pieces of scalloped edging. With right sides together, stitch the raw edging of this edging to the cuff along the long outer edge and the two short edges, easing through the corners. Open to the right side, press, trim this seam and overcast. Repeat with other cuff, and set aside the cuffs and collar.

Revers: Even the raw edge of 10" (13-1/2") of scalloped edging. With wrong sides together, French seam the scalloped edging to the fabric on the outer and lower edges of the revers. Gather the tiniest bit of edging going around the corner so that it will be full enough to lie flat when pressed. Press seam toward the revers and top stitch.

With right sides together, stitch revers to the front pieces. Trim the seam and overcast. Leave the last 1/2" open until you complete the bottom edging, finishing later. Turn to the right side and press. Stitch the back to the front/revers at the shoulders with a French seam.

Stitch two gathering rows at the top of the sleeves to curve, not to gather. With right sides together, stitch the sleeve into the armhole. Trim and overcast the sleeve. Stitch a gathering row at the bottom of the sleeve, pull up to 2-5/8" (4-5/8") and bind off. French seam from the bottom of the garment to the bottom of the sleeve. With the wrong side of the cuff against the right side of the sleeve, baste the cuff to the sleeve. With right sides together, stitch the bias sleeve binding to the sleeve. Trim the seam to 1/8". Turn the binding to the inside of the sleeve, turn under the raw edge and blind stitch. Turn the cuff up over the bottom of the sleeve.

Even the raw edge of the remaining scalloped edging, and French seam this to the entire bottom edge of the fronts and back. Complete the bottom 1/2" of the revers/front seams. Press the French seam up and top stitch the bottom edge. Turn the revers to the right side and press to a sharp edge along the seam line. You may wish to tack a couple of stitches at the edge of the revers to hold them in place.

With the wrong side of the collar against the right side of the jacket, stitch the collar in place. Turn under the short ends of the bias neck facing 1/4" at each end and press. With the right side of the facing against the right side of the collar, stitch on the facing. Turn to the wrong side, turn under the raw edge and blind stitch. Close with a 3/16" mother-of-pearl button and thread loop. The finished length of the jacket is 6-1/8" (8-1/4"), measured from the front shoulder seam.

The combing jacket for the 12-inch doll is made of Swiss batiste trimmed in Swiss embroidery.

The 18-inch Rohmer wears her antique cotton percale combing jacket trimmed in antique Swiss embroidery. Note that the fullness of the bottom of the jacket allows it to flow over the wide petticoats.

Combing Jacket from *La Poupée Modèle*, November 1864
12-inch Doll

Bias Pieces

Neck Facing ....3/4" x 4-1/2"
Cuff Binding ....2 (3/4" x 2-1/4")

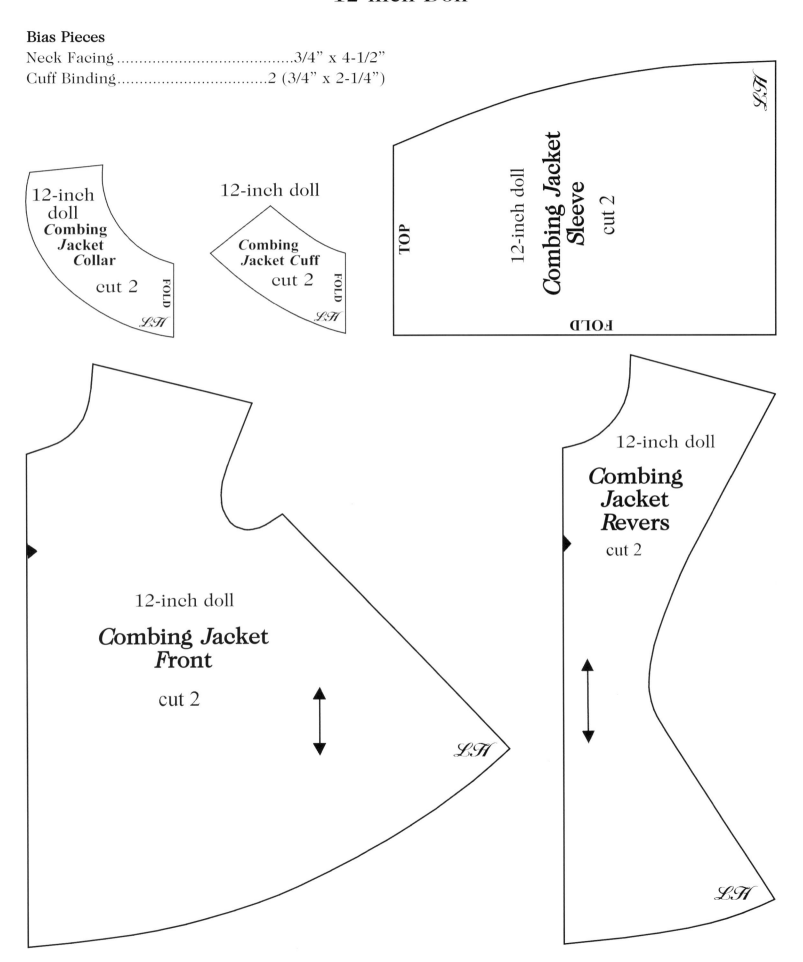

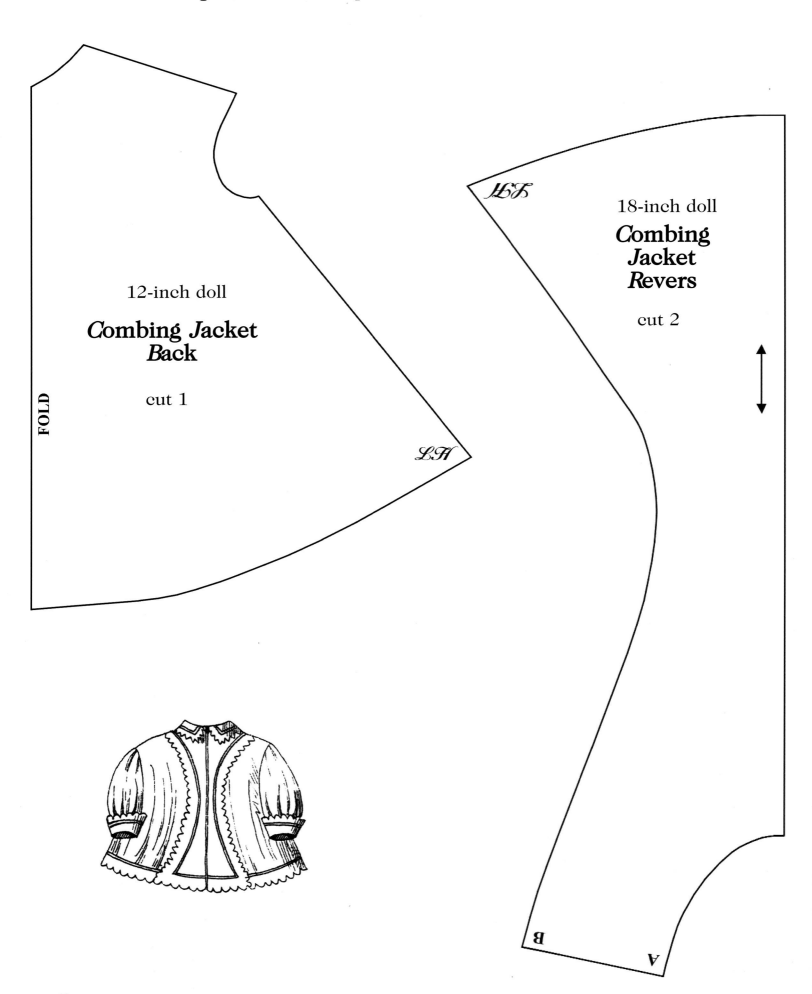

12-inch doll

Combing Jacket
Back

cut 1

FOLD

LH

LF

18-inch doll

Combing Jacket Revers

cut 2

LF

B

A

Combing Jacket from *La Poupée Modèle*, November 1864
18-inch Doll

Bias Pieces

Neck Facing ....3/4" x 5-3/4"
Cuff Binding................................2 (1/2" x 4-1/4")

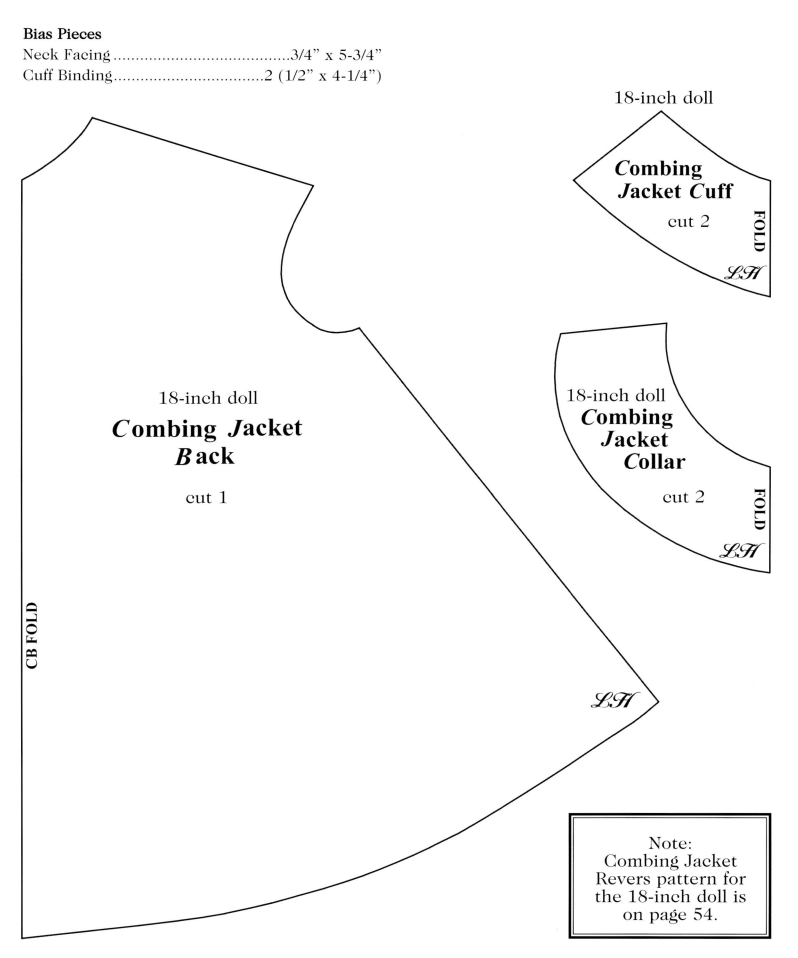

18-inch doll

Combing Jacket Cuff

cut 2

FOLD

LH

18-inch doll

Combing Jacket Collar

cut 2

FOLD

LH

18-inch doll

Combing Jacket Back

cut 1

CB FOLD

LH

Note:
Combing Jacket
Revers pattern for
the 18-inch doll is
on page 54.

Combing Jacket from *La Poupée Modèle*

November 1864 - 18-inch Doll

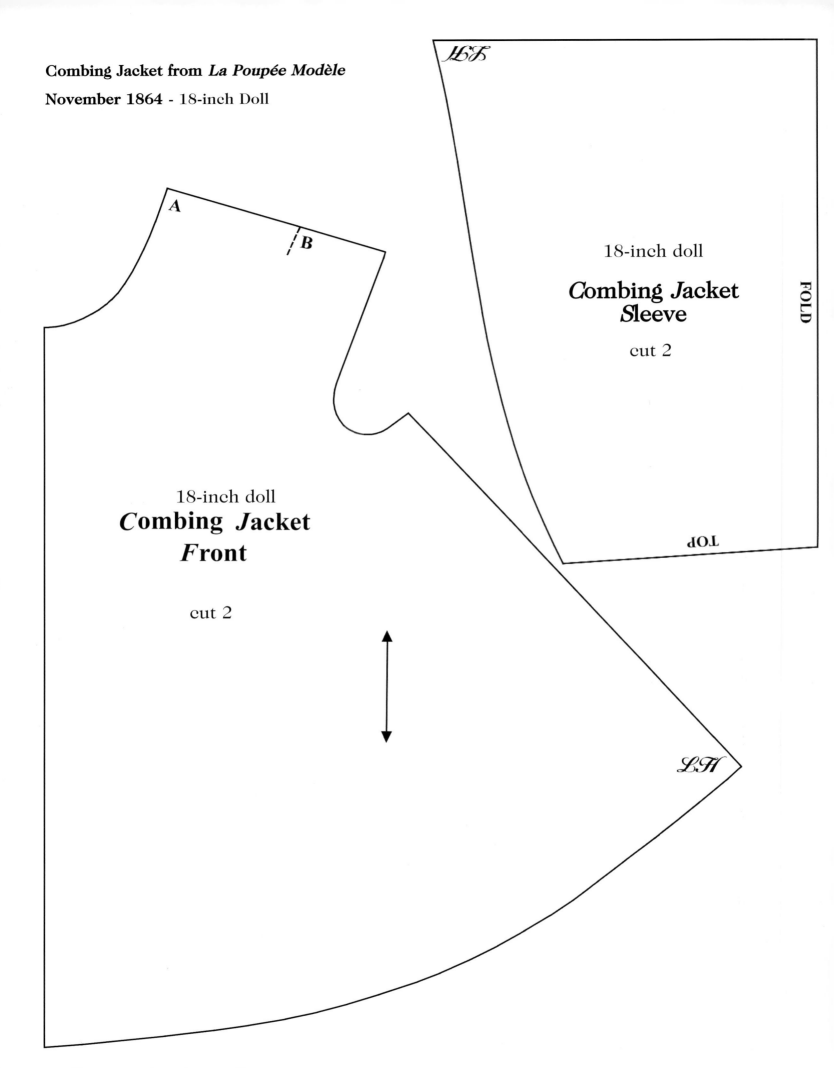

A

B

18-inch doll

Combing Jacket Sleeve

cut 2

FOLD

TOP

18-inch doll

Combing Jacket Front

cut 2

Peignoir from La Poupée Modèle, August 1870

Materials

Swiss cotton batiste (shown) or cotton voile: 9" x 36" (24" x 54")

3/8" Valenciennes lace edging: 2-1/4 yards (2-1/4 yards)

1/2" Valenciennes lace edging: 2/3 yard (none)

3/4" Valenciennes lace edging: 3/4 yard (none)

Stranded embroidery floss, DMC cotton or silk (shown): two yards of three colors

3/16" Mother-of-pearl button: 1

Fine embroidery thread to match

#9 Sharp needle for embroidery and #10-#12 crewel needle

It is interesting to note that when Mlle Péronne presented a pattern, the drawn illustration was usually for Lily, the #4 French fashion doll. In the text she offered a simpler version that was more appropriate for smaller dolls. Following her method, I have used the illustrated version for the 18-inch doll and the simpler version for the 12-inch doll. The pleating for the larger garment is beautiful, but not practical when rendered in a small size. For the smaller doll, Mlle Péronne suggested using varying widths of the same lace.

General construction for both sizes: (If you are making the pattern for an 18-inch doll, cut the pleating pieces first, as listed on the pattern page.) Cut two backs, two fronts, two back sleeves and two front sleeves. (For the 18-inch doll, cut a piece of bias neck facing 3/4" x 6".)

French seam the center back seam, shoulder seams and side seams. Press the side and shoulder seams toward the back and the back seam to one side. French seam both the front and back seams of the sleeves. Stitch two rows of gathering stitches 1-1/2" (2") on either side of the top of the back piece. With right sides together, ease—do not gather—the sleeves into the armholes. The shorter seam of the sleeve is on the top; the longer seam is on the bottom. After stitching, trim and overcast. The bottom seam lines up with the side seam and the upper seam is just forward of the shoulder seam. When all the embellishments have been added to these peignoirs, close with a 3/16" mother-of-pearl button and thread loop. The thread loop should be long enough to extend beyond the lace or pleating edge. The finished length of the peignoir is 7-1/4" (11-1/4").

Embellishment additions for 12-inch pattern: Roll and whip the entire outside edge of the peignoir, including the neck and sleeves. Gather the 3/4" lace edging to fit the bottom of the peignoir by pulling the heavy thread in the heading until it fits the lower edge. Distribute the gathers evenly. Stitch on with a running stitch so that the heading of the lace overlaps the hemmed edge on the right side. Cut two pieces of 3/8" lace edging 10" each; gather to fit each side of the front, and apply as you did the previous lace. Next, with a running stitch, stitch the 3/8" lace straight from the neck down the front, across the bottom edge, finishing at the neck on the other side. The headings of the two laces should overlap. Edge the sleeves with the gathered 1/2" lace and then repeat with the 3/8" lace, again overlapping the heading of the gathered lace as you did with the outside of the garment. Then stitch a row of 3/8" lace straight around the neck edge.

The version of the batiste peignoir for the 12-inch doll is trimmed in three widths of the same ivory lace, and then embroidered.

Smiling Empress Eugenie wears the antique voile 18-inch peignoir. As described by Mlle Péronne, it shows the three graduated widths of fine voile pleating that trim the edges of the garment, as well as a narrow lace and pastel embroidery. Opposite page: A close view of the peignoir for the 12-inch doll pictured on page 57 shows the three embroidery stitches used.

Embroidery: The embroidery design uses three colors and three stitches. A straight stitch is done in pale green to represent the vine (two strands); the detached Lazy Daisy (four stitches, one strand) is done in pale lavender for the flowers, and French knots (two strands) are done in pale gold for the center of the flower. These are stitched down the front on both sides, across the bottom and the sleeves of the peignoir. The green "line,"—the straight stitch—is stitched on top of the overlapped headings of the lace. See page 22 in Chapter 1 for instructions and diagrams.

Embellishment additions for 18-inch pattern: See pattern sheet for sizes for the neck, front, bottom and sleeve strips. Hand hem all pieces of pleating, turning the raw edge to the wrong side 1/8" and press, turn a second time 1/8" and press. Then hem with a running stitch and press again. Pleat the strips with 1/8" pleats by hand or using a commercial pleater. When pleating is finished, the size of the pieces are: neck, 1/2" x 6", front, 2(3/4" x 9-3/4"), bottom, 1-3/8" x 30", and sleeves 2(1" x 11-1/4"). Attach the front pleating as follows: With wrong sides together, stitch the 1/4" seam. The raw edges of the seam will be on the right side. Repeat with the bottom, sleeves and other side of the front. Stitch the 3/8" lace flat over the raw edges of the fronts, sleeves and bottoms. Stitch from the neck, down the front, across the bottom and up the other side, ending at the neck. Repeat with the sleeve edges. Press well. With right sides together, stitch the pleating to the raw neck edge. Turn under the short ends of the bias neck facing 1/4" on each end and press. With right sides together, stitch the bias over the pleating. Trim this seam to 1/8". Turn the bias to the wrong side, turn under the raw edge and blind stitch.

Embroidery: This embroidery design uses three colors and three stitches. A straight stitch is done in pale green to represent the vine (six strands), detached Lazy Daisy (six stitches, three strands) is done in pale aqua for the flowers, and French knots (three strands) in light peach for the center of the flower. These are stitched down the front on both sides, across the bottom and the sleeves. The green "line"—the straight stitch—is stitched on top of the heading of the narrow lace. See page 22 in Chapter 1 for instructions and diagrams.

Peignoir from *La Poupée Modèle*, August 1870 - 12-inch Doll

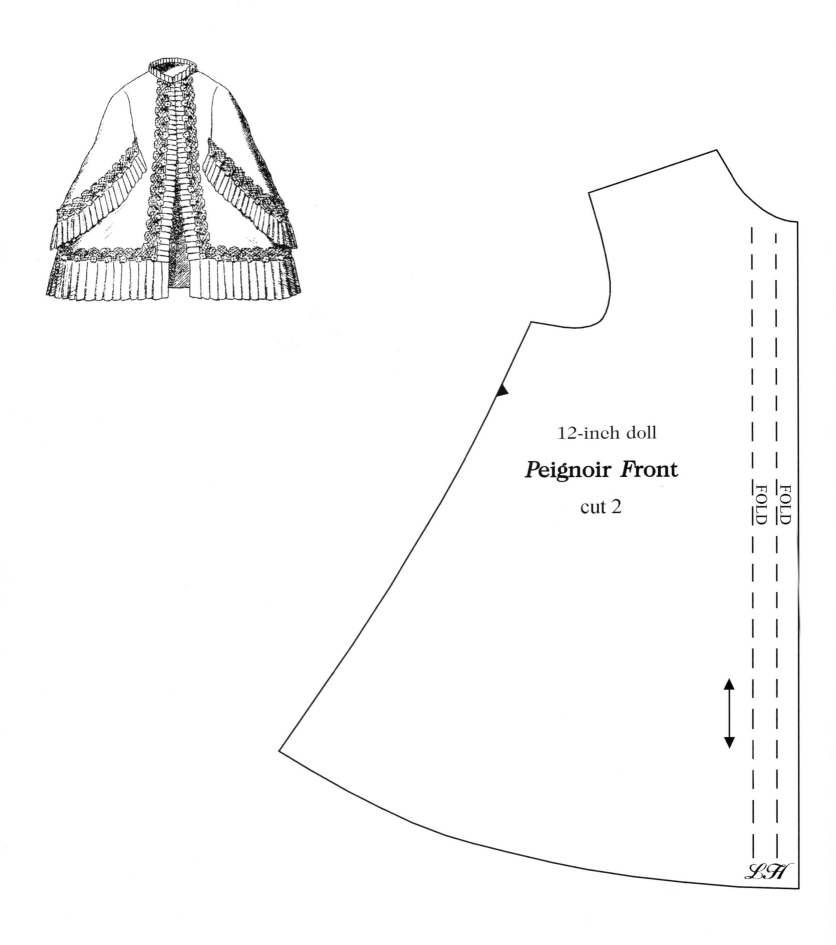

12-inch doll

Peignoir Front

cut 2

FOLD
FOLD
FOLD

LH

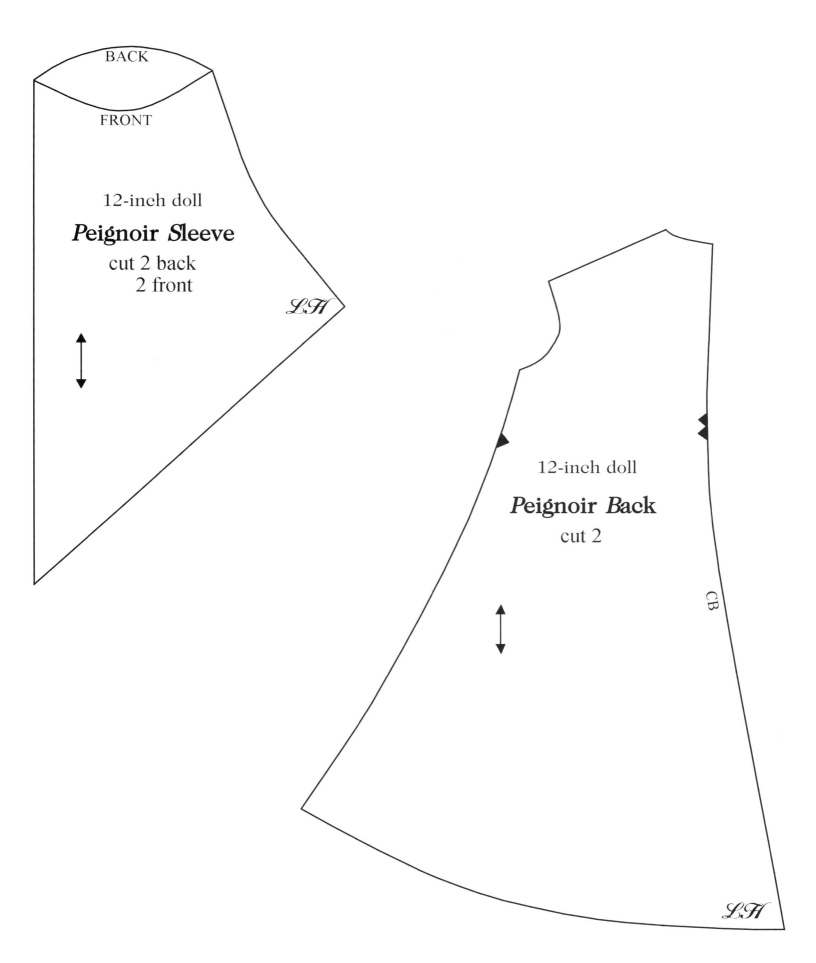

BACK

FRONT

12-inch doll

Peignoir Sleeve

cut 2 back
2 front

LH

12-inch doll

Peignoir Back

cut 2

CB

LH

Peignoir from *La Poupée Modèle*, August 1870 - 18-inch Doll

Straight Pieces

Neck Facing	3/4" x 18"
Front Pleating	2 (1" x 30")
Sleeve Pleating	2 (1-1/4" x 30")
Bottom Pleating	1-5/8" x 96"

Bias Piece

Neck Facing	3/4" x 6"

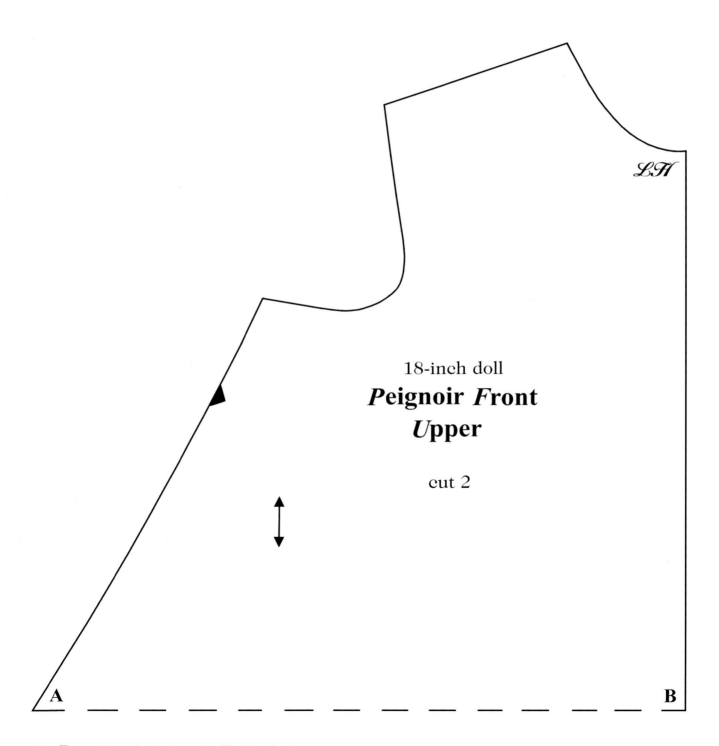

LH

18-inch doll
Peignoir Front Upper

cut 2

A   B

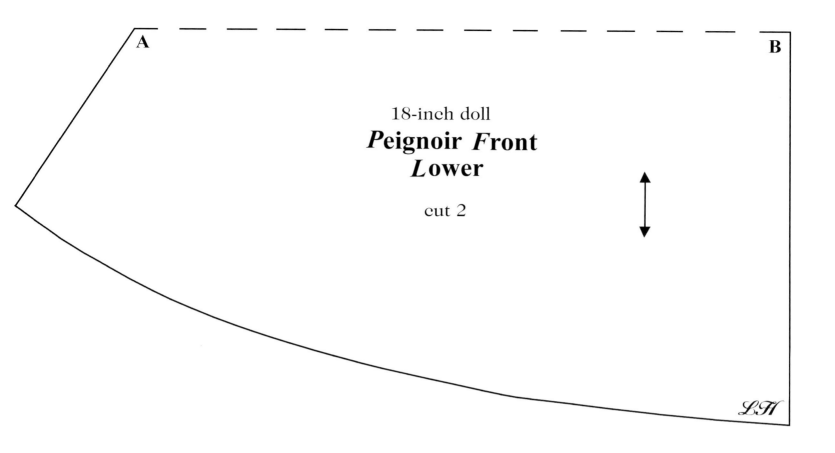

18-inch doll
**Peignoir *Front*
*Lower***

cut 2

A

B

LH

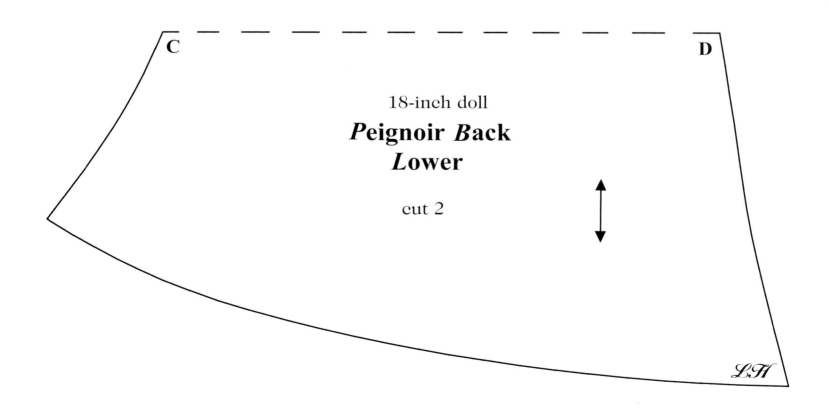

18-inch doll
**Peignoir *Back*
*Lower***

cut 2

C

D

LH

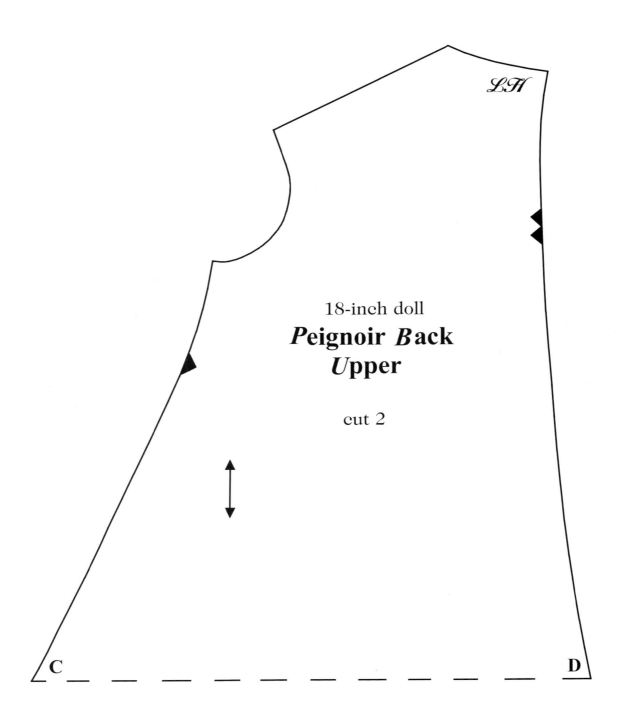

LH

18-inch doll
Peignoir *B*ack
Upper

cut 2

C   D

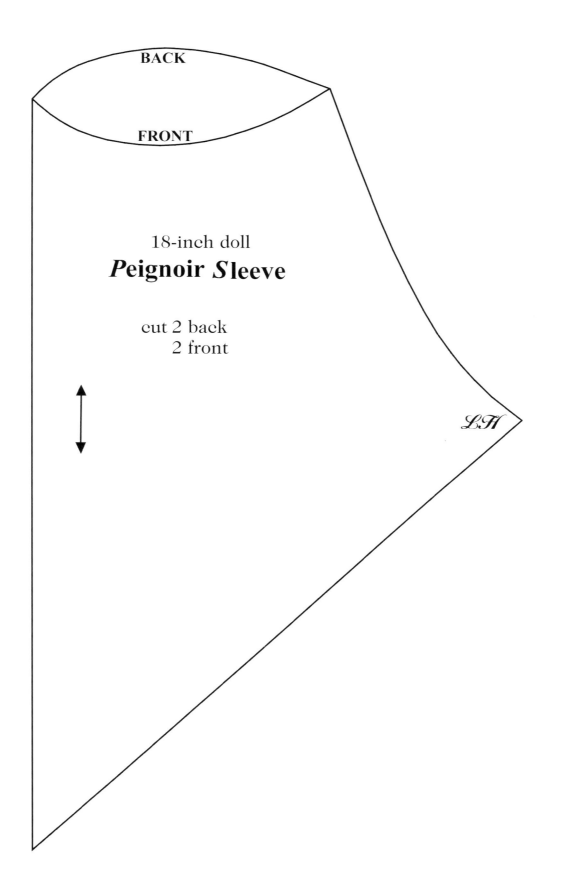

BACK

FRONT

18-inch doll
Peignoir Sleeve

cut 2 back
2 front

LH

Formal Chemise and Petticoat

Materials

Swiss cotton batiste (shown): 10" x 40" (24" x 54")
3/8" Valenciennes lace edging: 27" (5/8" embroidered insertion or galloon (shown): 2/3 yards)
1-1/4" Swiss embroidered edging: 2 yards
  (2-1/2": 3 yards)
3/16" Mother-of-pearl buttons: 2
Fine embroidery thread to match
#10-#12 Crewel needle

These two pieces were designed from antique garments meant to be worn under the formal gown
shown on pages 156 and 157 in Chapter 3. Bearing
only straps on the shoulders, the chemise can be worn
under any low-cut gown.

Preparation of folded edging: Following the directions for
the Basic Undergarments on page 28, prepare 24" (34") of
folded edging for the petticoat before cutting out the other
pattern pieces. These strips will cover the raw edges of the
embroidered edging when finishing the petticoat.

Chemise: Cut one front and one back on folds. Slash the
center front to the dot. Roll and whip these raw edges.
Turn the top edges of the front and back to the right side
and press to a sharp edge. Roll and whip the armholes.
Edge the underarm portions with 3/8" lace (embroidery)
with the edge side of the lace even with the rolled hem.
French seam the side seams and press toward the back.
Roll and whip the bottom edge and press.

If you use lace for the 12-inch pattern: Cut four pieces
of lace 2-1/4" each and, butting the straight sides together, whip them together. Secure these to the front and back
of the chemise to form the shoulder straps. Cut two pieces
of lace 3" each; butt, whip and stitch across the top edge
of the chemise back, covering the raw edge of the fabric
and bottom edges of the shoulder straps. First turn under
the lace edges 1/4". Cut four pieces of lace 1-3/4", butt two
of each together and stitch across the two fronts, first
turning under the raw edges 1/4".

If you use embroidery for the 18-inch pattern: Cut two
pieces 3" each for the straps. Secure these to the front and
back of the chemise to form the shoulder straps. Cut one
piece 4-1/2", turn under the raw edges 1/4" and stitch
across the top edge of the chemise back, covering the raw
edge of the fabric and bottom edges of the shoulder straps.

Cut two pieces 2-1/4", turn under the raw edges and stitch
across the two fronts. Close the center front with a 3/16"
mother-of-pearl button and thread loop. The chemise is
6" (9-1/2") long, measured from the shoulder straps.

Petticoat: Cut one front on fold, two backs and the waistband on fold. French seam the side and center back
seams. Leave the center back open 2-1/2" (3") at the top,
turn under this seam allowance, roll and whip. Turn under
the waistband 1/4" at center back and press. Stitch two
rows of gathering stitches at the top of the petticoat and
pull up to fit the waistband. With right sides together,
stitch the waistband to the skirt. Turn under the raw edge
of the waistband, turn to the wrong side, and blind stitch.
Roll and whip the bottom edge of the petticoat.

Cut a piece of Swiss embroidery 36" (1-1/2 yards) long.
Even the top raw edge. French seam the short ends. Stitch
two rows of gathers at the top of the embroidery, and pull
up to fit the bottom edge of the skirt. Stitch the embroidery
to the skirt from center back to center back with the
embroidered edge falling 1/4" (1/2") below the bottom of
the skirt. Stitch a piece of the folded edging across the front
of the skirt from side seam to side seam only, covering the
raw edge. Cut two pieces of Swiss
embroidery 18" (27") each, gather as
above, and stitch to the back portion of the skirt, side seam to
side seam, turning under 1/4"
at the seams. The embroidery
overlaps only 1/4". Finish by
stitching the remaining piece of
the folded edging across the
back of the skirt from side
seam to side seam. Finish
the skirt with a 3/16"
mother-of-pearl but-
ton and thread
loop. The petti-
coat measures
7" (11-5/8")
from center
front.

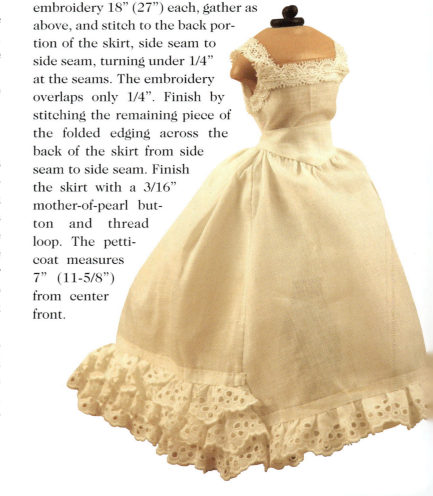

These two additional pieces, the chemise with small straps over the shoulders and the long petticoat with multiple flounces in the rear, have been added to provide the proper undergarments for Lily's and Linette's evening gowns.

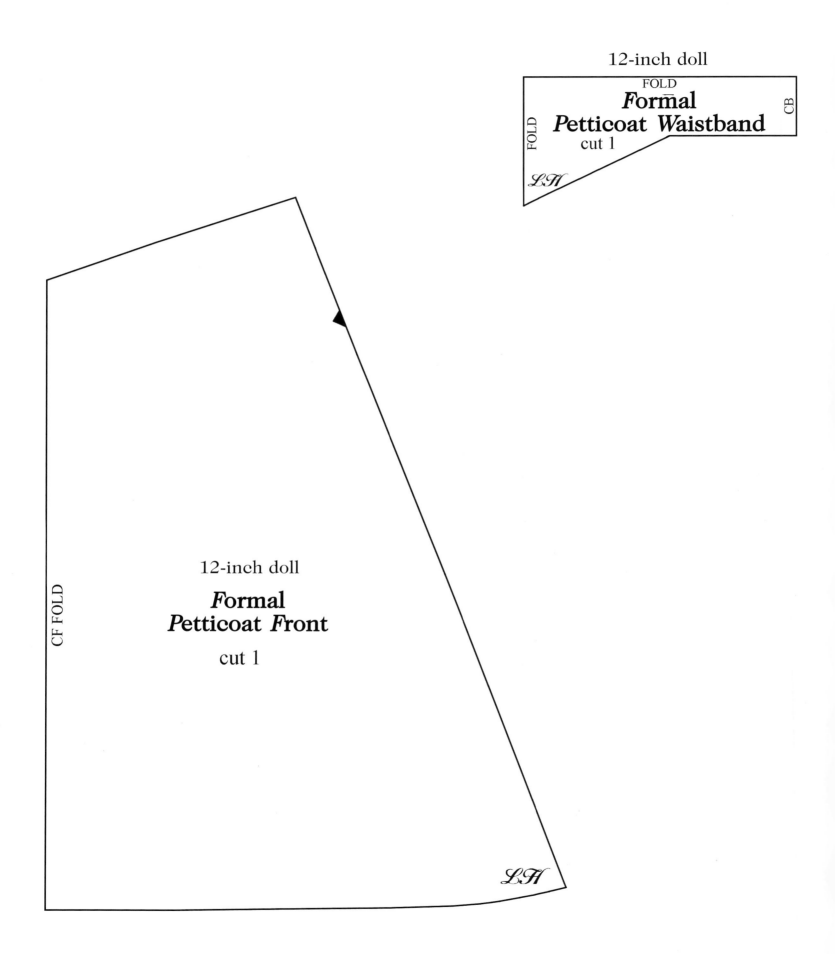

12-inch doll

FOLD

Formal
Petticoat Waistband

cut 1

FOLD

CB

𝓛𝓗

CF FOLD

12-inch doll

Formal
Petticoat Front

cut 1

𝓛𝓗

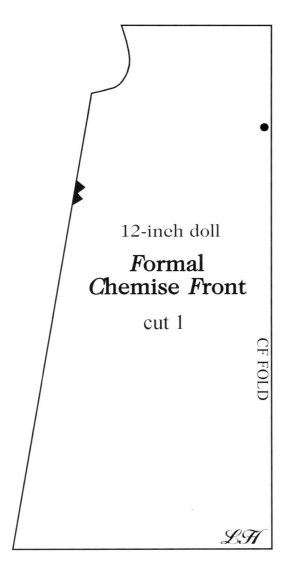

12-inch doll

**Formal
Chemise Front**

cut 1

CF FOLD

LH

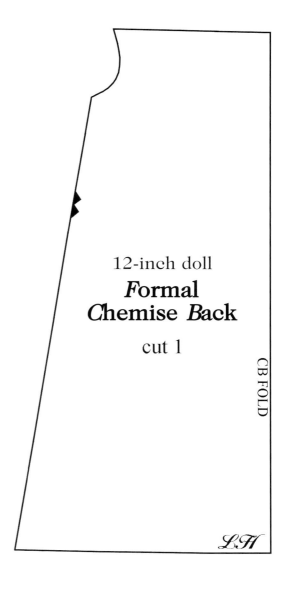

12-inch doll

**Formal
Chemise Back**

cut 1

CB FOLD

LH

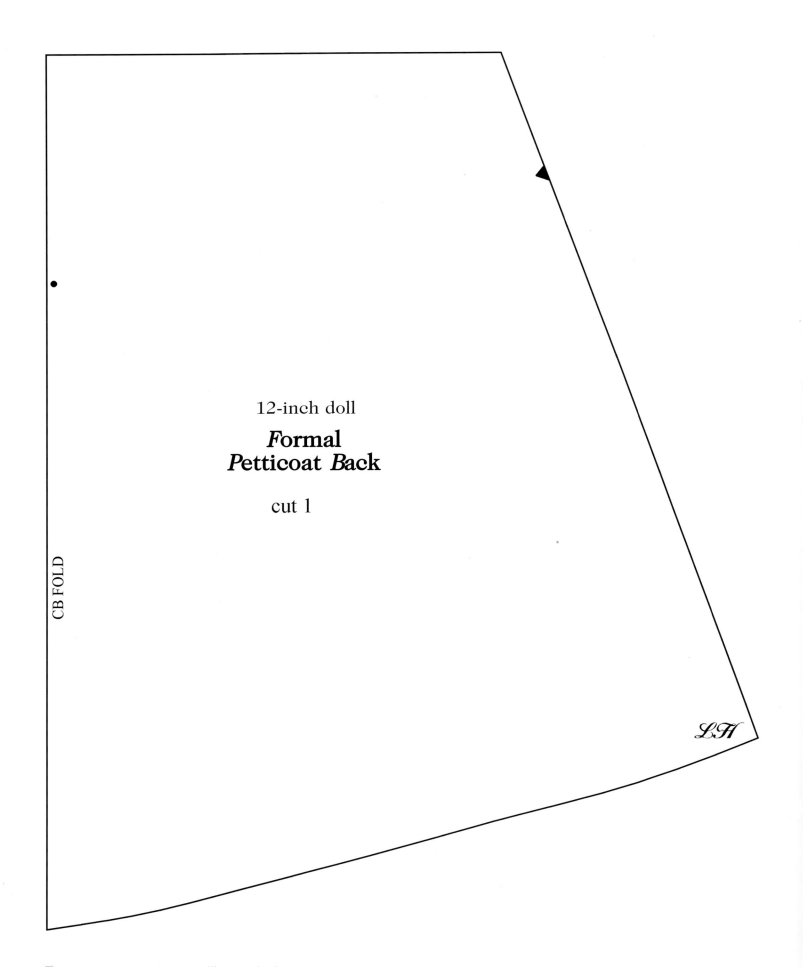

12-inch doll

**Formal
Petticoat Back**

cut 1

CB FOLD

LH

Formal Chemise and Petticoat - 18-inch Doll

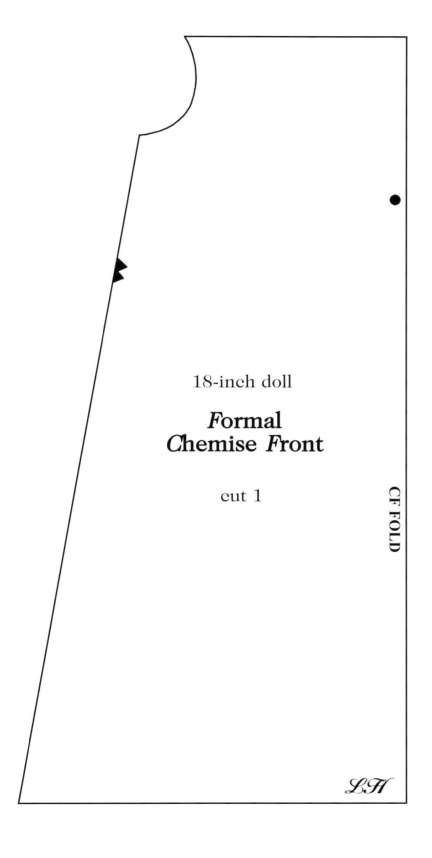

18-inch doll

Formal
Chemise Front

cut 1

CF FOLD

LH

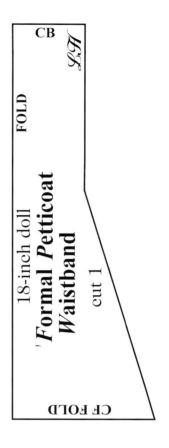

CB

FOLD

LH

18-inch doll

Formal Petticoat
Waistband

cut 1

CF FOLD

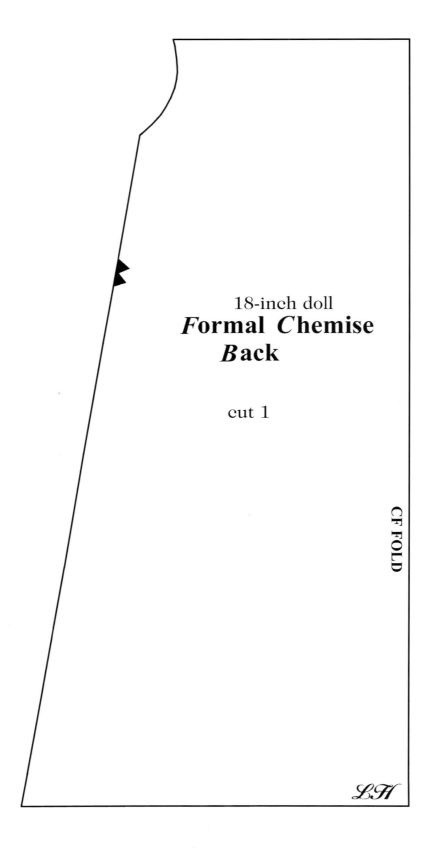

18-inch doll
Formal Chemise Back

cut 1

CF FOLD

LH

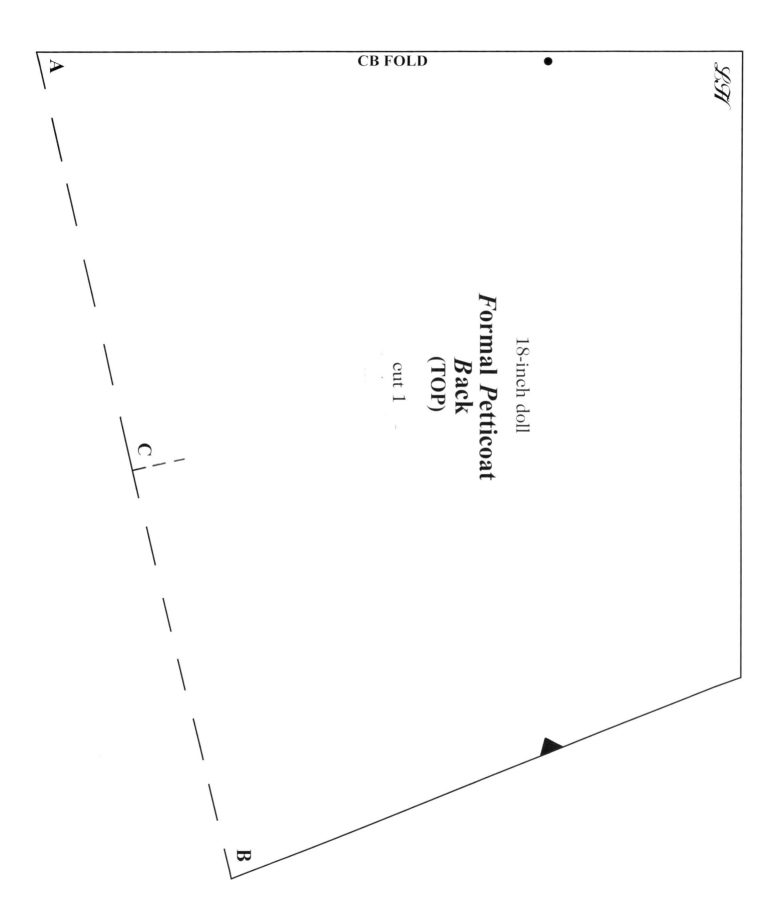

CB FOLD

18-inch doll

Formal Petticoat
Back
(TOP)

cut 1

A

B

C

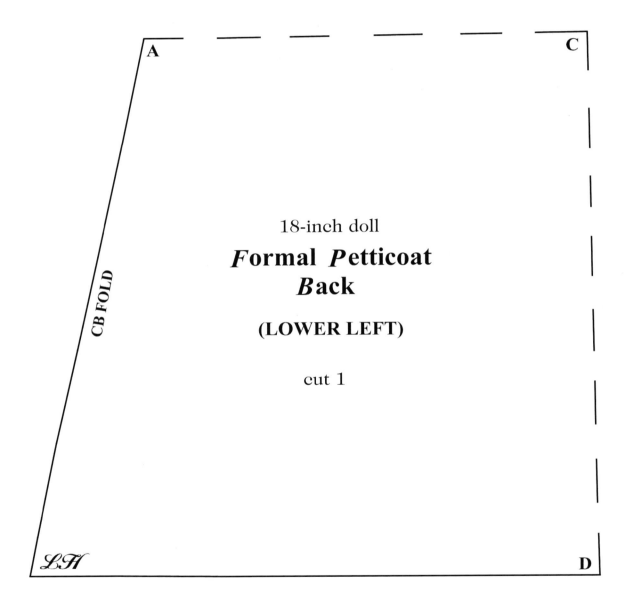

A

C

CB FOLD

18-inch doll

***Formal Petticoat
Back***

(LOWER LEFT)

cut 1

LH

D

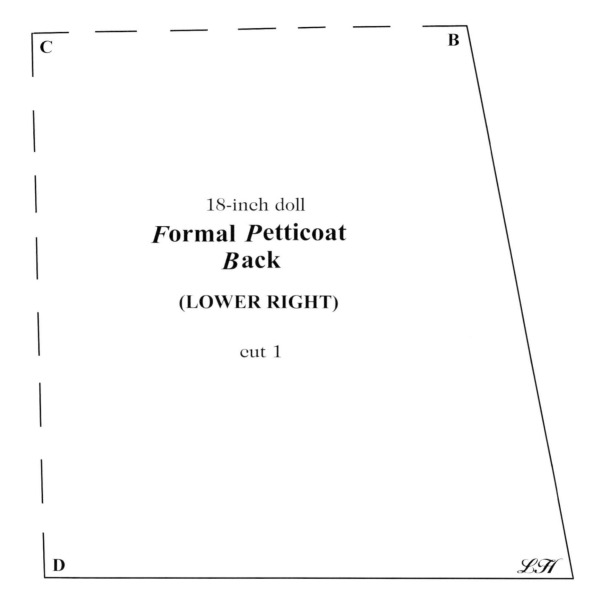

C

B

18-inch doll
Formal Petticoat Back

(LOWER RIGHT)

cut 1

D

LH

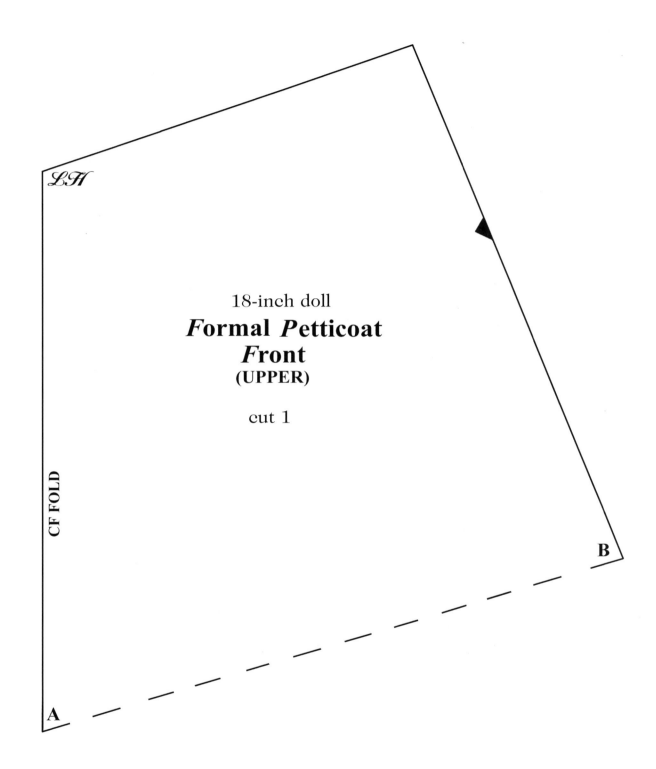

LH

18-inch doll
**Formal Petticoat
Front**
(UPPER)

cut 1

CF FOLD

A

B

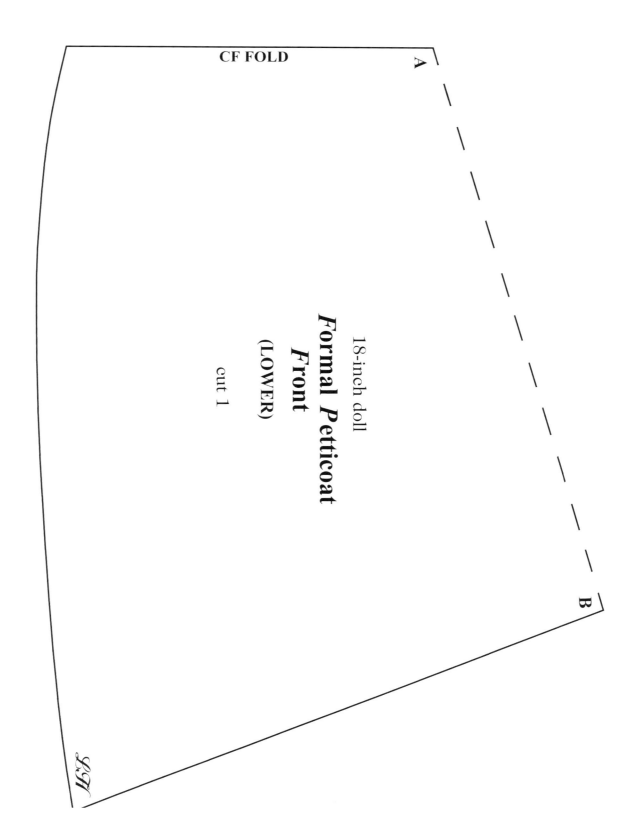

CF FOLD

A

18-inch doll
*Formal Petticoat
Front*
(LOWER)

cut 1

B

CF

Night Bonnet from La Poupée Modèle, November 1864

Materials

Swiss cotton batiste (shown): 7" x 9" (9" x 18")
3/8" Valenciennes lace edging: 18" with scallops,
   1-1/2 yards if all lace trim (none)
Fine embroidery thread to match
#10-#12 Crewel needle

The photograph below right of the 12-inch doll wearing the bonnet shows the ties and bavolet trimmed in machine-made scallops. These can be done on any computerized sewing machine using the smallest and plainest of the scallop stitches. The scallops were stitched with a rayon embroidery thread, which has a nice gloss. An alternative method is to trim the entire bonnet with the Valenciennes lace edging. The 18-inch doll is shown on the opposite page wearing the bonnet as seen in the illustration on page 80. These strips were cut with a nineteenth-century hand-cranked cutter with a scallop pattern. They can also be cut with pinking or scalloping scissors to achieve the same effect. If you trim with the fluted strips, cut these before cutting the rest of the pieces. The size of every doll head and wig is different. It would be prudent to first cut out the bonnet body from scrap fabric to determine if the size of pattern needs to be enlarged or reduced.

Night Bonnet: Lightly starch the fabric and cut out the body. Stitch two gathering rows along the back edge, A to B to A. Place the bonnet body on the doll with its wig in place; pull up to fit and tie off. Roll and whip the front edge of the bonnet.

Cut out the bavolet and ties, if you plan to trim them. If you are using the scallop pattern on the sewing machine, lightly draw the patterns on the larger piece of fabric and stitch the scallops. Then cut them out, taking care not to cut into the stitches. Stitch two rows of gathering stitches at the top edge of the bavolet and pull up to fit the lower edge of the bonnet, A to B to A. With wrong sides together, stitch the bavolet to the bonnet with a scant 1/8" seam. Trim. Place right sides together and stitch again. Press this seam up and stitch to lie flat.

If you are trimming with lace for the 12-inch doll: Cut two pieces of lace 9" each. Gather to fit the front edge of the bonnet, stitching the heading of the lace with a running stitch to the rolled hem. Gather the second piece of lace in the same manner. Stitch to the front of the bonnet,

overlapping the headings of the lace. Cut a piece of lace 9". Gather to fit the bottom of the bavolet and stitch on. Cut two pieces of lace 13-1/2", gather to fit around the ties and stitch on.

If you are trimming with fluted edgings for the 18-inch doll: Cut one piece of batiste 1-1/2" x 14" for the front ruffle. Trim both sides with scallop or pinking scissors. The finished piece should measure 1" x 14". Stitch two rows of gathering stitches down the center of the bonnet, pull up to fit the front edge of the bonnet, and stitch on. Cut two pieces of batiste 5/8" x 18" for ties. Trim one side with scallop or pinking shears. With wrong sides together, stitch the fluted edged fabric to a tie with a scant 1/8" seam. Trim. Stitch with two rows of gathering stitches and pull up to fit a tie. With right sides together, stitch again. Press the seam toward the fabric and top stitch it flat. Repeat with the other tie. Cut a piece of batiste 3/4" x 17" for the bavolet trim. Trim one side with scallop or pinking scissors. Stitch with two rows of gathering stitches to fit the bavolet bottom and sides. Attach to the bavolet bottom and sides as you did the ties.

Linette's ivory batiste night bonnet is trimmed in a narrow Valenciennes lace edging, suitable for a 12-inch doll.

The 18-inch Huret's bonnet de nuit is of fine antique batiste trimmed in self-fabric flounces, which have been scalloped on an antique cutting machine.

Night Bonnet from *La Poupée Modèle*, November 1864
12-inch Doll

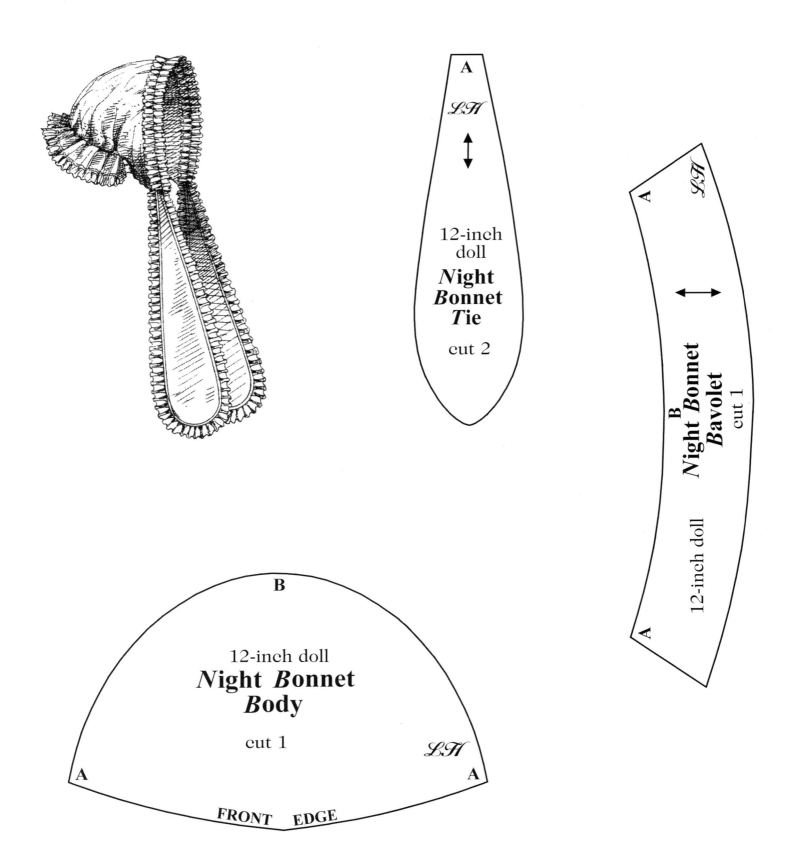

A

LH

12-inch
doll
**Night
Bonnet
Tie**

cut 2

A

LH

B
**Night Bonnet
Bavolet**
cut 1

12-inch doll

A

B

12-inch doll
**Night Bonnet
Body**

cut 1

LH

A

A

FRONT   EDGE

Night Bonnet from *La Poupée Modèle*, November 1864
18-inch Doll

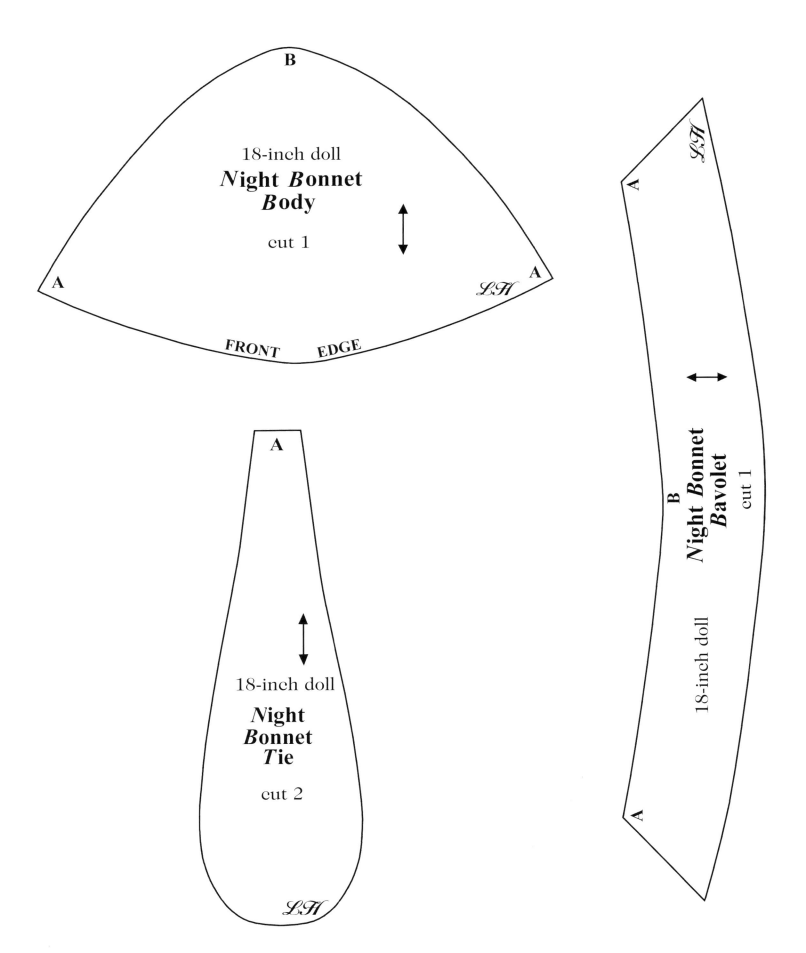

18-inch doll
Night Bonnet Body

cut 1

B

A

A

LH

FRONT EDGE

A

LH

A

B
Night Bonnet Bavolet
cut 1

18-inch doll

A

18-inch doll
Night Bonnet Tie

cut 2

LH

CHAPTER 3

DRESSES

By substituting pleats for gathers, exchanging sleeve shapes and varying the length of skirts and jackets, a seamstress can multiply the French fashion doll's ensembles.

F

insertion

insertion

h

Chemisette Front
cut 1

LH

Collar
cut 1 dress
1 lining

18-inch doll

Summer Soutache Dress
from La Poupée Modèle, September 1870

Materials

Swiss cotton piqué, birdseye (shown), waffle or
    lined: 12" x 27" (18" x 45")
Swiss cotton batiste (shown) or fine cotton lawn:
    9" x 13" (12" x 18")
1 mm Cotton soutache: 10 yards (15)
1/4" Valenciennes lace edging: 3/4 yard (40")
1/4" Cotton twill tape: 7" (10")
Size "0" hooks and eyes: 4 (5)
Fine embroidery thread to match
#10 and #22 Crewel needles, 1 each

This white piqué dress with red soutache was one of the most popular dresses of the period for summer. It is seen with many pattern variations; the two other most popular versions are white piqué with either black or white soutache. The dress was not lined.

Cut one skirt front, two skirt sides, one skirt back, two sleeves, one bodice front, two bodice backs, one collar, one belt and one basque of cotton piqué. Cut one bias skirt hem facing, one bias neck facing, two sleeves, one collar, one belt and one basque of cotton batiste. Stitch the hem facing pieces so that the final measurement is 24" (31-1/2").

Soutache pattern and marking: When marking the soutache pattern, use a #1 pencil or quilt marking pencil. It's best to use a light box, but taping the design and fabric to a window also works well. The seam allowance is 1/4", but everyone stitches their seam allowances differently, so the pattern has to be adjusted as you go. If you are new to soutache patterns, you may wish to draw the entire skirt pattern on a large piece of paper first. The lowest point of the design should be 1/2"(3/4") from the bottom of the skirt. Draw the pattern for the single motif at center front and center back first. This centers the design on the dress. Then continue drawing the design on the front and side pieces, once they have been put together. You must reverse the design on the pattern sheets for the back. The flowers point away from the center front on the front of the skirt and toward the center back on the back of the garment. After you have drawn the front and sides, continue to draw the lines.

The sleeves, basque and belt are much easier; the drawing can be done at one time before or after you have cut the pieces. Directions for stitching the soutache can be found on page 25 in Chapter 1.

Skirt: With right sides together, stitch the side fronts to the front piece, and overcast. Apply the soutache pattern to these three pieces. Repeat this by stitching the back piece to the side pieces and marking. Stitch the soutache. Slit the center back down to the dot, as shown

Linette wears the 12-inch piqué dress embellished with red soutache and the Auvergnate bonnet shown on page 200. The walking stick with the dog's head was made by Alice Leverett.

on the pattern. Turn the raw edge of the opening to the wrong side 1/8" and blind stitch. Press the skirt well. With right sides together, stitch the hem facing to the bottom of the skirt from center back to center back. Turn the facing to the wrong side, turn under the raw edge 1/4", press the facing up, and blind stitch. Press the skirt well and set aside.

Bodice: Stitch the darts in the front and back pieces of the bodice, as shown on the pattern and press toward center back. Stitch the shoulder seams, overcast and press toward the back. Fold and press in center back on fold lines as shown on the pattern and blind stitch.

Stitch the soutache design on the sleeves. With right sides together, stitch the bottom edges of the sleeves and lining together. Turn to the right side and press. Baste the lining of the sleeve to the piqué at the top of the sleeve. With right sides together, stitch the sleeve into the armhole, trim and overcast. If there is any extra fullness in the sleeve, gather this into the top of the sleeve. Trim, overcast and press. With right sides together, stitch from the bottom of the bodice to the bottom of each sleeve. Trim, overcast and press. Stitch the 1/4" lace edging on straight to the bottom of each sleeve.

Stitch the soutache design on the collar. With right sides together, stitch the center back and outside edges of the collar and lining together. Turn and press. With the wrong side of the collar against the right side of the dress, stitch the collar to the dress. Turn the short ends of the neck facing to the wrong side and press. With right sides together, stitch the neck facing to the collar/bodice. Turn the facing to the wrong side, trim, turn under the raw edge seam allowance and blind stitch. Press. Stitch the same lace edging to the outside edge of the collar straight, but ease it through the corners.

With right sides together, stitch the bodice to the skirt, easing in any extra fullness in the skirt as you stitch. Press this seam up. Turn the short ends of the twill tape to the wrong side, press and stitch the tape over this seam, center back to center back. Close the bodice with three hooks and three thread eyes. The first is at the neck, the second is at the waist, and the third is halfway between them.

Basque and belt: Stitch the soutache design on the basque. With right sides together, stitch the lining to the basque on the sides and bottom. Turn to the right side and press. Edge each side and bottom with the same lace, straight,

but ease through the corners. Stitch the soutache design on the belt. Finger press the seam allowance to the wrong side and then press with an iron. Repeat with the lining. Pin the lining to the wrong side of the belt and blind stitch. Turn under the raw edge of the basque and stitch it to the belt on the wrong side, as indicated by the stars on the pattern piece. The belt is closed with a hook and thread eye. The basque rests at center back with the hook and eye slightly to the right.

Lily presents a back view of the 18-inch dress, fashioned from antique birds-eye piqué, and of the Auvergnate bonnet.

Walking her dog on a summer day, Lily is sure to carry her Huret parasol.

Summer Soutache Dress from *La Poupée Modèle*, September 1870
12-inch Doll

Bias Pieces

Neck Facing ....3/4" x 8"
Skirt Hem ....1-1/2" x 24"

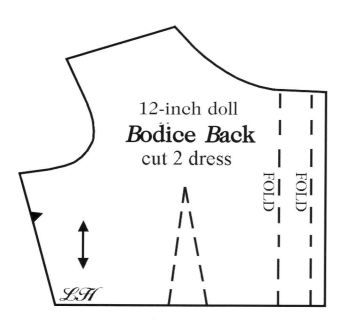

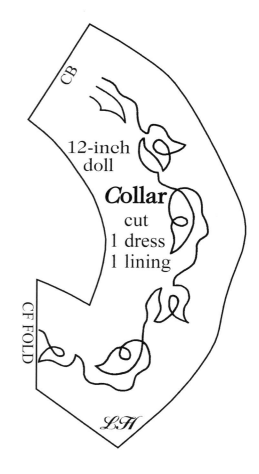

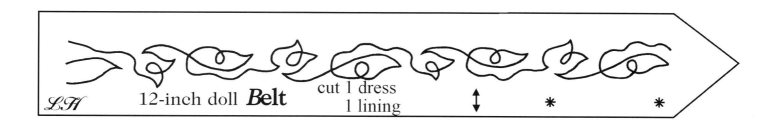

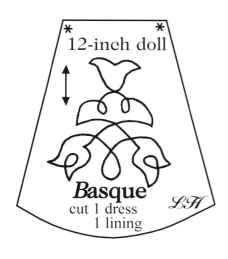

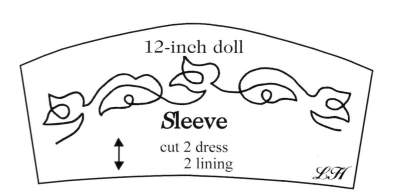

Summer Soutache Dress from *La Poupée Modèle*, September 1870 - 12-inch Doll

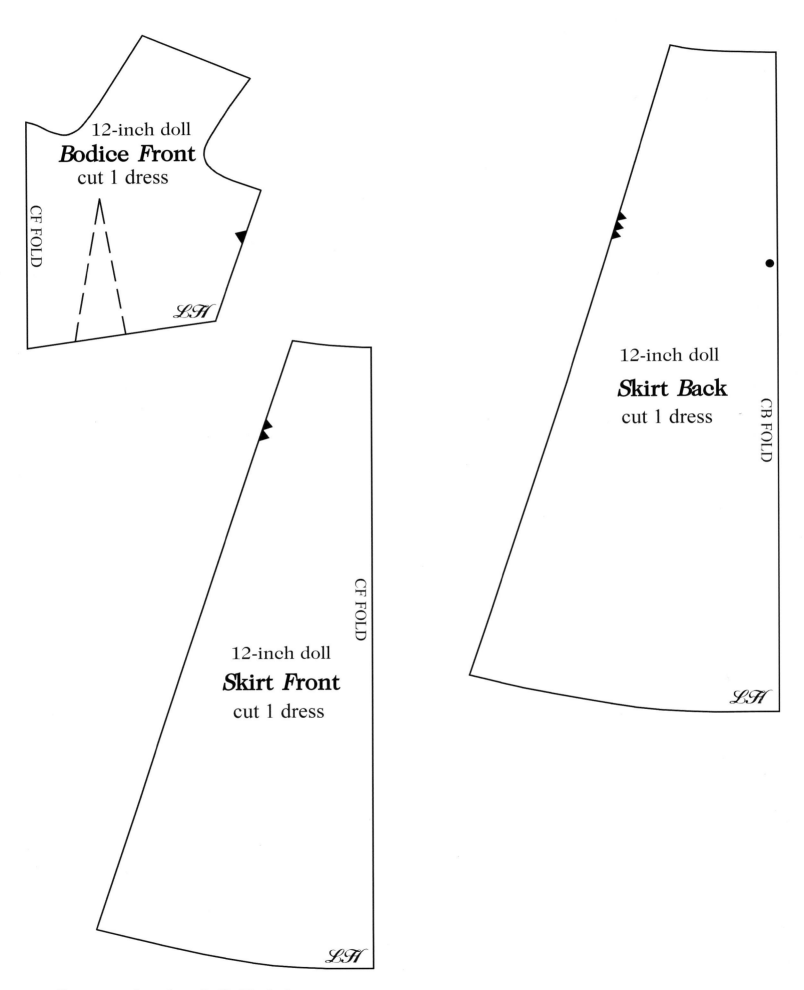

12-inch doll
Bodice Front
cut 1 dress

CF FOLD

LH

12-inch doll
Skirt Front
cut 1 dress

CF FOLD

LH

12-inch doll
Skirt Back
cut 1 dress

CB FOLD

LH

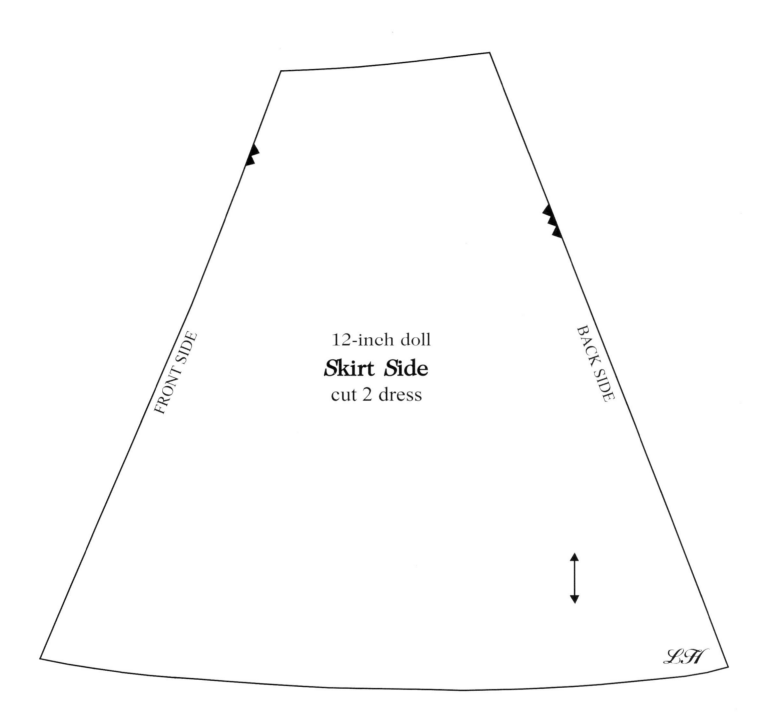

FRONT SIDE

12-inch doll

Skirt Side

cut 2 dress

BACK SIDE

LH

12-inch doll
Front Pattern

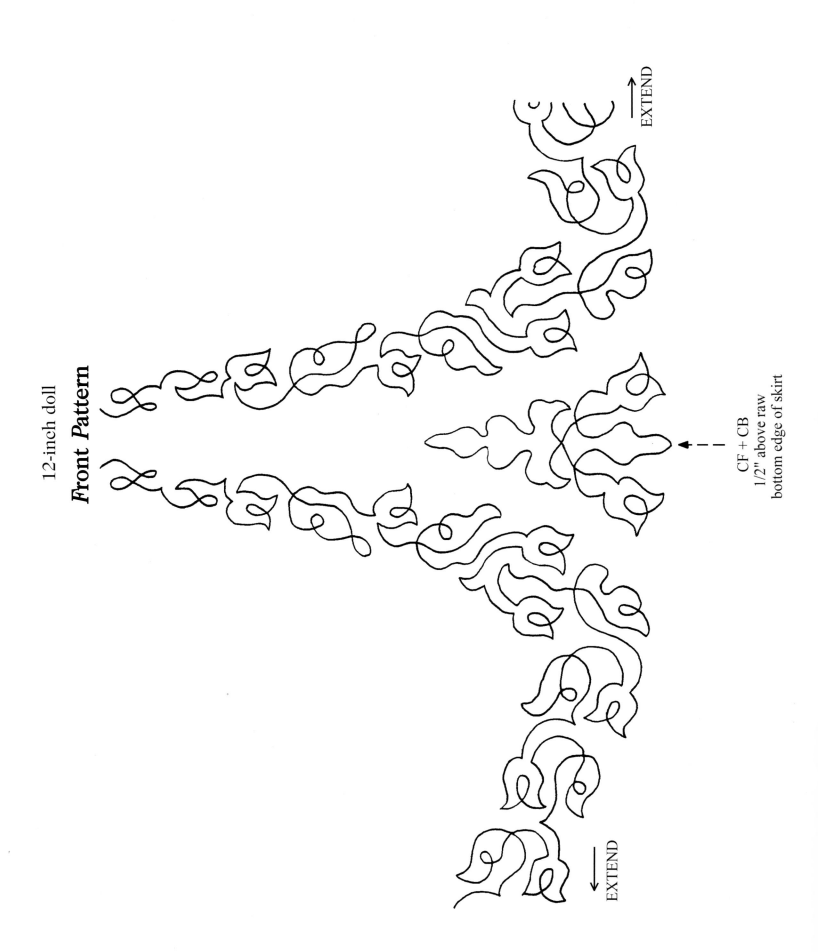

EXTEND

CF + CB
1/2" above raw
bottom edge of skirt

EXTEND

Summer Soutache Dress from *La Poupée Modèle*, September 1870
18-inch Doll

Bias Pieces

Neck Facing ....3/4" x 10-1/2"
Skirt Hem ....1-3/4" x 31-1/2"

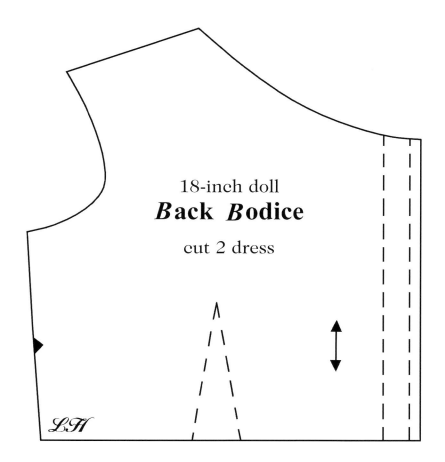

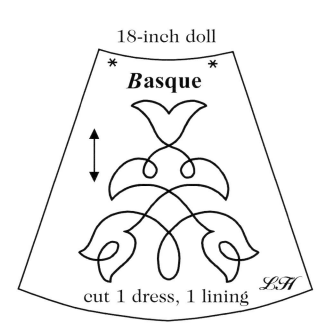

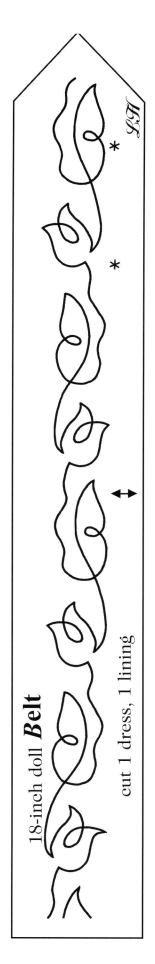

Summer Soutache Dress from *La Poupée Modèle*, September 1870 - 18-inch Doll

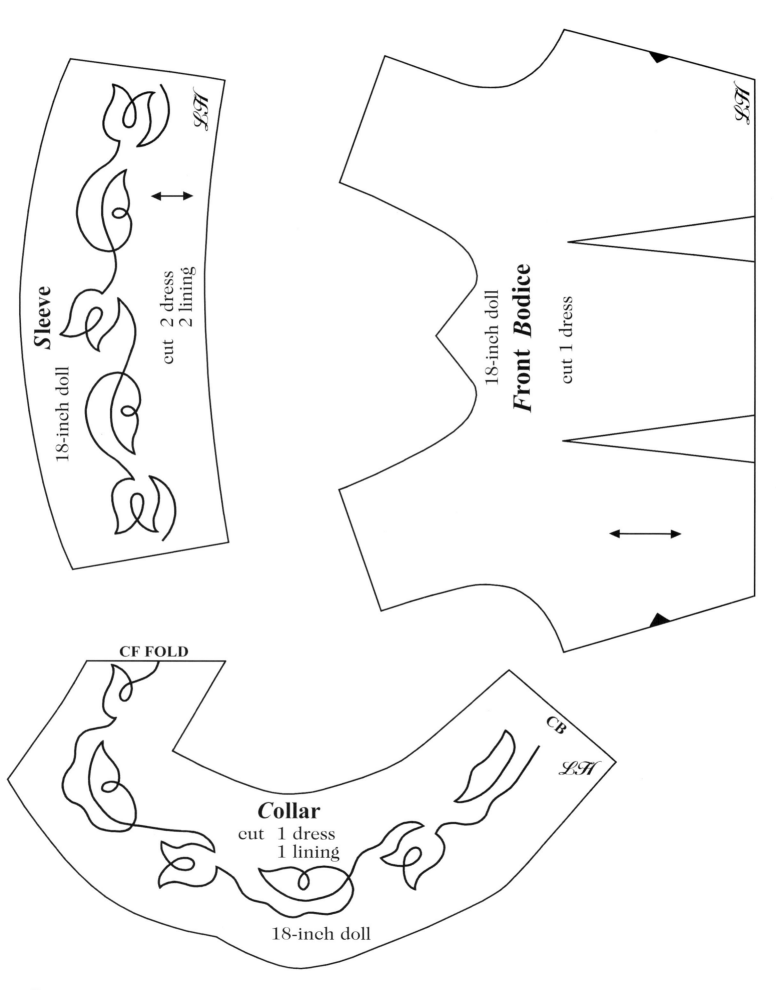

Sleeve

18-inch doll

cut 2 dress
2 lining

LH

Front Bodice

18-inch doll

cut 1 dress

LH

CF FOLD

CB

LH

Collar

cut 1 dress
1 lining

18-inch doll

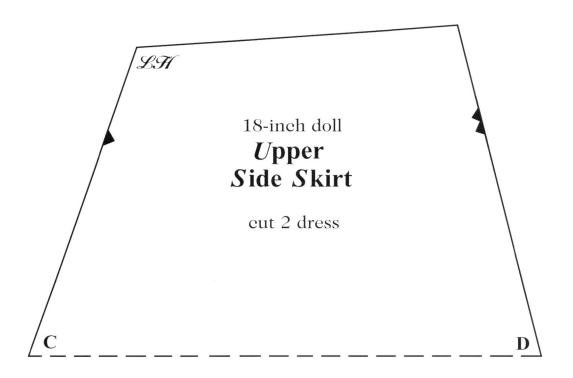

LH

18-inch doll
*Upper
Side Skirt*

cut 2 dress

C   D

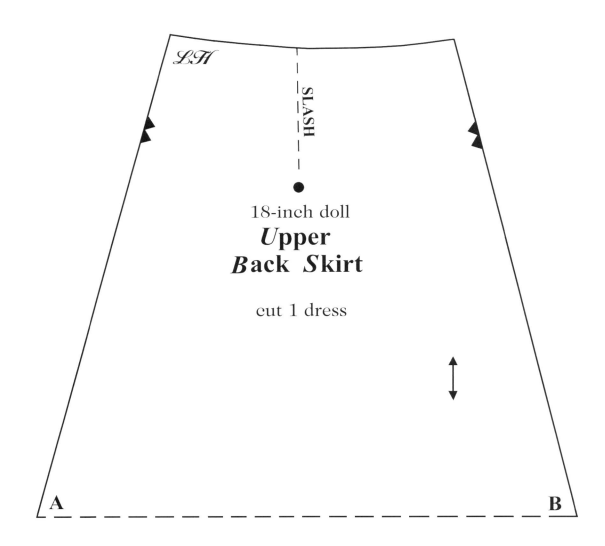

LH

SLASH

18-inch doll
*Upper
Back Skirt*

cut 1 dress

A   B

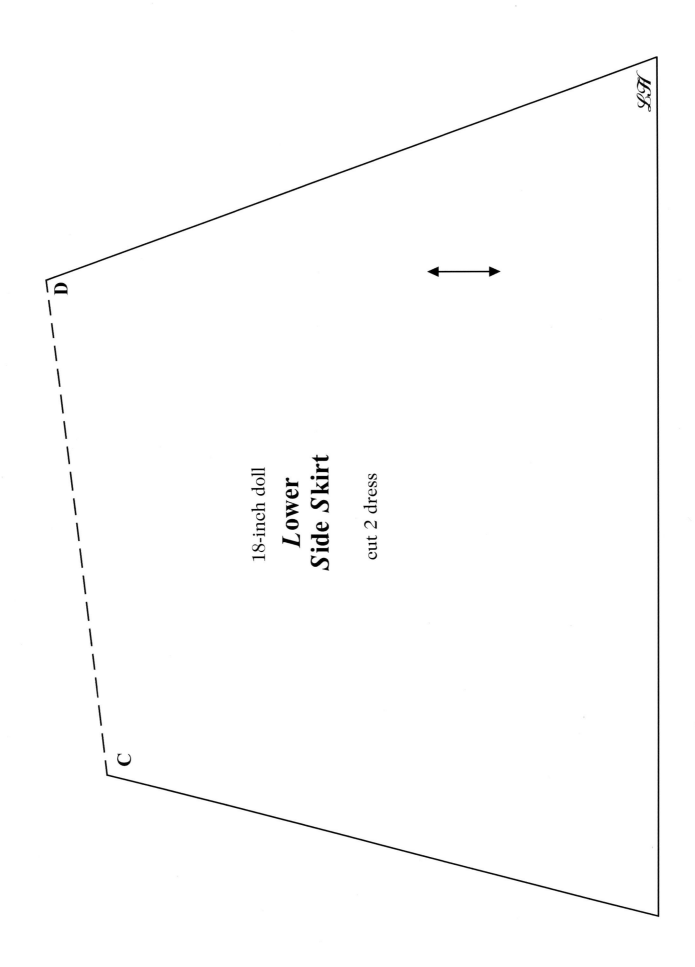

18-inch doll
Lower
Side Skirt
cut 2 dress

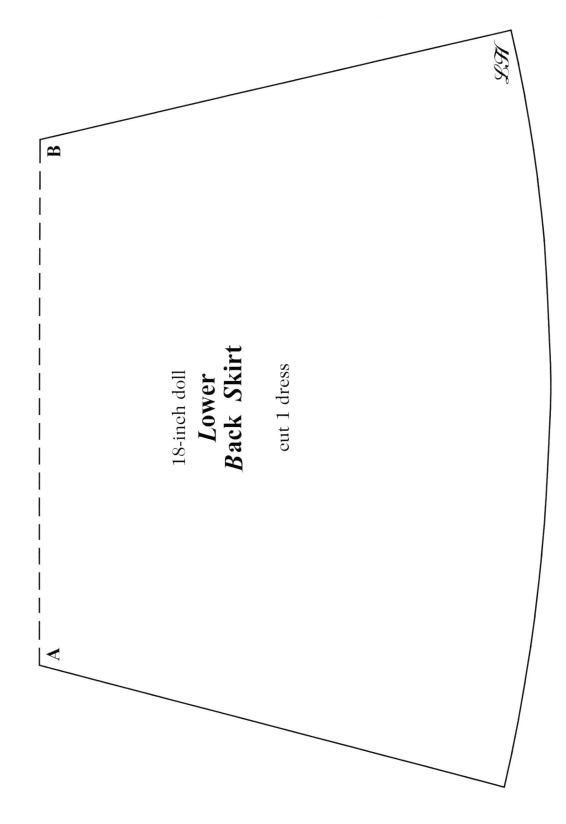

B

A

18-inch doll
Lower
Back **Skirt**

cut 1 dress

LH

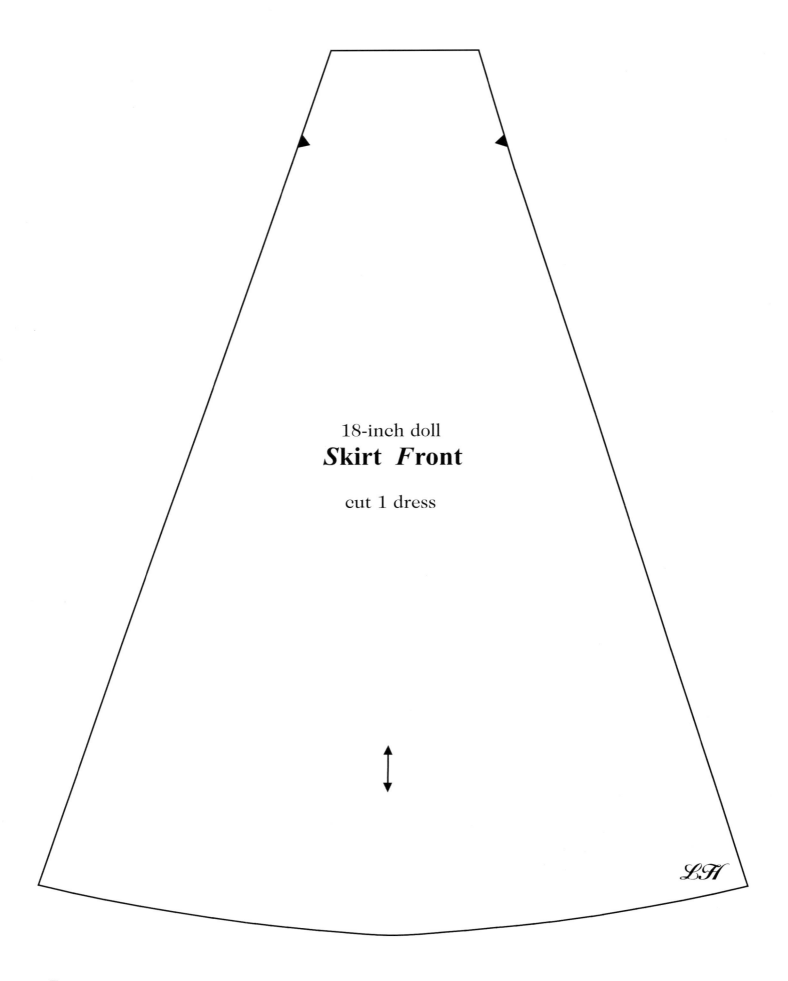

18-inch doll
Skirt Front

cut 1 dress

LH

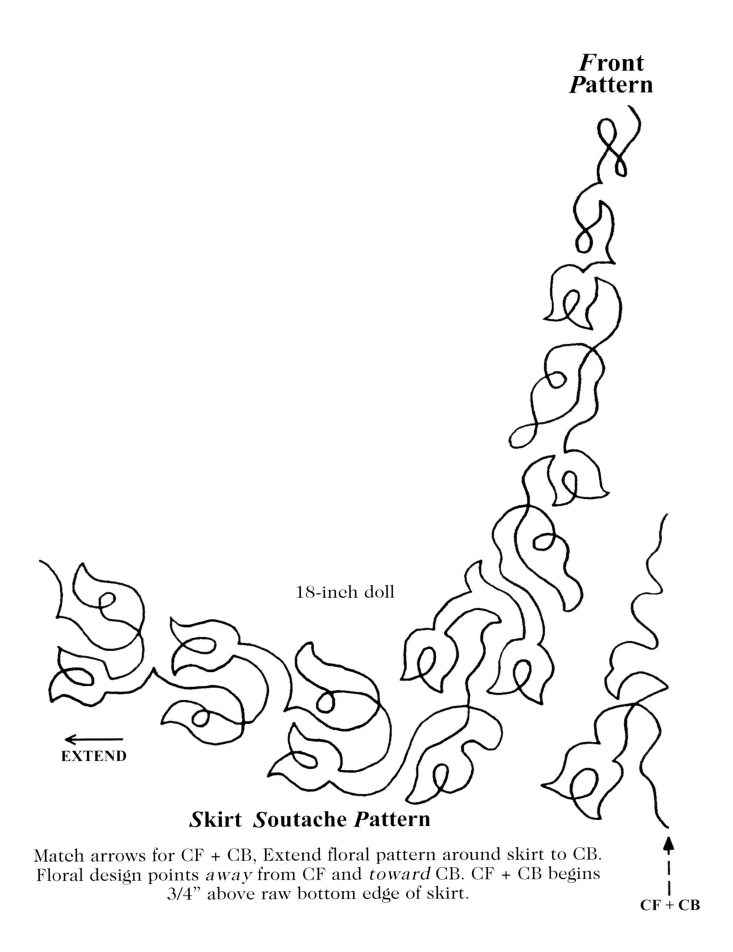

Front Pattern

18-inch doll

EXTEND

Skirt Soutache Pattern

CF + CB

Match arrows for CF + CB, Extend floral pattern around skirt to CB.
Floral design points *away* from CF and *toward* CB. CF + CB begins
3/4" above raw bottom edge of skirt.

Summer Soutache Dress from *La Poupée Modèle*, September 1870 - 18-inch Doll

**Front
Pattern**

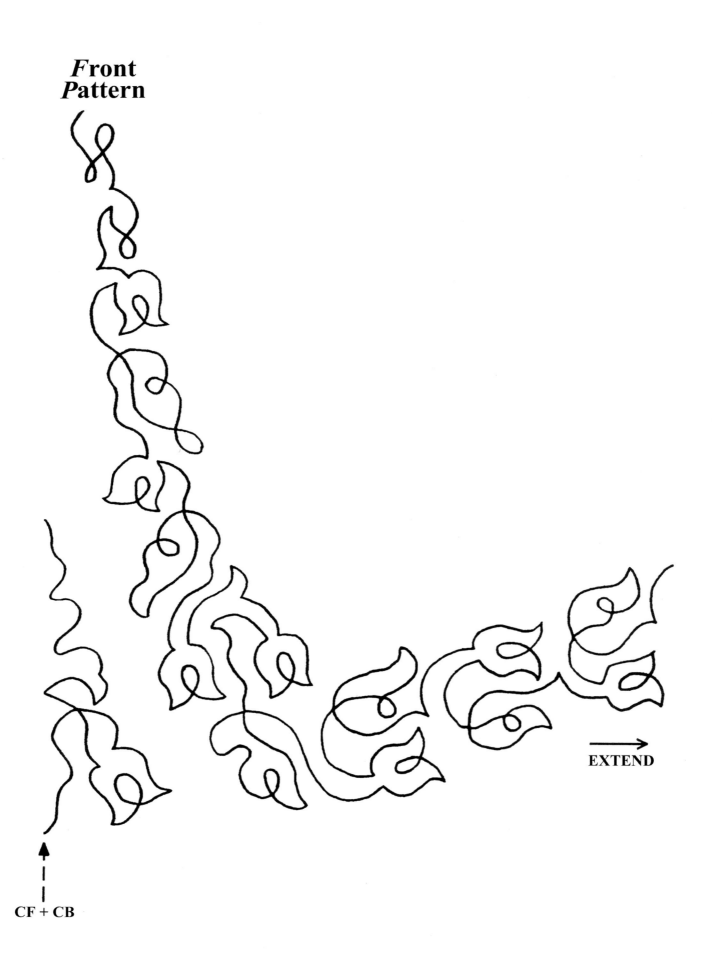

EXTEND

CF + CB

Swiss Dress and Chemisette
from La Poupée Modèle, May 1865 and March 1868

Materials

Silk taffeta (shown), cotton voile (shown): 7" x 45"
    (16" x 45")
Swiss cotton batiste for lining: 7" x 45" (9" x 12")
Silk batiste (shown), English cotton voile (shown),
    or Swiss batiste: 8" x 14" (9" x 18")
1/4" Insertion lace for chemisette: 7" (3/8": 9")
3/8" Valenciennes lace edging for chemisette: 1
    yard (1-1/4 yards)
1/8" Beading lace for chemisette: 1/2 yard (21")
2 mm Silk ribbon: 1/2 yard (21")
1/4"" Velvet ribbon: 2 yards (1/4" taffeta: 4 yards)
5/8" Taffeta ribbon: none (18")
1/2" Insertion lace for skirt: 22" (none)
1/2" Silk ribbon for skirt: 22" (none)
1/4" Cotton twill tape: 7" (10")
3/16" Mother-of-pearl buttons: 3 (4)
Size "0" Hooks and eyes: 2
Fine embroidery thread to match
#10-#12 Crewel needle

This skirt with bretelles was a great favorite of the era because of the many fabrics and trims that could be used. This was a time when many ornate braids, ribbons, fringes and other edgings were available for multiple bands. The skirt could be gathered, knife- or box-pleated. When made of a silk or heavier fabric, it was frequently lined, as on the 12-inch pattern. When made of a fine voile or other sheer silk or cotton fabrics, the skirt was unlined; the lining was used only on the waistband and bretelles. The 18-inch doll wears a skirt of antique cotton voile. Each of these two skirts has been trimmed with different combinations of lace and ribbon. Directions are given for a 12-inch doll's dress that is lined and for an 18-inch doll's dress that is unlined. The skirt is designed to be cut from one piece of fabric, and then adjusted so that the back of the skirt is longer than the front. This is to accommodate the fullness of the petticoats and hoop so that the skirt hangs evenly in the back. Instructions for this are given on page 24 in Chapter 1.

Skirt: Cut one skirt 7-1/2" x 22" (12" x 45"), two bretelles and a waistband of the skirt fabric. Cut one skirt 6-3/4" x

22" (none), two bretelles and a waistband of lining fabric. Place the wrong side of the skirt fabric against the wrong side of the lining fabric, with top edges even, and treat as one. See page 24 in Chapter 1 for instructions on how to cut the skirt/lining so that it is longer in the back than it is in the front. Stitch the center back seam, leaving open 2-1/2" (3") at the top. Trim, overcast and press the seam open. Turn under and blind stitch the opening. Turn up the hem 1/4" (3/4"), press, turn up again 1/2" (1") and press again. Blind stitch the hem. At this point, the skirt measures 6-1/4" (9-1/2") at center front. Turn the entire top edge under 1/4" (1/2") and press to sharp edge.

To embellish the 12-inch skirt: Measure up from the bottom edge 1-1/2" and stitch the 1/2" insertion lace from center back to center back. This lace has been backed with a 1/2" silk ribbon. This is called "creating a transparency of lace." Stitch this on both the top and bottom edges. On either side of the insertion lace stitch a row of 1/4" velvet ribbon on both the top and bottom edges.

To embellish the 18-inch skirt: Measure up from the bottom edge 1" and stitch the 1/4" ribbon from center back to center back. Measure up 1/2" and stitch another band. There is 1/4" between the two rows.

To pleat the 12-inch skirt: This skirt has a total of five box pleats. The center front, 1-1/2", is straight and there is a box pleat at the center back. Find the center front and measure 3/4" to either side. Fold the first box pleat here, and repeat at center back. The pleats will overlap completely. Place another pleat on either side halfway between the front and back pleats. The skirt top should measure 5-1/2". Adjust if necessary. Baste across the top edge.

To pleat the 18-inch skirt: This skirt has a total of five box pleats. Measure 1" on either side of center and make the first double pleat. Make a double pleat at the center back on either side of the opening. Make another pleat on each side, measuring the fabric first to allow an equal amount for both pleats. The depth of each pleat is about one inch. Adjustments will be necessary to get the skirt to fit the curved waistband. Some of the pleats will overlap. When the pleats have been pinned, baste across the top of the waistband.

Waistband: With right sides together, stitch the top edge and the two short ends of the waistband and the lining. Turn and press to a sharp edge. Stitch the velvet (taffeta)

Linette wears the 12-inch Swiss
dress of antique striped silk
taffeta. The skirt has a band of
antique insertion lace edged with
antique velvet ribbon, which is
repeated on the bretelles.

ribbon to the top edge. Stitch one row across the top edge of the ribbon with a running stitch. Stitch the 1/4" twill tape over the bottom raw edge of the waistband overlapping 1/8". Press this to the wrong side with 1/8" of the dress fabric showing on the wrong side. Beginning at the center front, stitch the skirt to the waistband, stitching through all pleat layers. Repeat with the other side. The needle should go through the very bottom of the tape, as in cartridge pleating. Remove basting stitches. Press seam up and trim. Stitch another row of velvet (taffeta) ribbon over the bottom of the waistband.

Bretelles: With right sides together, stitch both of the long edges of the bretelles to the lining. Turn to the right side and press to a sharp edge. Stitch the velvet (taffeta) ribbon on both of the long edges with a running stitch. Place the skirt on the doll, over the underwear, and pin the bretelles in place. The bottom of the waistband should be at the doll's waist. The bretelles should overlap the waistband by about 1/2". Blind stitch them to the waistband on both short ends. Tie two bows of velvet (taffeta) ribbon and stitch to the shoulder of the bretelles.

Close the skirt with two hooks and eyes. Stitch them at the top and bottom of the waistband so that the waistband

meets, but does not overlap. The eyes should extend about 1/8" beyond the fabric and the hooks should be about 1/8" inside the band. The finished length of the dress from the front shoulder is 8-5/8" (13-1/2")

Chemisette: Cut the fronts and backs as straight pieces, embellished with lace and tucks, and then cut them with the pattern pieces. Cut two sleeves, one waistband 1" x 6-1/4" (1" x 9"), two cuffs 1" x 2-7/8" (1" x 3-1/4"), two shoulder pieces, one front piece 3" x 4-1/2" (4" x 9") and two back pieces 3" x 3-1/2" (4" x 9"). Prepare the fronts and backs as follows.

Fronts: There are nine tucks and two insertion lace pieces on the front. Fold the fabric to find the center front. Stitch 1/16" (1/8") tuck down the center front. Measure 3/16" (1/4") on either side and stitch two more 1/16" (1/8") tucks. Measure over 1/4" on either side and stitch 1/4" (3/8") insertion lace from top to bottom. Measure over 1/8" (1/4") and stitch a set of three tucks to the left and right of the insertion lace. Press the tucks away from the center front and cut out the front pattern piece using this prepared piece.

Backs: *For the 12-inch doll:* Fold in the center backs as shown on the fold lines, and press. Measure 3/8" in from

This antique ivory chemisette features the 1/16" tucks, matching antique insertion and lace edging with a tiny beading strung with silk ribbon.

the folded edge and stitch a 1/16" tuck. Measure 3/16" over for the second tuck, and 3/16" for the third. *For the 18-inch doll:* Fold in the center backs as shown on the fold lines and press. Measure 3/8" in from the folded edge and stitch a 1/8" tuck. Measure 1/4" over for the second tuck. Repeat until you have stitched five tucks. *For both sizes:* stitch the second back, reversing the fold and the tucks. Press the tucks towards center back. Stitch the second back, reversing the fold and the tucks. Press the tucks toward the center back.

Cut out two backs from the back pattern piece. Blind stitch the center back folds. French seam the shoulder pieces, with front and back matching c-d and e-f. Gather the top of the sleeves to fit the armhole. With right sides together, stitch the sleeve into the armhole, trim and overcast. Gather the bottom of the sleeve to fit the cuff. With right sides together, stitch the cuff to the sleeve.

Turn the cuff to the wrong side, turn under the raw edge and blind stitch. With right sides together, French seam from the bottom of the blouse to the bottom of the sleeve.

Turn under the short ends of the waistband 1/4" on each end and press. With right sides together, stitch the waistband to the blouse, easing in any extra fullness. Turn the waistband to the wrong side, turn under the raw edge, and blind stitch. Cut two pieces of lace edging 4" (5"), and gather to fit the cuff. Stitch on two rows, butting the headings together in the middle of the cuff. Cut two pieces of 1/8" insertion lace strung with 2 mm ribbon 2-1/2" (4") and stitch them over these headings. Repeat with the other cuff. Cut two pieces of lace edging 9" (12") each. Turn the neck edge 1/8" to the right side, gather the lace to fit this edge and apply these two pieces as you did the cuffs. Stitch the insertion/ribbon over these headings. The finished length of the chemisette measured from the front shoulder is 3-1/4" (3-5/8").

Attired in a Swiss dress of sheer antique cotton muslin patterned with small blue flowers, the 18-inch Huret prepares for tea with friends. Bands of matching antique silk taffeta trim the skirt and bretelles.

Swiss Dress and Chemisette
from *La Poupée Modèle*, May 1865 and March 1868
12-inch Doll

Straight Pieces

Dress Skirt ....7-1/2" x 22"
Dress Skirt Lining...............................6-3/4" x 22"
Chemisette Waistband..........................1" x 6-1/4"
Chemisette Cuffs ....2 (1" x 2-7/8")

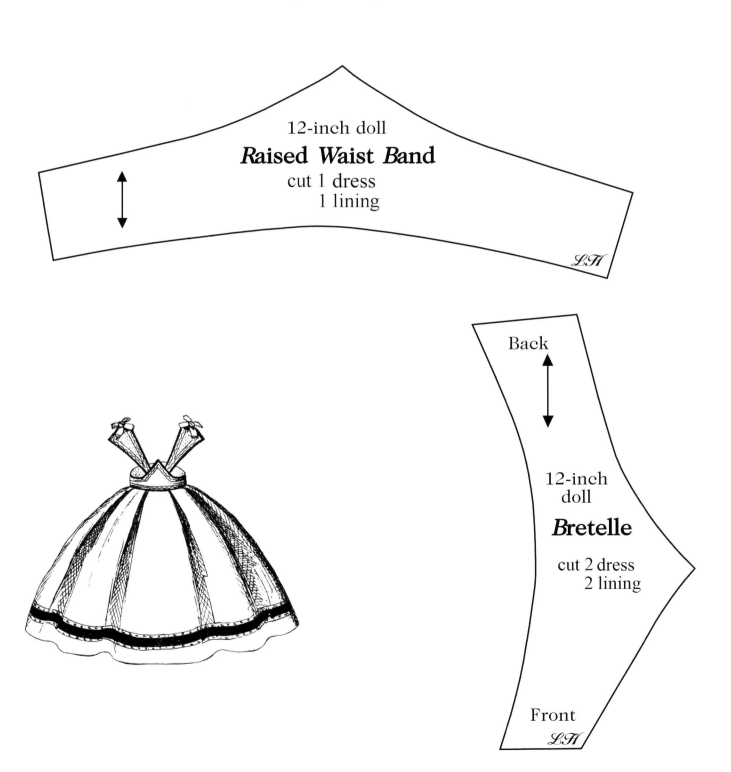

12-inch doll
Raised Waist Band
cut 1 dress
1 lining

LH

Back

12-inch
doll

Bretelle

cut 2 dress
2 lining

Front
LH

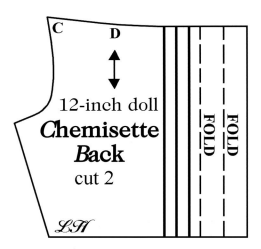

C   D

12-inch doll
**Chemisette
Back**
cut 2

FOLD
FOLD
FOLD

LH

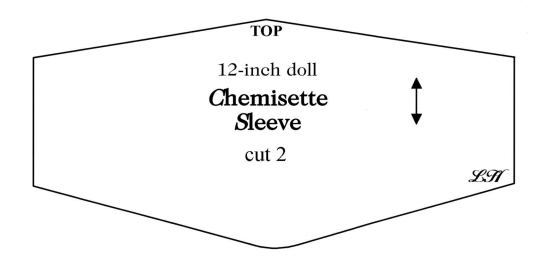

TOP

12-inch doll
**Chemisette
Sleeve**

cut 2

LH

12-inch doll

C   D

**Shoulder
Piece**
cut 2

E   F

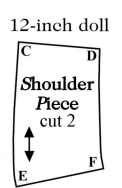

12-inch doll

E F   F E

Front
cut 1

INSERTION

INSERTION

LH

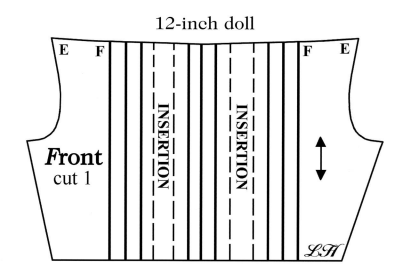

Swiss Dress and Chemisette
from *La Poupée Modèle*, May 1865 and March 1868
18-inch Doll

Straight Pieces

Skirt	12" x 45"
Skirt Lining	10-1/4" x 45"
2 Cuffs Chemisette	1" x 3-1/4"
Waistband Chemisette	1" x 9"

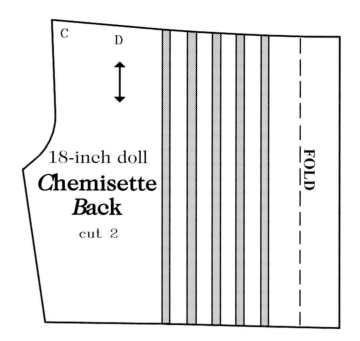

18-inch doll
Chemisette Back
cut 2

C D

FOLD

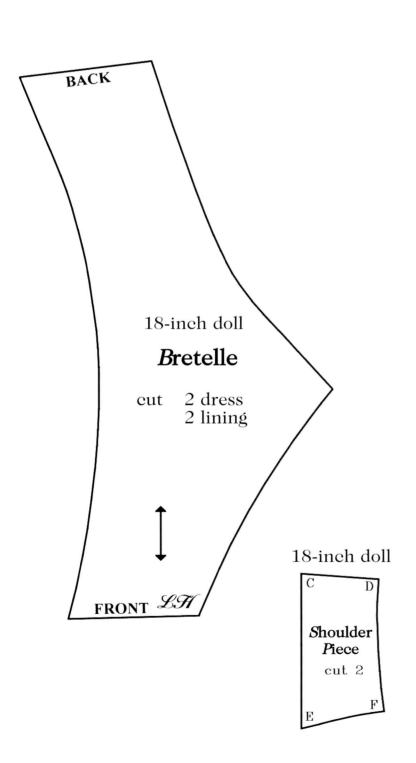

BACK

18-inch doll
Bretelle

cut   2 dress
      2 lining

FRONT *LH*

18-inch doll
Shoulder Piece
cut 2

C D

E F

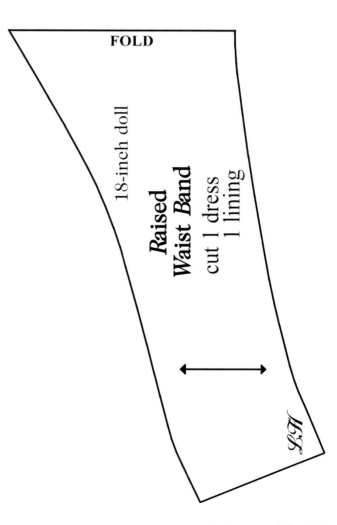

FOLD

18-inch doll
Raised Waist Band
cut 1 dress
1 lining

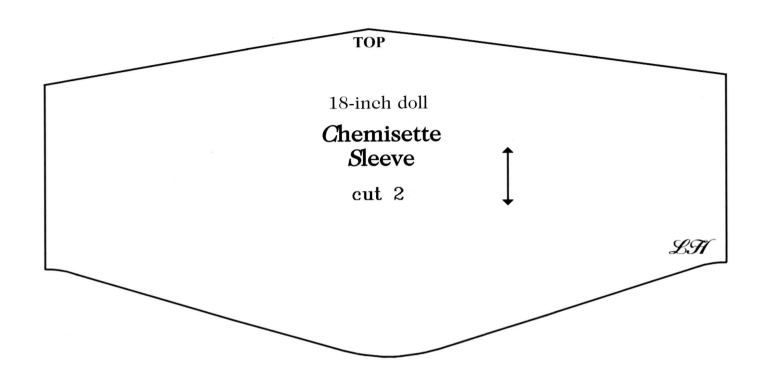

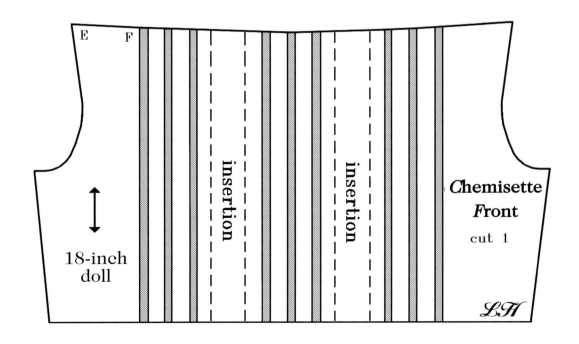

Summer Dress from La Poupée Modèle, *August 1866*

This summer dress can be made from a variety of fabrics. It is lined except when using sheer silks or voile. The sleeves are not lined in either of the examples. The 18-inch doll wears an antique striped fabric; the 12-inch doll wears a faithful reproduction of the same fabric. Before the reproduction was made, the pattern of the fabric was reduced 50 percent so that both the vertical and horizontal stripes would be in proper scale for the 12-inch doll. This dress can be worn alone, with the neckline outlining the shoulder plate of the doll or, as shown, with a sleeveless chemisette to fill in the neckline. A French fashion doll should have at least one silk chemisette in her wardrobe!

Cut one skirt 7-3/4" x 27" (12" x 38-1/2"), one front bodice, two back bodices, two sleeves, one collar front, two collar backs, two cuffs and a bias neck facing 3/4" x 9" (3/4" x 13"). From the lining fabric, cut one skirt 7" x 27" (10-3/4" x 38-1/2"), one front bodice, two back bodices, one collar front and two collar backs.

Skirt: Place the wrong side of the linings against the wrong side of the dress fabric and treat as one piece. Take the skirt pieces, and with the top edges even, shape the skirt as described on page 24 in Chapter 1. With right sides together, stitch the center back seam, leaving the top edge open 2-1/2" (3"); trim and overcast. Turn under that seam allowance and narrow hem. Turn the bottom edge of the skirt under 1/8" (1/4") and press. Turn under again 1/2" (1") and press. Blind stitch this hem. Beginning at center back, stitch three (four) rows of 1/16" (1/4") ribbon around the skirt. The first row is 1/2" (1") up from the bottom hemmed edge and each row after that has a 3/16" (1/4") space before the next one. This should be stitched with a running stitch, one stitching row per ribbon, at the very top edge of the ribbon. Turn the top edge of the skirt to the wrong side 1/4" (1/2") and press.

To pleat the skirt: Find the center front and measure 3/4" (7/8") on either side. Fold 4 (6) pleats, each one measuring 5/8" (1"), pleating away from center front on each side. This will form a box pleat at the center back opening. Adjust the pleats so that they measure 6-1/4" (9") at the top edge. Baste these pleats across the top edge.

Bodice: Place the wrong sides of the three bodice pieces for the dress and lining together. With right sides together, stitch the shoulder seams, trim, press towards the back and overcast. Stitch two rows of gathering stitches at the top of each sleeve and pull up to fit the armholes. With right sides together, stitch the sleeves into the armholes, trim and overcast. As you stitch, allow most of the fullness of the sleeve to be at the top of the sleeve. Gather the bottom of the sleeves to fit the cuffs. With right sides together, stitch the cuffs to the bottom of the sleeves. Turn the cuff to the wrong side, turn the raw edge under and blind stitch. The finished cuff should measure 1/4" (1/2"). With right sides together, stitch from the bottom of the bodice to the bottom of the sleeve, trim and overcast. Turn the short ends of the 3/8" twill tape to the wrong side 1/4" on each end and stitch the tape to the bottom of the bodice, overlapping the taffeta 1/8". Turn the tape to the inside of the bodice so that 1/8" of the dress fabric is showing on the wrong side and press. Stitch the top of the tape to the inside of the bodice through the lining. Stitch the top of the skirt to the bottom of the twill tape, piercing the top edge of the skirt with the needle, then going into the twill tape at the very bottom. Stitch two rows of 1/16" grosgrain ribbon (1/4" velvet) around the waist: the first at the bottom of the bodice, the second 1/4" (3/8") above. Stitch two rows of 1/16" grosgrain (1/4" velvet) ribbon on the cuffs: one at the bottom of the cuff, the second at the top.

Collar: With right sides together, stitch the front collar of the dress fabric to the backs, and press toward the back. Repeat with the linings. With right sides together, stitch the collar to the collar lining down the center back and across the entire outside edge. Trim, turn to the right side

Lily wears a summer dress of antique silk taffeta. The vertical black stripes are woven into the fabric. Matching velvet bands the skirt, bodice and sleeves. The modest neckline features a chemisette of antique silk gauze.

and press. Stitch two (three) rows of 1/16" grosgrain (1/4" velvet) ribbon on the collar, the first at the outer edge, next (rest) spaced 1/8" apart. With the lining of the collar against the right side of the dress, baste the collar to the dress. Turn the short ends of the bias collar facing 1/4" to the wrong side. With right sides together, stitch the facing, collar and dress together. Turn the facing to the wrong side, turn under the seam allowance and blind stitch. Close the back with three hooks and thread eyes. The first is at the top of the dress, the second is at the waist and the third is at the bottom of the collar. Stitch the thread eyes opposite the hooks. The finished dress measures 8-3/8" (13-1/2") from the front shoulder.

Chemisette: Cut one back, two fronts, two collars and one bias neck facing 3/4" x 4-1/4" (3/4" x 5-1/2"). Fold under twice, following the lines on the pattern of the center front, press and blind stitch. French seam the shoulder seams. Narrow hem the sides of the front/back. With right sides together, stitch the two short ends of the collar and the outside edge with a 1/8" seam. Carefully trim this seam to 1/16". Turn to the right side and press. Whip on the 1/8" (1/4") lace to these stitched edges straight. Pin the collar to the neck and stitch with a basting stitch. Turn under the short ends of the bias facing 1/4" each to the wrong side, and press. With right sides together, stitch the bias facing to the neck. Turn the facing to the wrong side, turn under the seam allowance and blind stitch. Close the neck of the chemisette with a mother-of-pearl button on one side and a worked button hole on the other. Turn the bottom edges of the fronts and back up 1/8" and press. Turn them up again 1/4" and press. Stitch this casing with a running stitch. Cut the 1/8" (1/4") twill tape in half. String one piece through the fronts and the second through the back. Tie the twill tape in a bow on each side of the doll's waist.

Linette wears a faithful reproduction silk taffeta fabric of the same material featured on the opposite page. The striped pattern has been reduced to the proper scale for her 12-inch size.

Summer Dress
from *La Poupée Modèle*, August 1866
12-inch Doll

Straight Pieces

Dress Skirt..7-3/4" x 27"

Dress Lining..7" x 27"

Sleeve Cuff...2 (1" x 2-3/4")

Bias Pieces

Dress Neck Facing ....3/4" x 9"

Chemisette Neck Facing....................3/4" x 4-1/4"

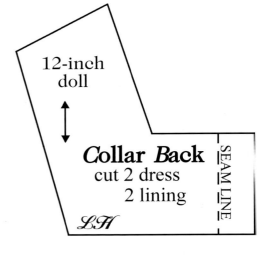

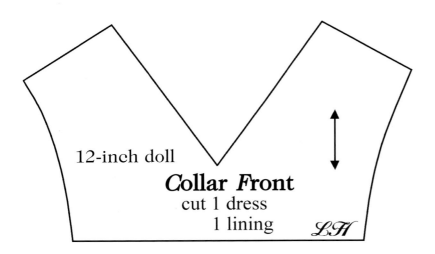

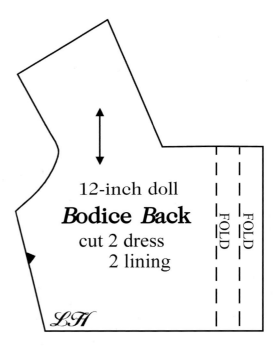

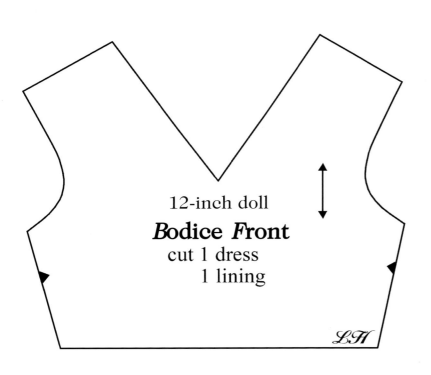

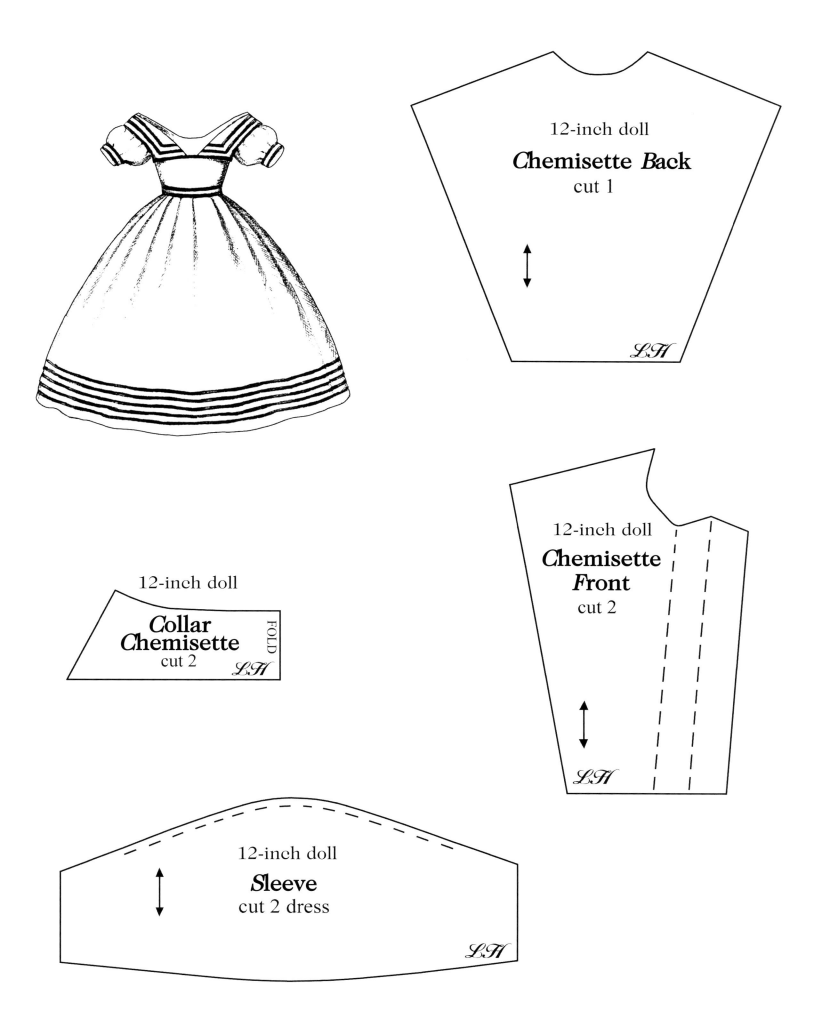

12-inch doll

Chemisette Back
cut 1

LH

12-inch doll

Chemisette Front
cut 2

LH

12-inch doll

Collar Chemisette
cut 2 *LH*

FOLD

12-inch doll

Sleeve
cut 2 dress

LH

Summer Dress
from *La Poupée Modèle*, August 1866
18-inch Doll

Straight Pieces

Dress Skirt ....12" x 38-1/2"
Dress Lining ....10-3/4" x 38-1/2"
Sleeve Cuff....................................2 (1-3/4" x 4")

Bias Pieces

Dress Neck Facing ....3/4" x 13"
Chemisette Neck Facing...................3/4" x 5-1/2"

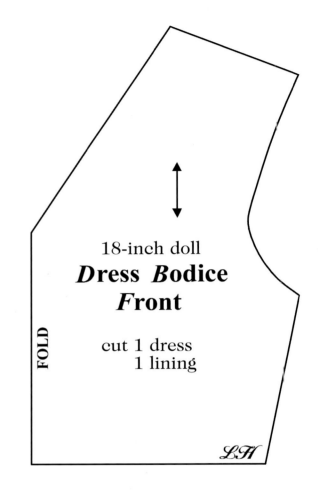

18-inch doll
Dress Bodice Front

cut 1 dress
1 lining

FOLD

LH

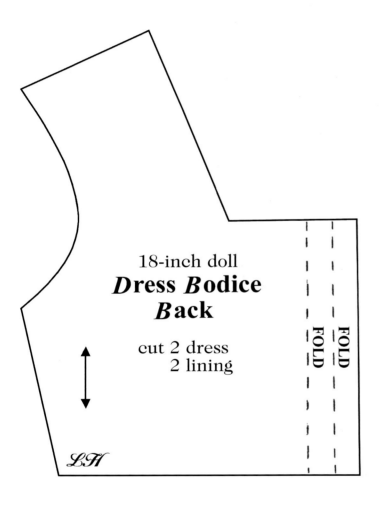

18-inch doll
Dress Bodice Back

cut 2 dress
2 lining

FOLD FOLD FOLD

LH

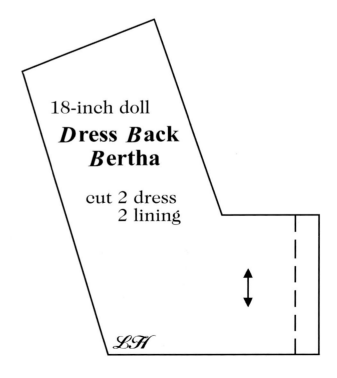

18-inch doll
Dress Back Bertha

cut 2 dress
2 lining

LH

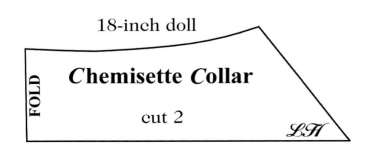

18-inch doll

FOLD

Chemisette Collar

cut 2

LH

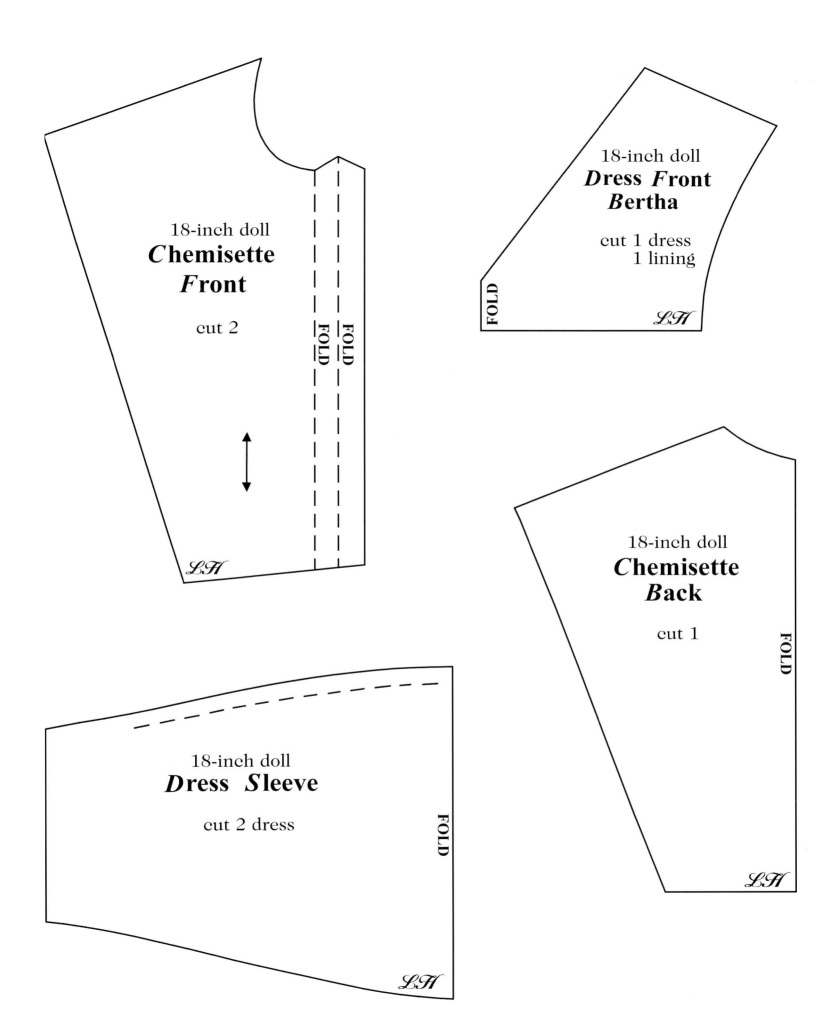

18-inch doll
Chemisette
Front

cut 2

FOLD
FOLD
FOLD

𝓛𝓗

18-inch doll
Dress Front
Bertha

cut 1 dress
1 lining

FOLD

𝓛𝓗

18-inch doll
Chemisette
Back

cut 1

FOLD

𝓛𝓗

18-inch doll
Dress Sleeve

cut 2 dress

FOLD

𝓛𝓗

Polonaise Dress from La Poupée Modèle, *October 1868*

T his dress, called the "Camargo" in the October 1868 issue of *La Poupée Modèle,* was "reminiscent of the costumes and panniers that were worn a long time ago," wrote Mlle Péronne in the directions in that issue of the magazine. The illustration shows matching fabrics for the polonaise and skirt, however, the samples are contrasting. The illustration also shows bias-cut pleated edging for both pieces, which is duplicated on both dresses pictured here. However, fringe and other trimmings would also be very effective.

Preparation of pleating: Cut 1" (1-1/2") strips on a true bias for the pleating. The dress for the 18-inch pattern shows them with a tiny hand-stitched hem; the 12-inch pattern's pleating has a wave cut from a hand-cranked antique cutting machine. Scallop or pinking scissors could also be used. The 12-inch pattern requires 3-3/4 yards; the 18-inch pattern requires 5 yards. The 18–inch pattern requires an additional 58" of 3/4" bias strips, to be stitched on as a heading for the pleats. Using a commercial pleater, prepare 15" (22") of pleating for the polonaise and 24" (36") of pleating for the skirt. Folding to the wrong side 1/4", press the strips for the heading under 1/4"; press the other raw edge under 1/4". Press the strips well and trim the raw edges to 1/8". You need 22" for the polonaise and 36" for the skirt. Set these aside.

Materials

Silk taffeta (shown) or fine wool for polonaise:
   8" x 45" (24" x 45")
Silk taffeta (shown) or fine wool for skirt: 8" x 30"
   (12" x 45")
Silk taffeta or other silk for pleating: 12" x 45"
Cotton batiste for lining: 16" x 45" (45" x 45")
Iron-on pellon for belt lining: 3/4" x 7"
   (1-1/4" x 10")
1/4" Valenciennes lace: 3/4 yard (1/2": 1 yard)
1/8" - 1/4" Grosgrain ribbon: 1-1/4 yards
1 mm Cotton cord: 9" (10")
3/8" Cotton twill tape: 4"
1/8" - 3/16" buttons: 6 (9)
Size "0" hooks and eyes: 7 (8)
Fine embroidery thread to match
#10-#12 Crewel needle

Skirt: For the 18-inch pattern, cut a 9" x 36" piece of lining and cut strips for the bias hem. You will need strips 2" wide and 37" long. Cut one front, two backs and one waistband 1" x 5-1/2" (1-1/4" x 9"). Cut one front and one back of lining fabric. Place the wrong sides of the lining against the wrong sides of the skirt fabric and treat as one piece. With right sides together, stitch the center back seam, leaving open 2-1/2" (3") at the top. Narrow hem this opening. With right sides together, stitch the side seams, overcast, and press towards the back. *Pleating the skirt:* Leave the front piece of the skirt straight. Beginning with each side seam, make three pleats about 5/8" (1") on each side, pleating toward the center back. This will result in a box pleat at the center back opening. Adjust until the top of the skirt measures 5" (8-1/2"). Baste the top of the skirt.

Turn the short ends of the waistband under 1/4" on each side and press. With right sides together, stitch the waistband to the skirt. Turn the raw edge to the wrong side, turn under this edge and blind stitch. Press the skirt. The pleats are not pressed in, but left to fall in soft folds.

For the 18-inch pattern, stitch the bias facing to the bottom of the skirt. With right sides together, stitch a 1/8" seam from center back to center back. Press up the bias to the wrong side. Turn the raw edge under 1/4", press again and blind hem. *For the 12-inch pattern,* turn up the hem of the skirt 1/4" and press. Turn up again 3/4" and press. Blind stitch this hem. Close the skirt with a hook and thread eye. Stitch the pleating at the bottom of the skirt so that it extends about 1/16" longer than the bottom edge from center back to center back. *For the 18-inch pattern,* stitch the bias fabric over the raw edge. *For the 12-inch pattern,* trim the raw edge of the pleating to 1/8" from the stitching. Stitch the 1/8" - 1/4" grosgrain ribbon over this raw edge. The finished length of the skirt is 6" (9") measured from center front.

Polonaise: Cut two fronts, two sides, one upper back, one lower back, two front facings 1" x 6-5/8" (1" x 10"), two upper sleeves, two lower sleeves, one neck facing on the bias 3/4" x 4-1/2" (3/4" x 5-1/2") and one belt 1" x 6-1/4" (1" x 10-1/4"). Cut two fronts, two sides, one upper back, one lower back, two upper sleeves and two lower sleeves for the lining. Cut one piece of iron-on pellon 1" x 6" (1" x 10-1/4"), and iron to the wrong side of the belt. Place the wrong sides of the fabric and lining together and treat as one piece. Mark the darts on both fronts, stitch and press toward the back. With right sides together, stitch the shoulder seams, overcast and press toward center back.

With right sides together, stitch the silk facings to the front edge. Press to the wrong side, turn under 1/4", press again and blind stitch. Narrow hem the bottom edge of the front pieces and hem up the sides 2-3/4" (4"). Whip on 1/4" (1/2") lace edging across the bottom and up the sides where it is hemmed. Stitch this lace on straight with the heading on the wrong side. Ease around the corners so that the lace lies straight.

With a small running stitch, stitch the 1/4" twill tape to the bottom of the upper back, overlapping the bottom edge of the fabric 1/8". Press up so that 1/8" of the taffeta is on the wrong side. Blind stitch the top of the tape to the lining of the upper back, taking care that the stitching does not show on the right side.

Turn the upper edge of the lower back/lining to the wrong side 1/4" (1/2") and press to a sharp edge. Cartridge pleat this edge as described on page 24 in Chapter 1.

With right sides together, stitch the sides to the back,

press to the back, trim and overcast. Narrow hem the bottom of the sides/back. Finish the sides and back of this polonaise with pleating and edging as shown on the skirt. Following the pleat lines on the pattern piece, fold in the three pleats on the side pieces. With right sides together, stitch the sides to the front, press to the back, trim and overcast.

Sleeves: See page 24 in Chapter 1 for construction of the sleeves. After stitching is complete, edge the bottom of each sleeve with the same lace. Stitch the lace straight with the heading of the lace even with the bottom of the sleeve. Stitch two rows of gathering stitches at the top of the sleeves to curve, not to gather. With right sides together, stitch the sleeve into the armhole of the bodice. The higher part of the sleeve is in the back. The underarm seam is even with the front/side seam; the top seam of the sleeve is even with the shoulder seam. Cut two pieces of lace edging 4" each, gather to 2" and stitch to the top of the sleeve.

Linette's fashionable 12-inch polonaise dress features a stripe over a solid green skirt. Note the antique buttons of silver and jade.

A profile view of Lily in the 18-inch polonaise dress shows the fullness gravitating towards the back.

Lily wears an 18-inch polonaise dress of antique shot-silk taffeta stripe and solid green with matching pleats cut on the bias. The buttons are self-covered fabric. Her skirt features the flat a-line front with the fullness gravitating toward the back. Her antique chain metal purse displays a tiny clock.

Take bias neck facing and 1 mm cord, and make fine piping. After stitching, trim the seam so that it measures 1/4" from the stitching to the raw edge. Leave the balance of the cording extending from both ends. With right sides together, cording on the outside, stitch to the neck edge. Pull the cord slightly as you stitch, curving as you go. Trim off the excess cord and turn raw edges under. Turn the raw edge to the wrong side, trim seam and blind stitch.

Stitch 5 (6) hooks, beginning at the neck edge and continuing down every 3/4" (1"). Stitch thread eyes on the other front just opposite the hooks. Stitch the buttons on the same side as the hooks, 6 (9) of them every 3/4" (1").

Optional: Antique buttons were used on the 12-inch pattern. Two-hole 3/16" buttons covered with fabric were used on the 18-inch fashion. Directions for making fabric-covered buttons appear on page 24 in Chapter 1.

Belt: The fabric belt/pellon measures approximately 7 (10-1/4") long. Finish the belt after the underwear and dress are completed, so that it fits snugly over the bodice and is not too loose. It rests between the second and third button in the front. When you have determined the proper finished length, add 1/2" for finished short ends and 1/4" for the overlap. Fold the short ends under 1/4" each and press. Carefully fold up the bottom edge 1/4" and press. Fold the top long edge down 1/4" and press. Whip this raw edge to the wrong side, taking care not to let the stitches show on the right side. Finish with a hook on one side and a thread eye on the other.

Front and back views of another version of the 18-inch polonaise dress show a skirt and polonaise with a simpler embellishment: a fine black silk fringe with matching velvet ribbon.

Polonaise Dress from *La Poupée Modèle*, October 1868 - 18-inch Doll

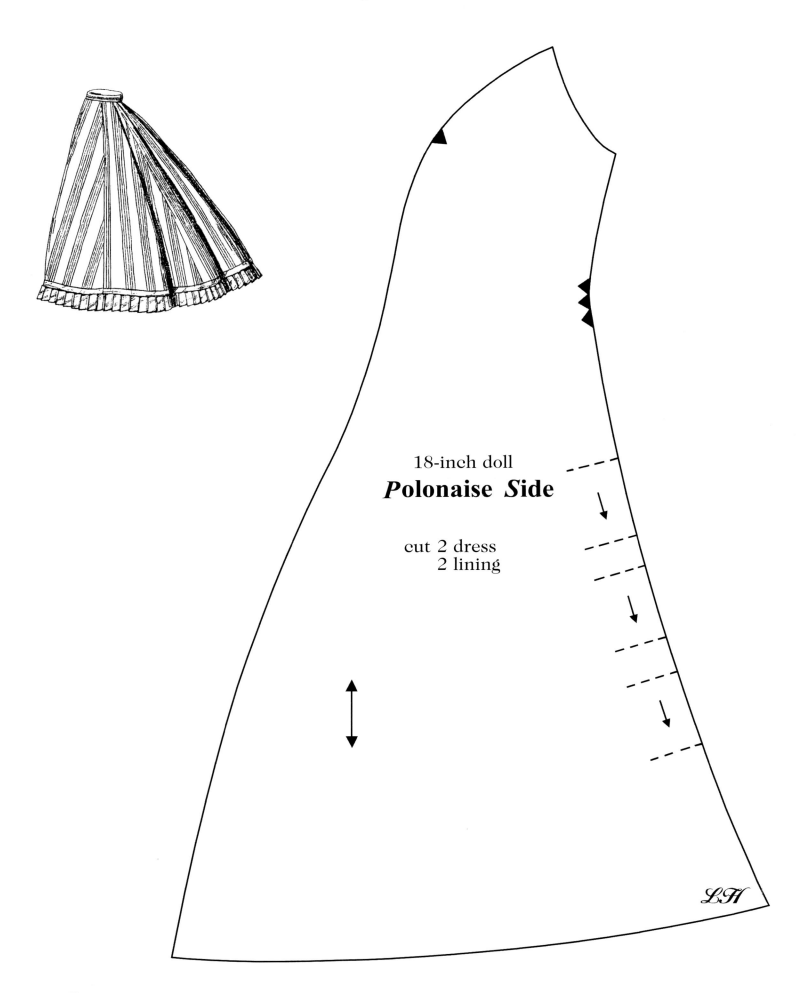

18-inch doll
Polonaise Side

cut 2 dress
2 lining

LH

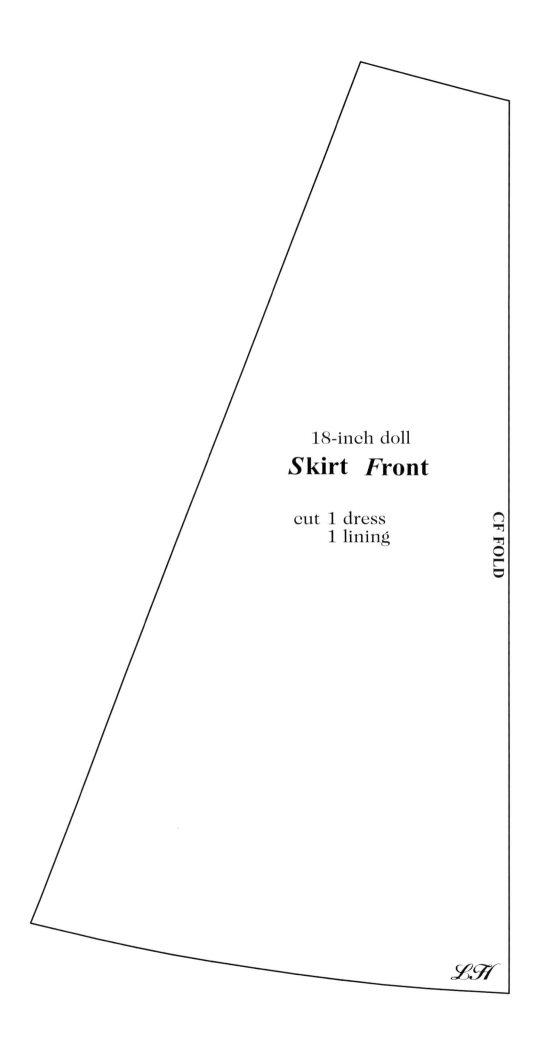

18-inch doll

Skirt Front

cut 1 dress
1 lining

CF FOLD

LH

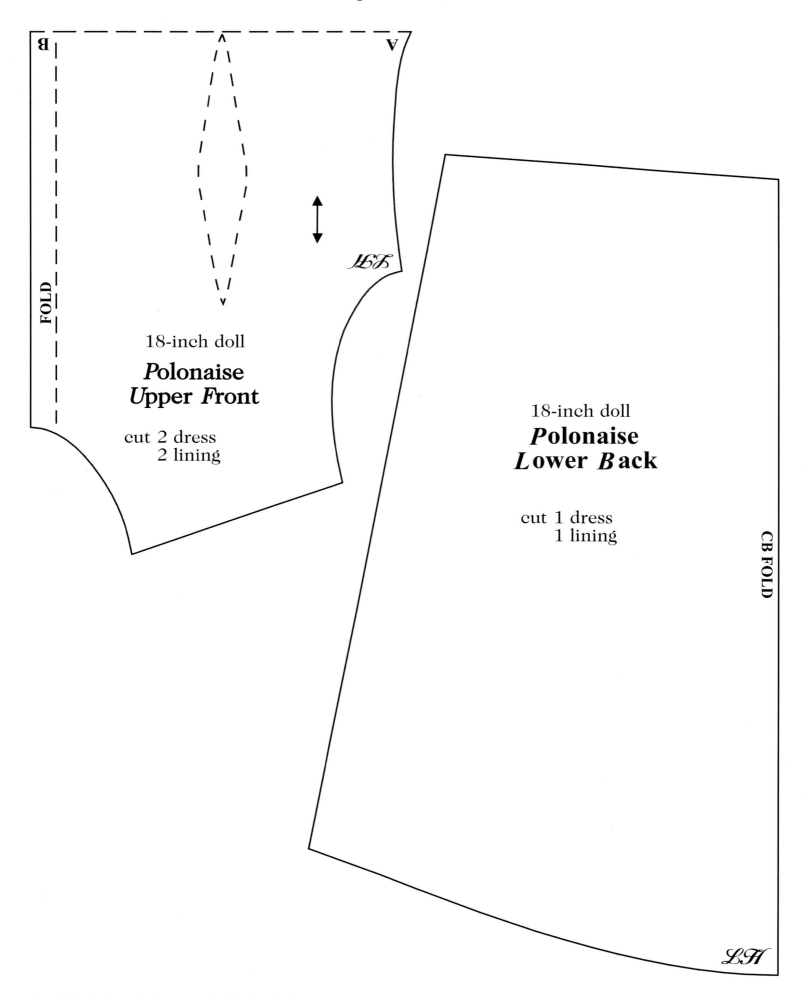

B

A

FOLD

18-inch doll

Polonaise
Upper Front

cut 2 dress
2 lining

LCF

18-inch doll

Polonaise
Lower Back

cut 1 dress
1 lining

CB FOLD

LH

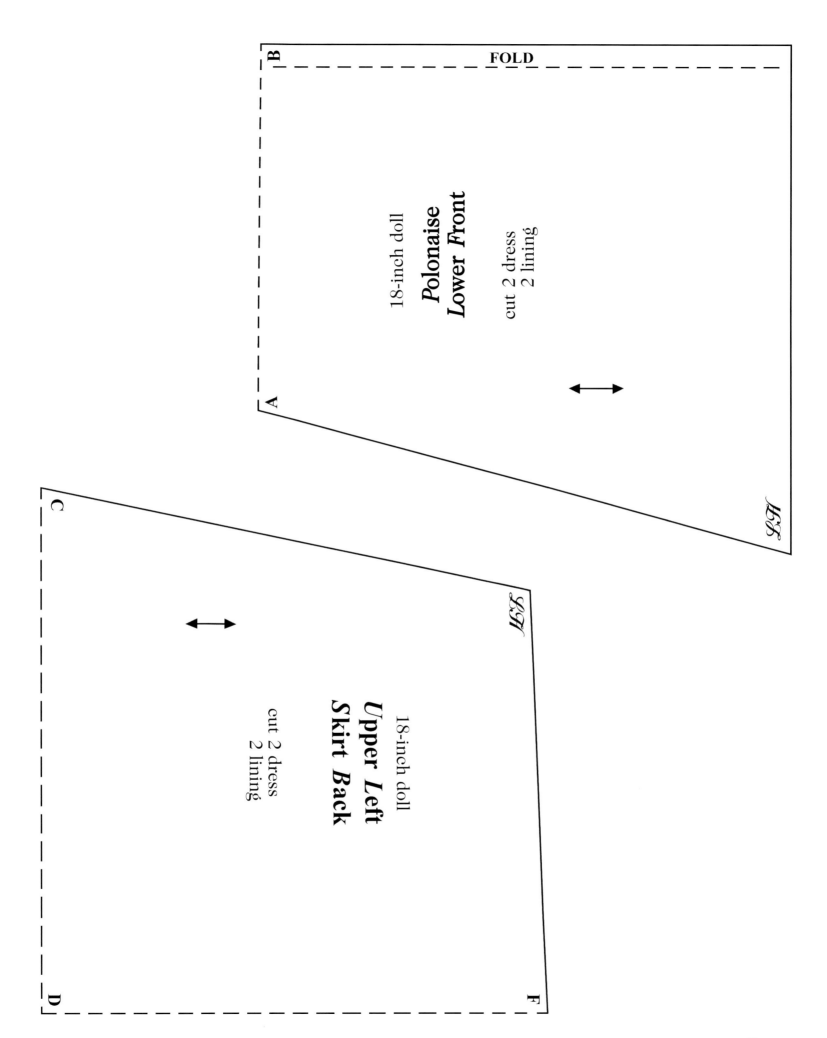

FOLD

B

Polonaise
Lower Front

18-inch doll

cut 2 dress
2 lining

A

$\mathscr{LGF}$

C

$\mathscr{LGF}$

Upper Left
Skirt Back

18-inch doll

cut 2 dress
2 lining

D

F

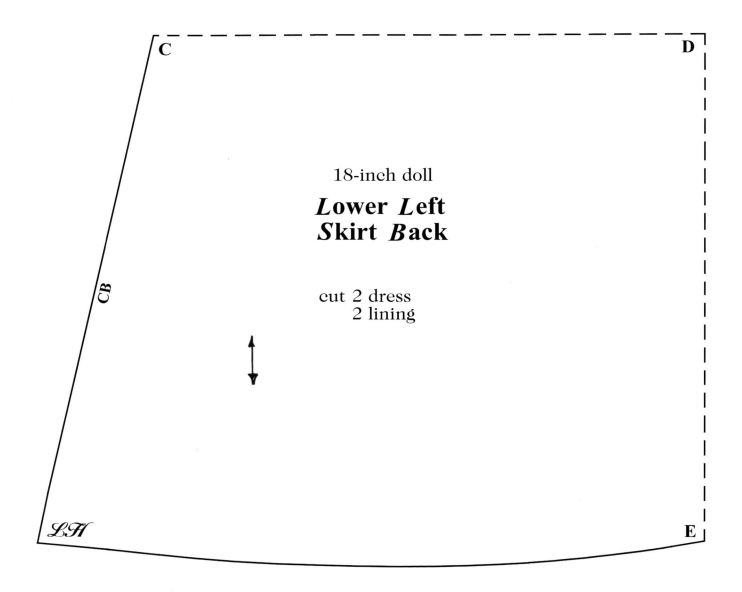

18-inch doll

Lower Left
Skirt Back

cut 2 dress
2 lining

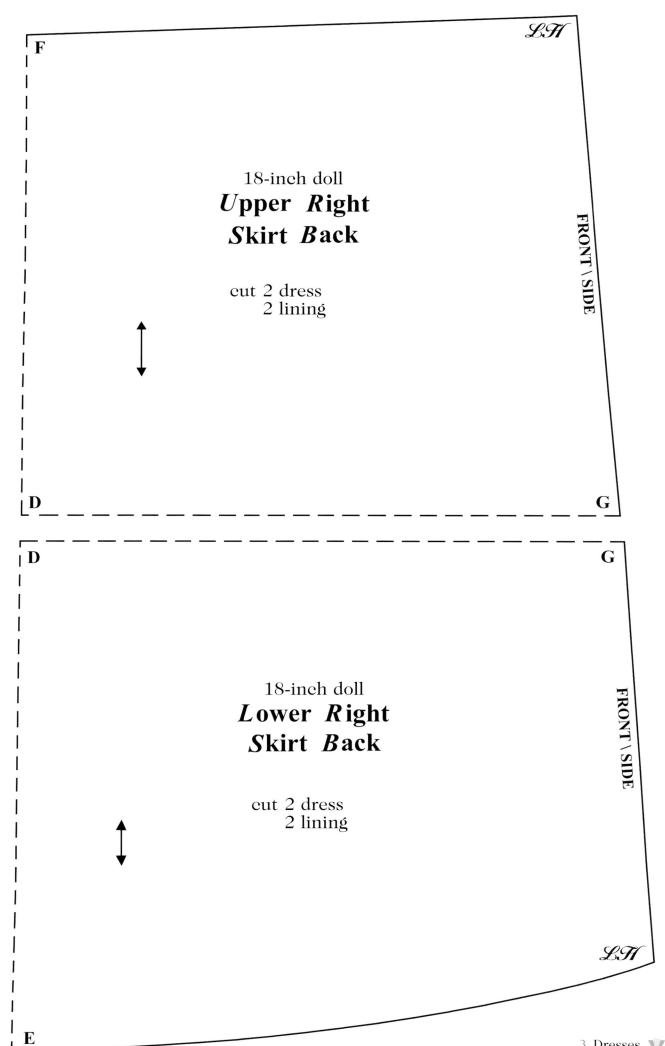

F

LH

18-inch doll
**Upper Right
Skirt Back**

cut 2 dress
2 lining

FRONT \ SIDE

D

G

D

G

18-inch doll
**Lower Right
Skirt Back**

cut 2 dress
2 lining

FRONT \ SIDE

LH

E

Mlle Bereux Soutache Dress, Circa 1865

Materials

Silk taffeta (shown) or other tightly woven silk or cotton: 16" x 45" (27" x 45")
Swiss cotton batiste or finely woven cotton lawn: 9" x 45" (18" x 45")
1 mm Cotton soutache: 9 yards (20 yards)
1/4" Cotton twill tape: 7" (3/8": 10")
Stranded embroidery thread silk (shown) or cotton: 1 yard (2 yards)
Fine embroidery thread to match
3/16" Mother-of-pearl buttons: 1 (1)
Size "0" Hooks and eyes: 3 (3)
#10 and #22 Crewel needle, 1 each

This dress was adapted from one shown in the Theriault's January 1995 *The Trousseau of Blondinette Davranches* auction catalog (page 30). The antique dress originated from the Parisian boutique of Mlle Bereux in the mid 1860s. Note that the soutache in both the 12-inch and the 18-inch dress patterns is 1 mm wide. The difference between the two dresses is the simplification of the pattern for the smaller size.

Skirt: Cut one skirt, 8-1/4" x 28" (12" x 45"), one front, two backs and one bias neck facing 3/4" x 7" (3/4" x 9"). Cut rectangles to be embroidered as follows: one 6" x 6" (8" x 8") and four 6" x 4" (8" x 6"). From the lining fabric cut one skirt 7" x 28" (10-3/4" x 45"), one front and two backs.

Turn the top edge of the skirt to the wrong side 1/4" (1/2") and press well. Place a pin at center front. Measure 3-1/2" (5-1/2") to the left and right and place a pin there. Measure down 3/8" (5/8"); this is where the soutache pattern begins. Before assembling the skirt, trace the patterns, beginning at these two spots. Then assemble the skirt as follows.

Place the wrong side of the skirt against the wrong side of the fabric and treat as one piece. Take the skirt pieces and, with the top edges even, shape the skirt as described on page 24 in Chapter 1. With right sides together, stitch the center back seam, leaving the top edge open 2-1/2" (3"). Trim and overcast. Turn under that seam allowance and narrow hem. Turn the bottom edge of the skirt under 1/4" and press. Turn under again 1" and press. Blind stitch this hem.

Stitch the two soutache designs on the front of the skirt.

See page 25 in Chapter 1 for instructions for stitching the soutache. This, and all other soutache patterns in the dress, are stitched in one continuous line. Following the directions on page 24 in Chapter 1, cartridge pleat the skirt and leave the thread ends long.

Remaining soutache pieces: Using the 6" x 6" (8" x 8") piece of fabric, trace the soutache and scallop designs of the collar on the fabric. Stitch the soutache on the collar. Using one strand of embroidery thread, such as DMC, stitch the scallops with a buttonhole stitch as shown on page 23 in Chapter 1.

Cut out the collar, taking great care not to cut any of the buttonhole stitches. Repeat this soutache pattern and buttonhole stitch scallops on the two sleeves and two panniers. Note that the sleeve and pannier patterns are labeled right and left.

Bodice: Take the three bodice and lining pieces, place wrong sides together and treat as one. Stitch the four darts into the front and back pieces. Press to the back. Fold under center backs as shown on the pattern, press and blind stitch. With right sides together, stitch, trim, press and overcast the shoulder and side seams. With right sides together, stitch the seams of the sleeves. Turn to the right side and press. With right sides together, stitch the sleeves into the armholes, trim, and overcast. Turn to the wrong side 1/4" of the twill tape, press and stitch it to the bottom of the bodice, overlapping 1/8". Press the bodice bottom up so that 1/8" of the bodice fabric shows on the wrong side. Blind stitch the top of the twill tape to the lining, taking care that the stitching does not show on the right side. Stitch gathering stitches across the top of the panniers and pull up the threads so that the panniers are eased to fit the bottom of the bodice. Each pannier goes from center front to the very edge of the opening at center back. Beginning at center front, stitch the panniers to the bodice on the wrong side at the very bottom edge of the twill tape. The length of the dress is 9" (13").

Assembly: Pull up the threads of the skirt pleating to fit the bottom of the bodice and tie off. Stitch the skirt to the bottom of the twill tape. Close the bodice with three hooks and thread eyes: the first at the neck, the second at the waist and the third halfway between them. Stitch one button halfway down the collar on one side: place a thread loop on the other side. On the samples this button is a 3/16" mother-of-pearl button that has been covered with fabric. See page 24 in Chapter 1 for these instructions.

The copy of the Mlle Bereux dress is a tightly woven, heavier antique brown silk to support the elaborate soutache pattern. The deep collar, overskirt and sleeves have a scalloped edging stitched in silk. The ensemble is displayed on the 18-inch Huret. Inset: This picture of the original Mlle Bereux dress appeared in *The Trousseau of Blondinette Davranches* by *Florence Theriault*. (Photo courtesy of Theriault's)

Mlle Bereux Soutache Dress, Circa 1865 - 12-inch Doll

Straight Pieces

Skirt ....8-1/4" x 28"

Bias Piece

Neck Facing ....3/4" x 7"

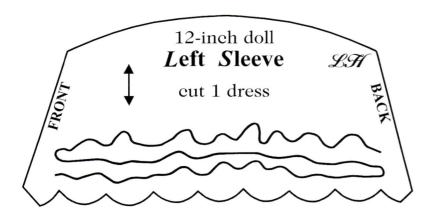

The soutache dress worn by 12-inch Linette is of antique Eugenie blue silk taffeta; the simplified soutache pattern befits her small size.

Left Front

12-inch doll

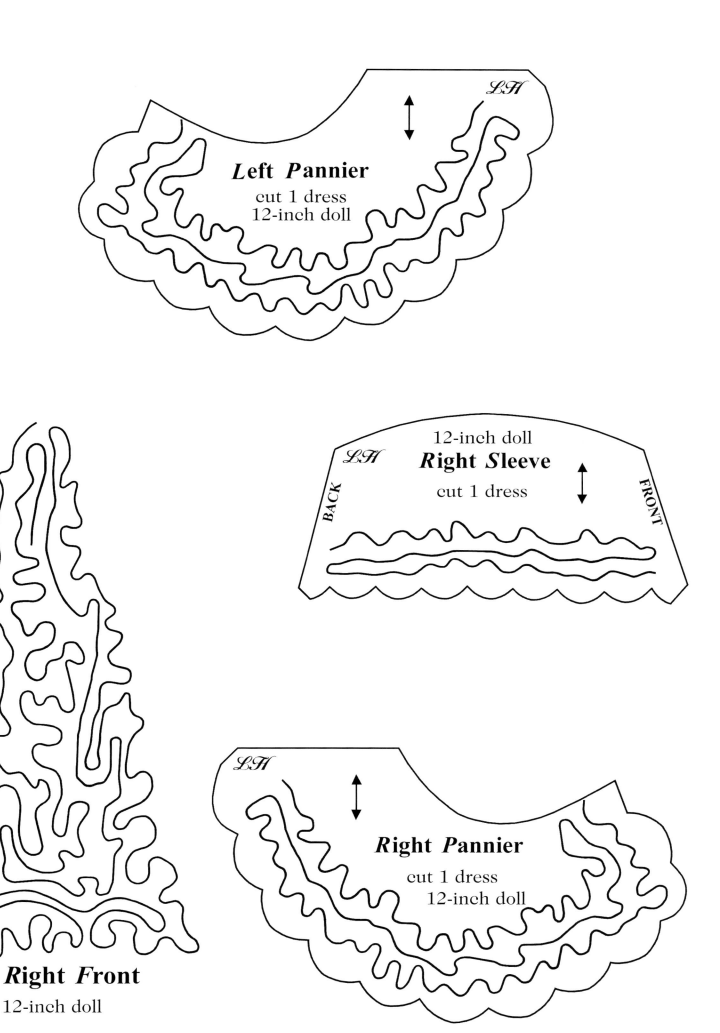

Left Pannier

cut 1 dress
12-inch doll

LH

12-inch doll
Right Sleeve

cut 1 dress

LH

BACK

FRONT

Right Front

12-inch doll

LH

Right Pannier

cut 1 dress
12-inch doll

Mlle Bereux Soutache Dress, Circa 1865 - 12-inch Doll

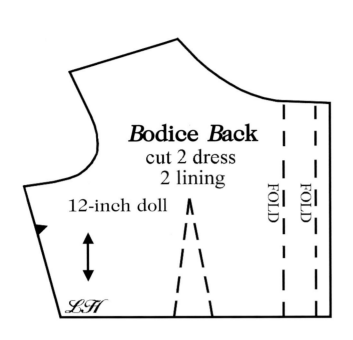

Bodice Back
cut 2 dress
2 lining

12-inch doll

FOLD FOLD

LH

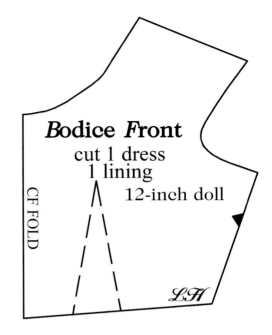

Bodice Front
cut 1 dress
1 lining
12-inch doll

CF FOLD

LH

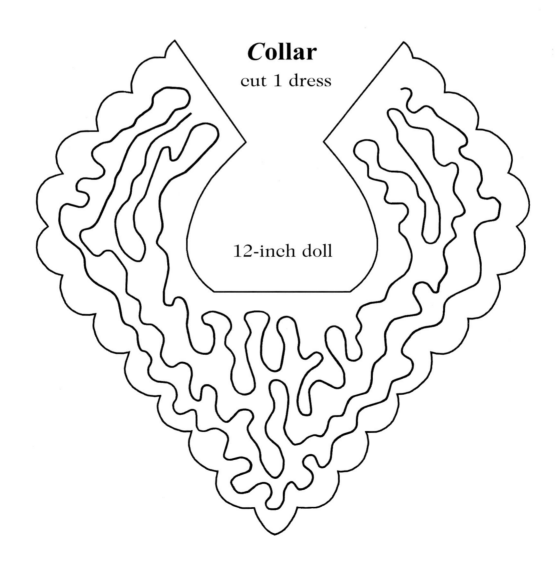

Collar
cut 1 dress

12-inch doll

Mlle Bereux Soutache Dress, Circa 1865 - 18-inch Doll

Straight Piece
Skirt ....12" x 45"

Bias Piece
Neck Facing ....3/4" x 9"

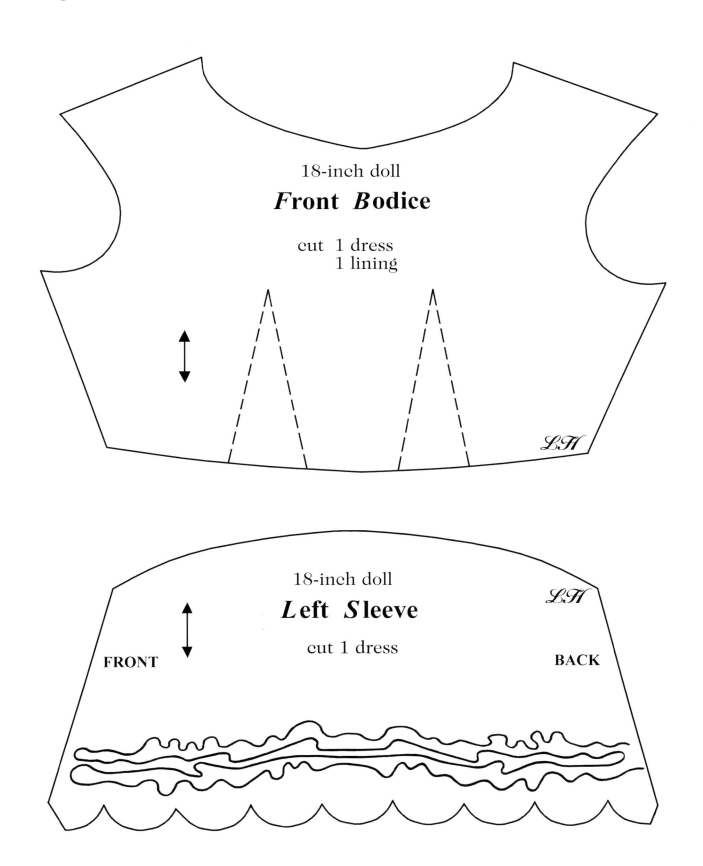

18-inch doll
Front Bodice

cut 1 dress
1 lining

LH

18-inch doll
Left Sleeve

cut 1 dress

LH

FRONT

BACK

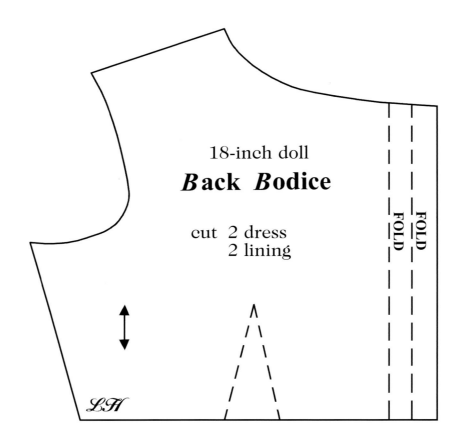

18-inch doll
Back Bodice

cut 2 dress
2 lining

FOLD
FOLD
FOLD

LH

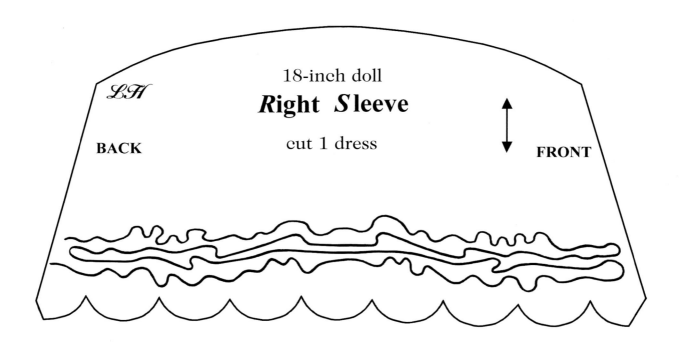

LH

18-inch doll
Right Sleeve

BACK

cut 1 dress

FRONT

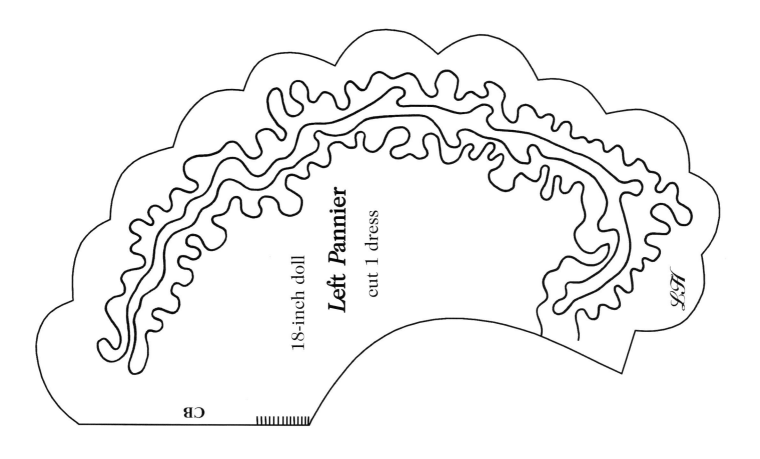

18-inch doll

Left **Pannier**

cut 1 dress

CB

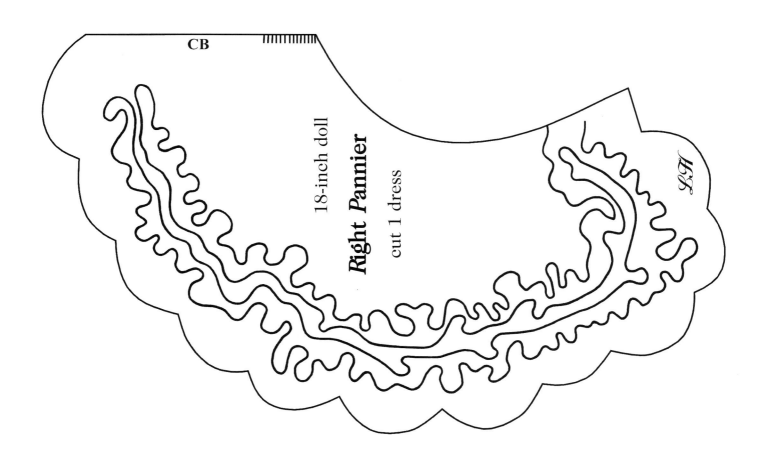

CB

18-inch doll

Right **Pannier**

cut 1 dress

18-inch doll
Left Side Skirt

Right Side Skirt

18-inch doll

18-inch doll
Collar

cut 1 dress

LH

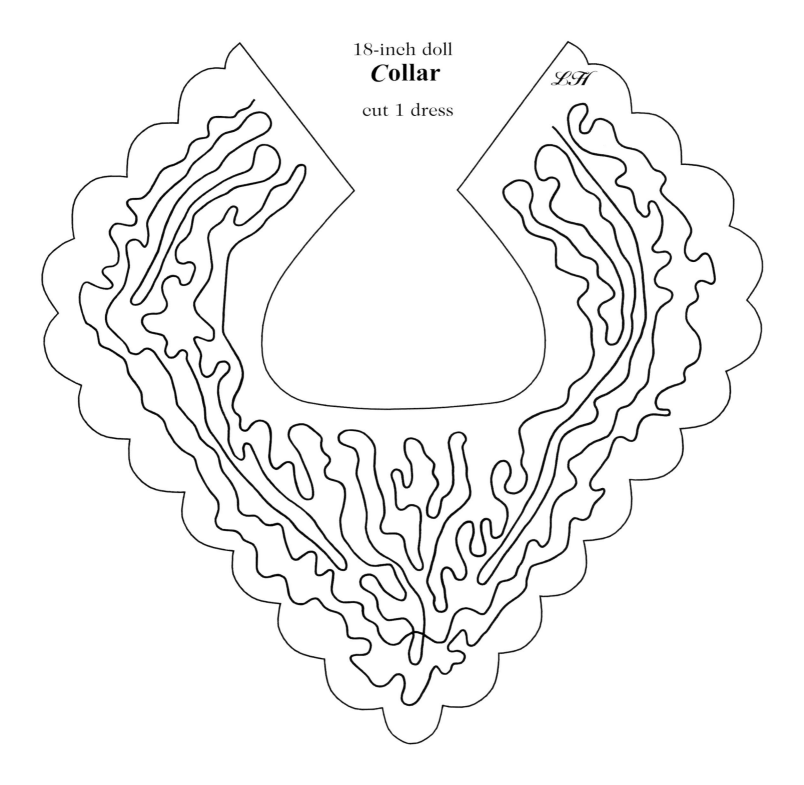

Demi-Season Ensemble
from La Poupée Modèle, March 1870

Materials

Silk taffeta (shown), wool (shown) for jacket: 6" x 24" (9" x 45")

Silk taffeta (shown), wool for skirt: 8" x 27" (14" x 45")

Silk taffeta (shown), cotton batiste for jacket lining: 10" x 14" (9" x 45")

Swiss cotton batiste (shown), cotton lawn for chemisette, skirt lining: 13" x 27" (19" x 45")

1/4" Insertion lace: 1-1/4 yards (3/8": 1-3/4 yards)

5/8" "Tom Thumb" silk fringe (shown): 1-1/2 yards (1" silk fringe (shown): 2-1/4 yards)

1 mm Cotton soutache: 4-1/2 yards (11 yards)

4 mm Silk ribbon: 1-1/4 yards (7 mm: 1-3/4 yards)

1/16" Grosgrain ribbon (shown): 1-1/2 yards (1/4" velvet ribbon: 2-1/4 yards)

1/8" Mother-of-pearl buttons: 5 (7)

Size "0" Hooks and eyes: 2

Fine embroidery thread to match

#10-#12 and #22 Crewel needle: 1 each

This ensemble—a wide skirt, full jacket with pagoda sleeves trimmed in soutache and chemisette—can be made in many ways. Silk taffeta is always appropriate and is shown on the 12-inch pattern. Wool and cotton are also good choices. Fine Swiss cotton batiste was the preferred fabric for the chemisettes, but English cotton voile, fine silk or Swiss wool challis were also seen. The use of colored ribbon under the lace was called a "transparency," and was used to highlight the lace patterns during this period. For lining the skirts, a heavier cotton batiste or lawn, lightly starched, makes a good lining. The antique skirts were most often lined in a glazed cotton. The color was frequently tobacco, but colored ones that matched the skirt were also used. This plaid skirt for the 18-inch pattern is lined in an antique green glazed cotton. Many different types of trims were used to decorate these skirts.

Skirt: Cut the skirt pieces as follows: one front, two sides, two backs and one waistband 1" x 5-1/2" (1-1/4" x 9-1/2"). Cut the lining pieces: one front, two sides and two backs. Put the wrong sides of the skirt fabric and lining together, and treat each fabric/lining as one piece. With right sides together, stitch the sides to the front, trim and overcast. Press seams toward the center back. Repeat by stitching the sides to the back, trim and overcast. Stitch the center back seam, leaving open 2-1/2" (3") at the top. Turn under the seam allowance and blind stitch the opening. Turn the entire top edge of the skirt to the wrong side 1/4"(1/2") and press to a sharp edge. Cartridge pleat the skirt sides and back. See page 24 in Chapter 1 for instructions for cartridge pleating. Leave the front of the skirt straight.

Turn the short ends of the waistband to the inside 1/4" and press. Fold the top and bottom long edges to the inside and press. Fold in half once more so that the raw edges are enclosed. Blind stitch the three open ends. Stitch the completed waistband to the cartridge pleating with the single fold at the top.

Turn the bottom edge of the skirt under 1/4" and press. Turn again 1/2" and press. Blind stitch this hem. Trim the bottom of the skirt with one row of silk fringe, beginning at center back. The bottom of the fringe should extend about 1/16" below the bottom of the skirt. (On the 18-inch skirt, the fringe begins 2" above the bottom of the skirt.) Stitch two rows of grosgrain ribbon: the first one 3/16" above the fringe and the second one 1/8" above the first. Close the skirt with a size "0" hook and thread eye. The skirt measures 6-1/4" (9-1/2") from center front.

Chemisette: Cut one front, two backs, two sleeves, four collars, two cuffs 1" x 2-1/2" (four cuffs: 3/4" x 3"), one waistband 1" x 6" (1" x 10") and, on the bias, one neck facing 3/4" x 3-3/4" (3/4" x 5-3/4"). Fold the center back fold lines under as shown on the pattern and press. Blind stitch. Add the ribbon/lace to the chemisette. Place the 4 mm (7 mm) silk ribbon under the lace insertion as shown on the pattern. It is stitched on with a tiny running stitch on both sides of the lace. Fold the front piece of the chemisette in half to find the center front. This is the placement for the first piece. Each succeeding piece is placed over 1/4". See the pattern pieces of the back and the front for placement. Repeat with the back pieces. After these are completed, stitch the shoulder seams with a French seam. Then stitch the ribbon/lace over the shoulder seam.

12-inch-pattern cuff: Gather the bottom of each sleeve to fit the cuff. With right sides together, stitch the cuff to the sleeve. Turn the cuff to the wrong side, turn under the raw edge and blind stitch.

The 18-inch Huret models
the demi-season ensemble of a
green wool jacket with
pagoda sleeves over a plaid silk
taffeta skirt embellished with
velvet ribbon and an elaborate
antique silk fringe.

18-inch-pattern cuff: Roll and whip the bottom 1-1/2" of each side of each sleeve. Gather the bottom of each sleeve to fit the cuff. With right sides together, stitch the cuff to the sleeve. Take a second cuff and, with right sides together, stitch the short ends and one long end of the cuff pieces. Trim and turn to the right side. Turn under the other long edge of the second piece and blind stitch to the sleeve.

Gather the top of the sleeve, two rows, to fit the armhole. Distribute the gathers on the top of the sleeve. With right sides together, stitch the sleeves into the armhole. Trim and overcast. French seam from the bottom of the sleeve (the top of the hemmed opening) to the bottom of the bodice. Add a row of ribbon/lace to the cuffs. Fold the waistband short ends to the inside and press. With right sides together, stitch the waistband to the bodice, easing the bodice as you stitch, if necessary. Turn the waistband to the wrong side, turn under the raw edge and blind stitch.

Collars: Make a pair of collars. With right sides together, stitch the center front, center back and lower edge of each collar using a 1/8" seam allowance. Place the wrong side of the collar against the right side of the bodice and baste together. The collars should meet in the front and allow a space in the back so that the center backs can be overlapped. Turn the short ends of the bias facing 1/4" to the wrong side and press. With right sides together, and the bias facing on top, stitch the facing to the collar/bodice. This is also a 1/8" seam allowance. Trim this seam, if necessary, turn the facing to the wrong side, turn under the raw edge and blind stitch. Close the chemisette with five 1/8" buttons on one side and thread loops on the other. For the 18-inch doll, place a thread loop at the top and worked buttonholes for the remaining four. The top button is at the neck, the bottom on the waistband, and the others spaced regularly in between. For the 18-inch pattern, stitch a button on one side of the cuff, a thread loop on the other. The chemisette measures 2-5/8" (4-3/8") from center front to the bottom of the waistband.

Jacket: Cut one back, two fronts and two sleeves from both

This full-sleeved chemisette of antique batiste features a transparency of ivory insertion over black silk ribbon.

The back of the jacket shows the single soutache designs and the intricacy of the antique silk fringe.

the jacket fabric and the lining. Construct each of these separately. For the jacket, with right sides together, stitch the shoulder seams and the side seams and press toward the back. Repeat with the jacket lining and set the lining aside. Draw two motifs on the jacket back, one motif on each front and one (two) on each sleeve, using a #1 pencil and a light box, or taping the fabric to a window. Place them on the jacket pieces exactly where they are on the pattern pieces. Do not draw the straight lines that are shown on the pattern pieces. Attach the soutache to the jacket following the directions on page 25 in Chapter 1. (There are additional soutache instructions on page 84 in this chapter.)

After completing the motifs, apply the straight lines to the back piece as shown on the pattern. These lines follow the curve of the side seam and are approximately 2-1/8" (3-1/8") long. They begin 1/2" from the bottom of the jacket. Stitch these, and then complete the outline strip around the jacket. The 18-inch pattern has two of these lines. The seam allowance is 1/4" and the soutache line is 1/8" in from the seam. Beginning at the center back of the neck, apply the soutache around the jacket and end in the same hole where you began at center back. Repeat with the lines at the bottom of the sleeves, beginning and ending at the seam. Press the jacket well.

With right sides together, stitch the bottom of the jacket fabric to the bottom of the lining. Press the seam toward the lining. Open up the lining and the jacket sleeve to the wrong side. Stitch from the top of the sleeve under the armhole down across the bottom of the sleeve/lining and back up to the top of the lining under the armhole. Turn the sleeve to the right side and finger press the seam and the bottom of the sleeve. Trim the lower edge of the sleeve with one row of fringe. The fringe should extend 1/16" (3/8") below the bottom of the sleeve. Begin and end stitching at the seam. Stitch two rows of gathering stitches across the upper sleeve and pull up to curve, not to gather. With right sides together, stitch the sleeve into the armhole. The sleeve seam matches the side seam of the jacket. For a nice finishing touch, bind the sleeves with a narrow piece of lining fabric that has been cut on the bias.

Stitch one row of fringe across the bottom of the jacket, extending the fringe 1/16" (3/8") below the bottom of the jacket. Close the jacket with a size "0" hook and thread eye. The jacket measures 4-1/4" (6-3/4") at center front.

Linette's ensemble of coordinated lavender-and-white plaid and solid silk taffeta features a simplified soutache pattern, and is trimmed in silk fringe and grosgrain bands of ribbon.

Demi-Season Ensemble from *La Poupée Modèle*, March 1870
12-inch Doll

Straight Pieces

Chemisette Cuff..1" x 2-1/2"

Chemisette Waistband..............................1" x 6"

Skirt Waistband ....1" x 5-1/2"

Bias Piece

Chemisette Neck Facing....................3/4" x 3-3/4"

Chemisette Front

cut 1

12-inch doll

LH

12-inch doll

Jacket Back

cut 1 dress

1 lining

12-inch doll

Chemisette Collar

cut 4

LH

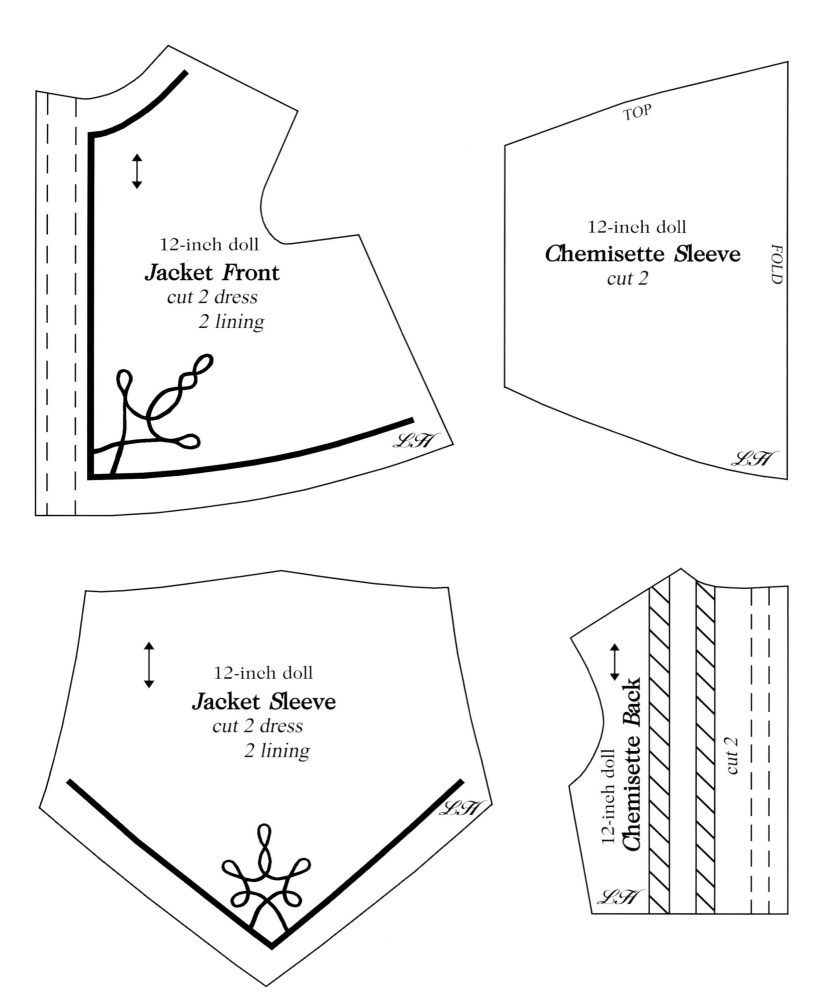

12-inch doll
Jacket Front
cut 2 dress
2 lining

LH

12-inch doll
Chemisette Sleeve
cut 2

TOP

FOLD

LH

12-inch doll
Jacket Sleeve
cut 2 dress
2 lining

LH

12-inch doll
Chemisette Back

cut 2

LH

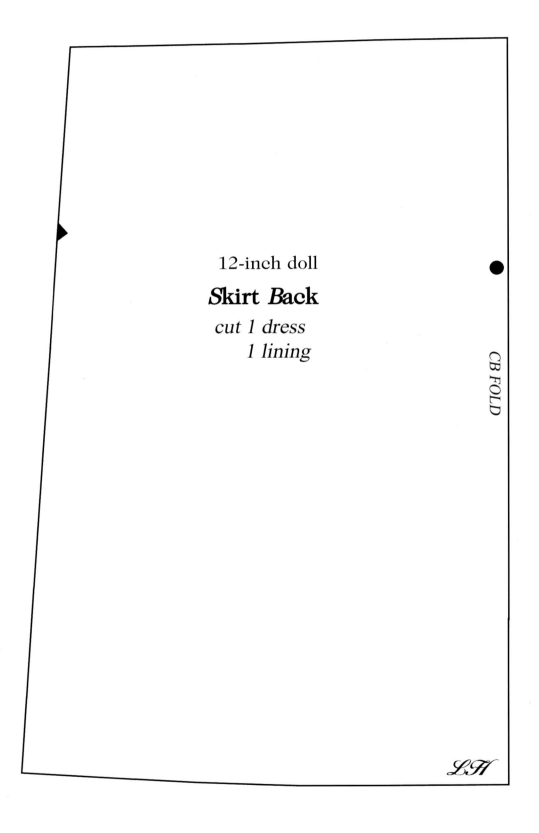

12-inch doll

Skirt Back

cut 1 dress
1 lining

CB FOLD

LH

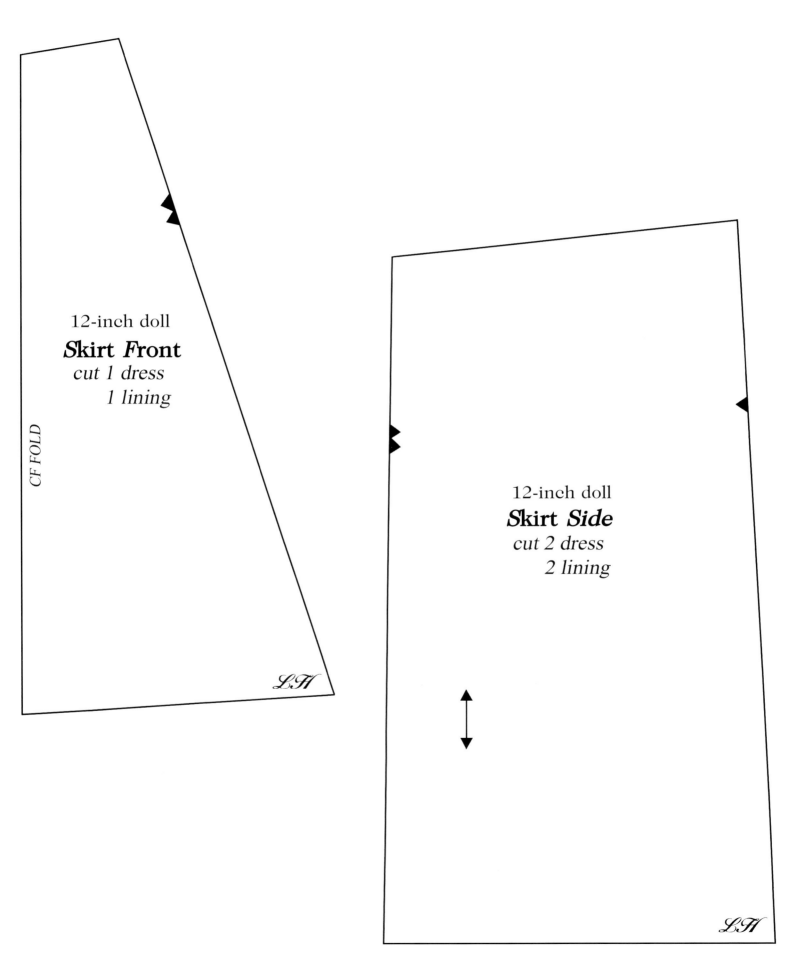

CF FOLD

12-inch doll
Skirt Front
cut 1 dress
1 lining

𝓛𝓗

12-inch doll
Skirt Side
cut 2 dress
2 lining

𝓛𝓗

Demi-Season Ensemble from *La Poupée Modèle*, March 1870
18-inch Doll

Straight Pieces

Skirt Waistband .... 1-1/4" x 9-1/2"

Chemisette Cuff .... 4 (3/4" x 3")

Chemisette Waistband .... 1" x 10"

Bias Piece

Chemisette Neck Facing .... 3/4" x 5-3/4"

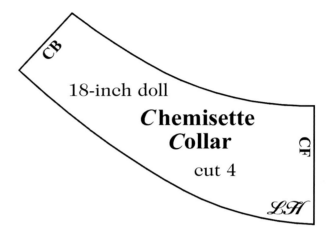

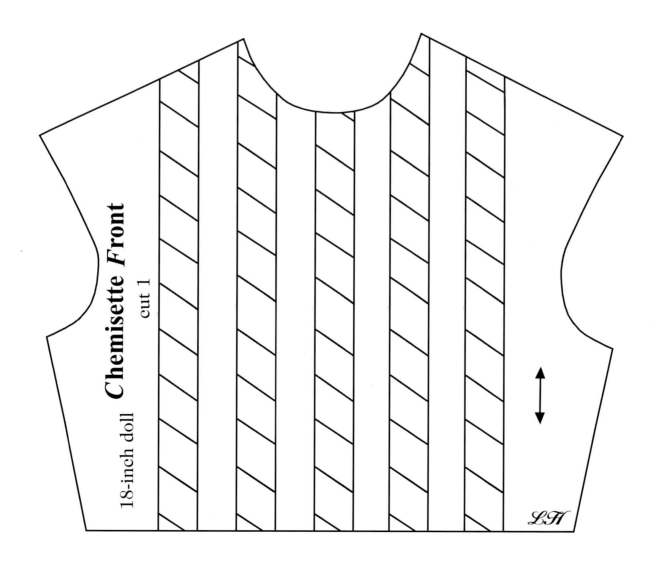

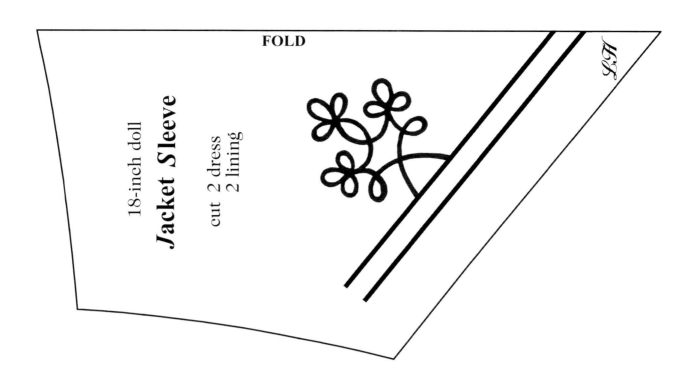

FOLD

18-inch doll
Jacket Sleeve

cut 2 dress
2 lining

LH

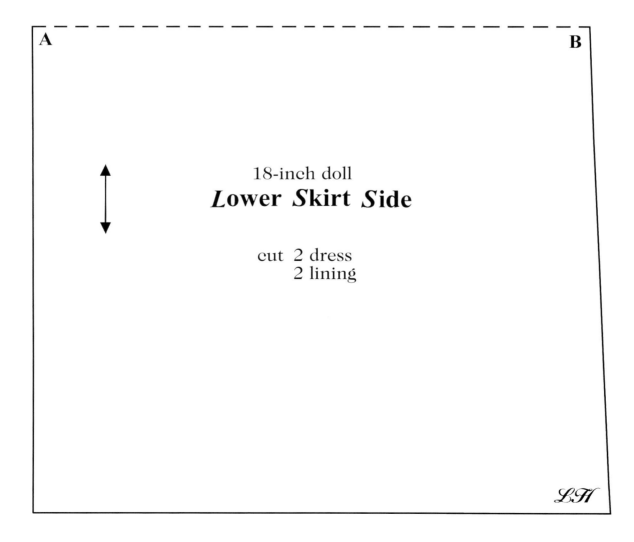

A

B

18-inch doll
Lower Skirt Side

cut 2 dress
2 lining

LH

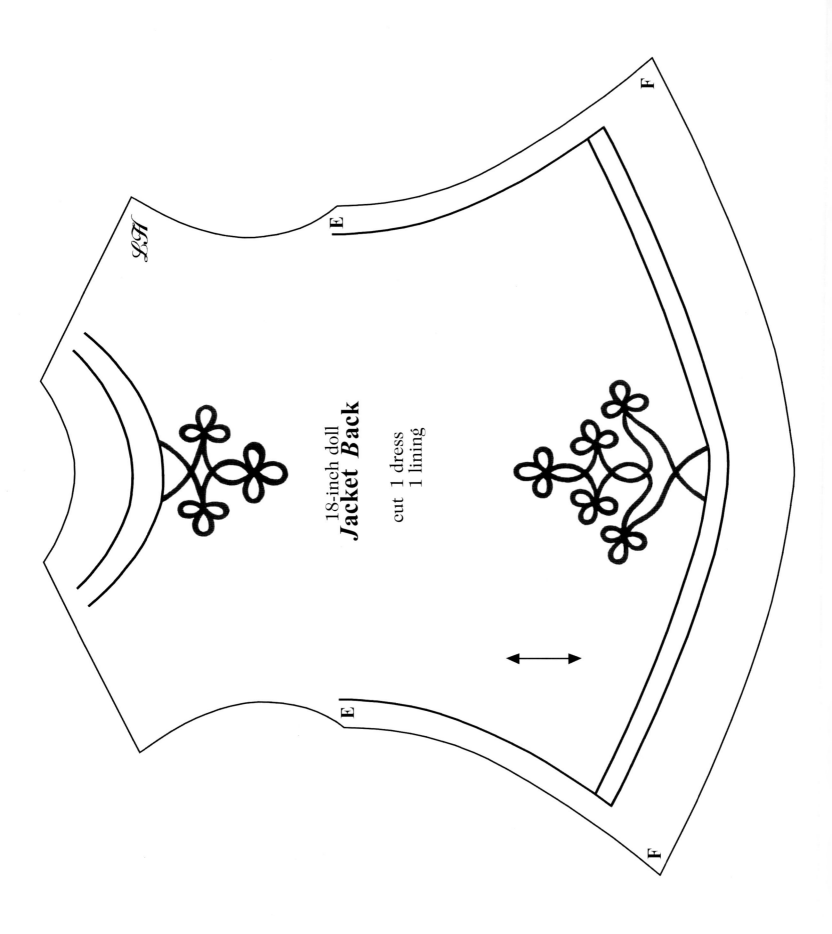

L.H.

18-inch doll
Jacket Back

cut 1 dress
1 lining

E

E

F

F

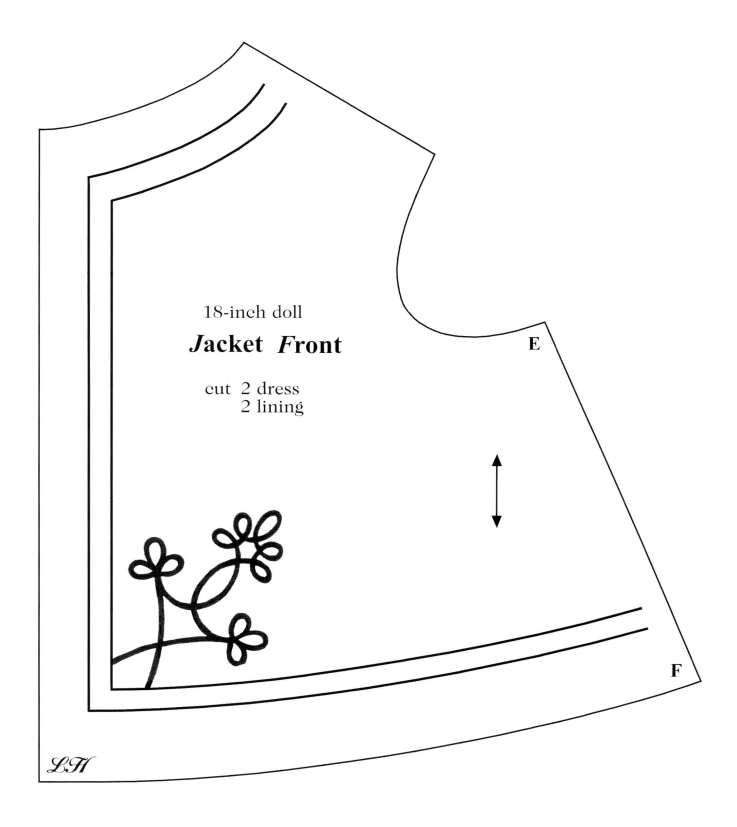

18-inch doll

Jacket Front

cut 2 dress
     2 lining

E

F

LH

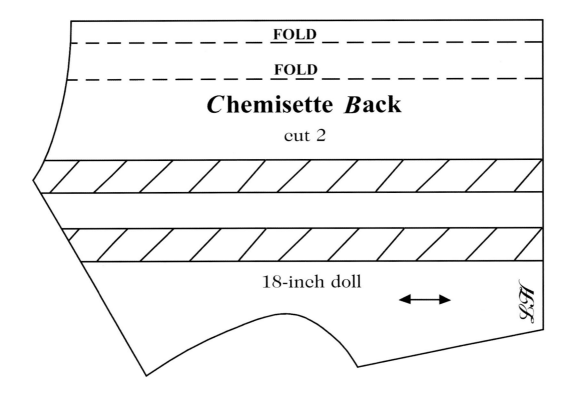

FOLD

FOLD

Chemisette *Back*

cut 2

18-inch doll

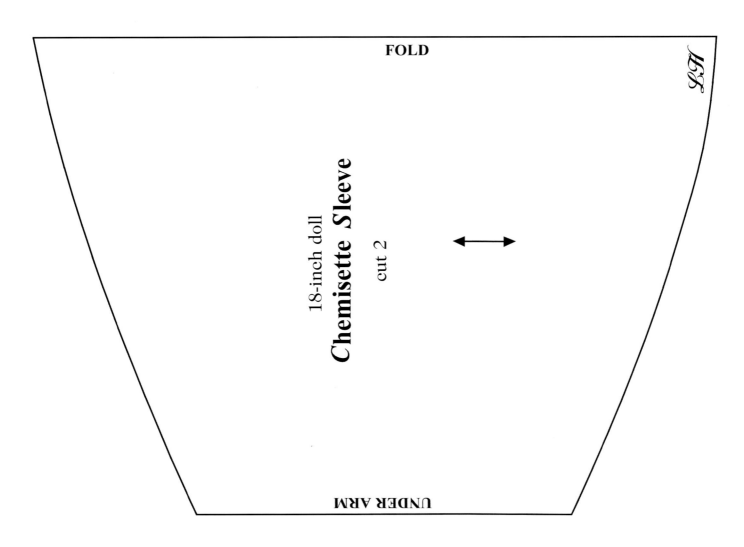

FOLD

18-inch doll
Chemisette *Sleeve*
cut 2

UNDER ARM

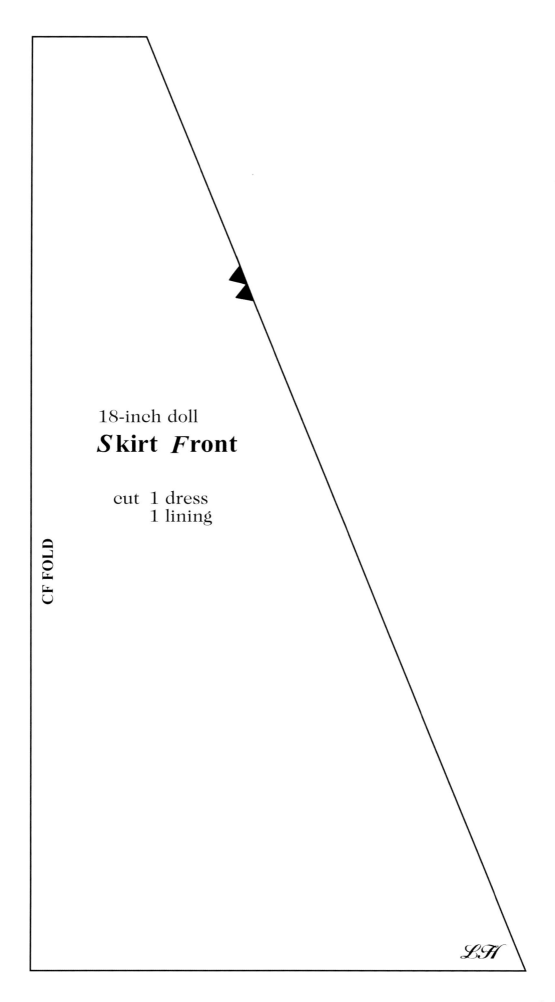

18-inch doll
Skirt Front

cut 1 dress
1 lining

CF FOLD

LH

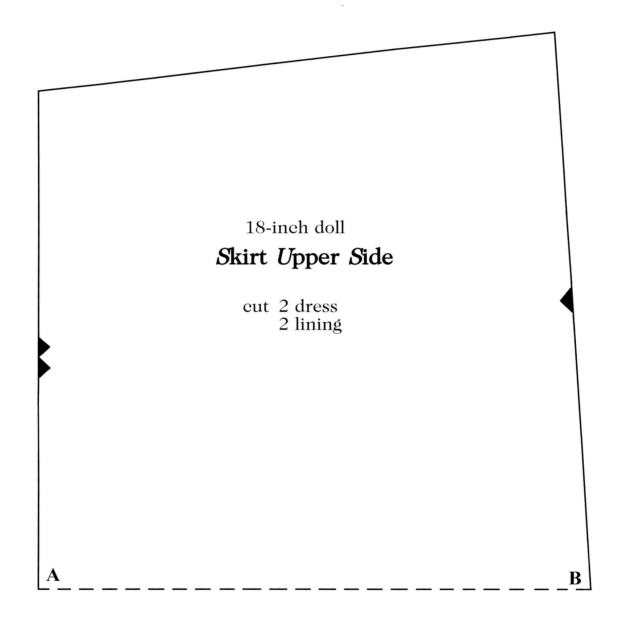

18-inch doll

Skirt Upper Side

cut 2 dress
2 lining

A

B

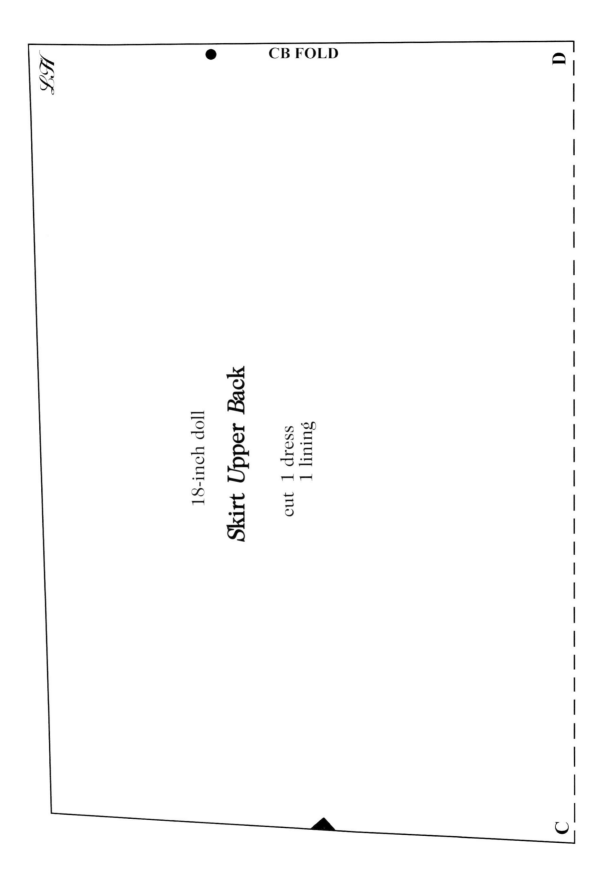

LH

● **CB FOLD**

D

18-inch doll

Skirt *Upper Back*

cut 1 dress
1 lining

C

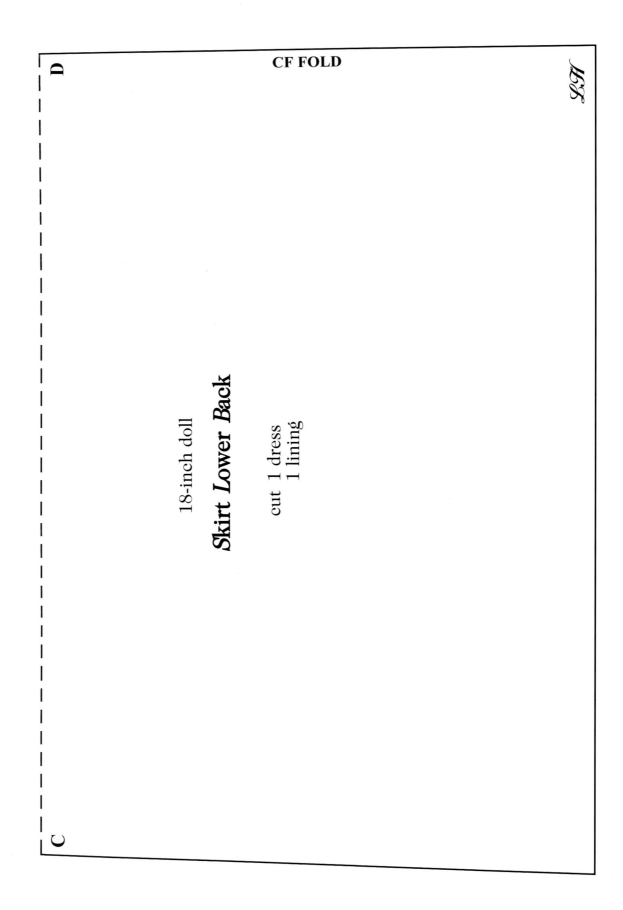

D

CF FOLD

LH

18-inch doll
Skirt *Lower Back*

cut 1 dress
1 lining

C

Evening Gown from La Poupée Modèle, April 1865

This is the only formal evening gown pattern shown during these years of *La Poupée Modèle*. Mlle Péronne explained to her readers the many different variations that will fulfill most of the styles seen during this period. There are certain constants. The skirt is always a little longer in the back, the bodice is boned, the neckline is cut low, the sleeves are short and often puffy, and the dress is in two pieces. The great variations in style are created by the fabric and trim. Layers of lace could make up the skirt and trim the bodice. Garlands of flowers often twist and turn on the skirt, and set off the neckline and sleeves. The possibilities are endless. The young lady of the period had many opportunities to attend balls; the high point of the year for young unmarried women in Paris was the St. Catherine's Ball.

Skirt: Cut from cotton netting: one skirt 10" x 32" (15" x 45"), one puffing strip 3-3/4" x 64" (5-1/2" x 90"), one front bodice, two back bodices, two sleeves and four bodice pleatings. Cut from silk taffeta: one skirt 10" x 32" (15" x 45"), one front bodice, two back bodices, two sleeves on the bias, one neck facing 3/4" x 7-1/2" (1" x 9") and one cording piece 1" x 6-1/2" (1" x 10"). The skirt is demi-trained. Place the netting for the skirt on top of the silk taffeta and, treating as one piece, cut the skirt as shown on page 24 in Chapter 1.

French seam the center back seam of the taffeta, leaving open 2-1/2" (3") at the top. Turn under the bottom edge of the taffeta 1/4" and press, turn under 1/2" again and press. Blind stitch this hem. French seam the center back seam of the net skirt, leaving open 2-1/2" (3") at the top. Prepare the puffing strip as follows: stitch the entire 64" (90") with four (five) gathering rows. This is easily done on a machine, but can be hand stitched. The top and bottom rows are 3/8" from the top and bottom of the strip. The second, third (and fourth) are 1" apart, leaving three (four) puffs. Gather all rows to fit the bottom edge of the skirt, and, with right sides together, stitch the bottom edge of the puff to the bottom edge of the skirt. In order to get this strip to lie attractively at the bottom of the skirt, stitch each succeeding row by scrunching the puff down and stitching by hand with a running stitch. In other words, each 1" puff line will lie from 5/8 to 3/4" above the bottom edge, which allows the strip to look "puffed." Begin and end at center back, turning under the raw edge of the strip at the end. Place the net skirt over the taffeta skirt, matching perfectly. Narrow hem the center back opening. Turn the top edge of the skirt to the wrong side 1/4"(1/2") and press. Cartridge pleat the top of the skirt. See directions for cartridge pleating on page 24 in Chapter 1.

Cut the waistband grosgrain ribbon 6-1/2" (9-1/2"). Turn under 1/4" at each short end. Stitch the skirt to the waistband following the directions on page 24 in Chapter 1. Embellish the skirt with eight ribbon and bead strips as follows. Cut eight pieces of ribbon 3" (4") each. Fold the bottom edge under 1/4" and press. Turn the top edge into a point edge using 1/4" for the point. Four of the ribbons are stitched at center back, center front and each side, evenly divided. Place the remaining four ribbons half way between these. The bottom of the ribbon is flush with the bottom of the net skirt. The top of the ribbon is a tiny bit above the top of the puff strip. This ribbon is stitched only to the net skirt. Tack the bottom edge, then stitch the rest on with five beads, evenly spaced. The length of the skirt is 9" (12-5/8") at center front.

Bodice: Lay out the front, back and sleeves of the bodice with the net on top of the taffeta. Treat each as one piece. Stitch two darts into the front of the bodice and press to center back. With right sides together, stitch the shoulder seams, overcast and press. Cut two pieces of 1/4" twill tape 2" (2-1/2") long. Stitch these on the bodice over the darts on each long side and at the top. Take care to go through only the taffeta layer. Leave the bottom edge of the twill tape open. Cut two bones so that they rest inside the twill tape, but do not extend past the stitching line at the bottom of the bodice, approximately 1-3/4" (2-3/4"). Insert these bones and tack at the opening. Turn under twice the seam allowances at center back, as shown on the pattern. Press. Blind stitch these seams. Insert a 2" (3") bone on the left side only, again not allowing the bone to extend beyond the seam allowance at the bottom. Tack closed.

On both layers of the sleeve, press the 1/4" seam allowance to the wrong side. Place the net on top of the taffeta. Gather the top row edges to fit the armhole, with most of the fullness at the top. With right sides together, stitch into the armhole, trim and overcast. With right sides together, stitch from the bottom of the sleeve to the bottom of the bodice, trim and overcast. Press these seams to center back. Gather two rows at the bottom of the sleeves. Pull up to fit the arm, taking care that you have left enough room to fit the sleeve over the doll's hand. Knot and bind off. When placing the bodice on the doll, push up the sleeves so that the fullness of the middle of the sleeves falls over the gathered edge.

Linette's 12-inch gown is ivory Swiss netting over ivory silk taffeta. The lavender trims are silk ribbon augmented with pearls and beads in the fringe. Lace edging was added to the bottom of the sleeve to cover her kid upper arms. Her fan was made by Alice Leverett.

Turn the short ends of the bias neck facing under and press. With right sides together, stitch the facing to the neck edge. Trim. Turn the raw edge to the wrong side, turn under and blind stitch. Make the cording for the bottom of the bodice as follows. Fold the taffeta bias in half so it measures 1/2" x 6-1/2" (1/2" x 10"), and place the cording in the middle. Stitch with a running stitch, taking care not to stitch the cording. The cord should extend at each end. Trim the completed cording so that it measures 1/4" from the stitching to the raw edge. With right sides and raw edges together, stitch the cording to the bottom edge of the bodice. Pull the cording slightly as you stitch so that it lies very flat and comes to a sharp point at the center of the bodice. Turn the raw edges to the wrong side and blind stitch them to the lining, taking care to go through only the taffeta layer.

Seam the four pieces of neck pleating, leaving the center back open. Turn under 1/4" and tack the two short ends. Turn under the top and bottom, as shown on the pattern, and press. Pleat this piece so that you have two or three pleats, as shown on the pattern piece. Steam press these. Tack this pleating from the center back to the center back along the top edge. Whip on the 1/4" (1/2") lace that you gather to fit the neckline and stitch so that only 3/16" (3/8") shows on the right side at the top. Cut three pieces of ribbon 1/8" (1-3/8"). Fold under 1/4" at the bottom edge, press in points at the top as you did the skirt, and attach these in the same manner at center front and each shoulder. There are 2 (3) beads on each ribbon.

Finish the bodice by beading a "fringe" on the pleated strip at the bottom edge as follows. Each string of the fringe is 1/8" apart. In order to center it properly, begin at center front and work to center back. As the fringe goes over the shoulders, reduce the number of beads to hang properly. When applying the beads, go through all of them, then come back through them again, except for the bottom bead. When anchoring the beads at the top of each strand, keep the thread rather loose so that when the beads fall, they move with the dress.

12-inch gown: Bead in the following sequence: pearl, crystal, pearl, bead cap, 3 mm crystal, pearl, crystal and pearl. Beginning with center front, 15 strands of the 8 beads, then 5 beads for about 7 strands, then 3 beads for about 10 strands, then 4 beads for about 7 strands, finishing with 8 beads to center back.

18-inch gown: Bead in the following sequence: crystal, 3 pearls, crystal, bead cap, 4 mm pearl, crystal. The number of strands should be approximately the same as on the 12-inch gown.

Close the bodice with five hooks, and five thread eyes on the other side. The finished length of the bodice at the center of the shoulder in front is 2-1/2" (4").

Wearing a two-piece gown of antique silk-screened tulle over silk taffeta, 18-inch Lily is off to the ball. The neckline features a heavily beaded fringe and blue velvet ribbon. She carries an antique ivory ball program; the silk crocheted gloves were made by Carrole Sharp.

Evening Gown from *La Poupée Modèle*, April 1865
12-inch Doll

Straight Pieces

Skirt ....10" x 32"

Skirt Puff Strip....................................3-3/4" x 64"

Bias Pieces

Neck Facing ....3/4" x 7-1/2"

Cording Piece ....1" x 6-1/2"

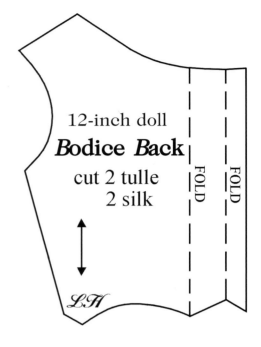

12-inch doll
Bodice Back
cut 2 tulle
2 silk

FOLD FOLD

LH

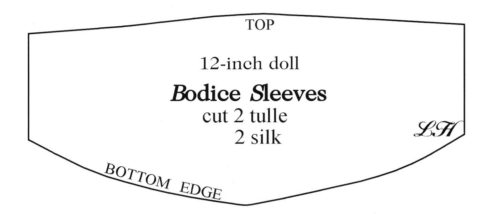

TOP

12-inch doll
Bodice Sleeves
cut 2 tulle
2 silk

LH

BOTTOM EDGE

Completed Pleating
12-inch doll

FOLD UNDER

12-inch doll
Neck Pleating
cut 4 tulle

LH

FOLD UNDER

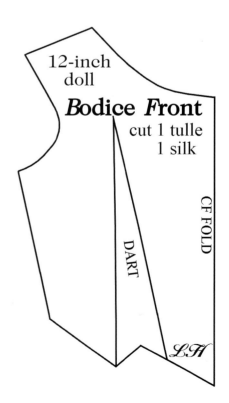

12-inch
doll
Bodice Front
cut 1 tulle
1 silk

DART

CF FOLD

LH

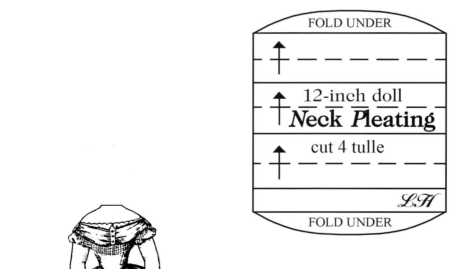

Evening Gown from *La Poupée Modèle*, April 1865
18-inch Doll

Straight Pieces

Skirt ....15" x 45"

Skirt Puff Strip...................................5-1/2" x 90"

Bias Pieces

Neck Facing ....1" x 9-1/2"

Cording Piece......................................1" x 10"

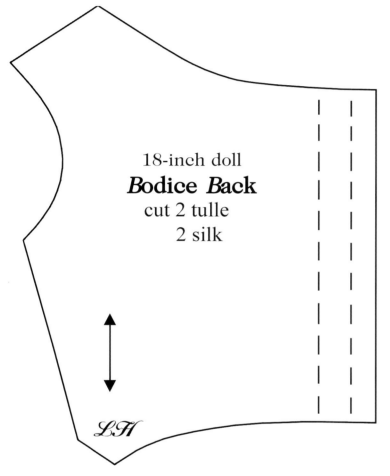

18-inch doll
Bodice Back
cut 2 tulle
2 silk

LH

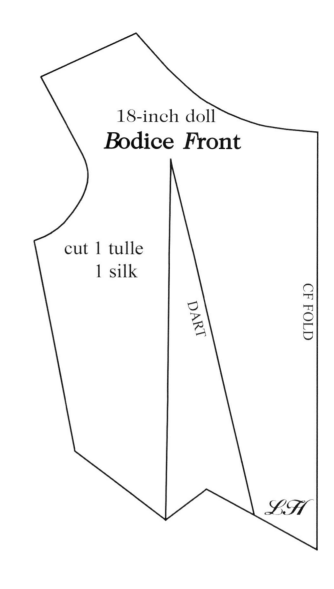

18-inch doll
Bodice Front

cut 1 tulle
1 silk

DART

CF FOLD

LH

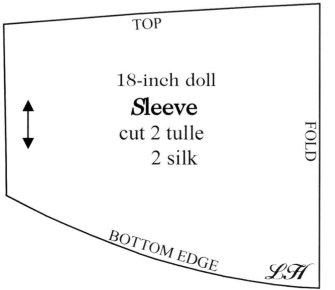

TOP

18-inch doll
Sleeve
cut 2 tulle
2 silk

FOLD

BOTTOM EDGE

LH

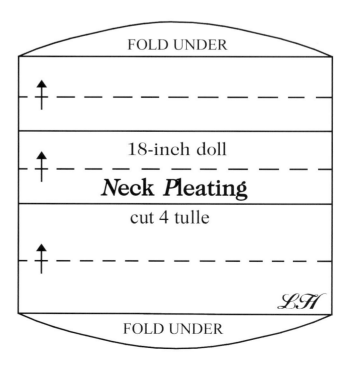

FOLD UNDER

18-inch doll

Neck Pleating

cut 4 tulle

LH

FOLD UNDER

CHAPTER 4
OUTERWEAR

The cape, best suited to augment the width of m'lady's skirts, was the predominant piece of outerwear during this era, but there were other practical and beautiful options, as well.

PART "C" - JOIN TO PART "B"

12-inch doll

Evening Cape

join 3 pieces together

cut 2 cape

2 lining

LH

Winter Ensemble with Soutache
from La Poupée Modèle, December 1871

Materials

Wool Challis (shown) or other fine wool (shown):
   10" x 54" (21" x 45")
Swiss batiste (shown), other cotton or silk (shown)
   for skirt lining and chemisette: 7" x 45 (9" x
   45")
Silk taffeta (shown), fine cotton or glazed cotton
   (shown) for coat/cape lining: 7" x 45 (9" x 45")
1/8" - 1/4" Lace beading (shown) or insertion lace
   (shown): 21" (27")
1/8" - 1/4" Lace edging (shown): 12" (18")
2-4 mm Silk ribbon: 1 yard (1-1/4 yards)
1 mm (2 mm) Soutache: 10 yards (15 yards)
3/4" Cotton or silk fringe: 48" (2-1/4 yards)
3/16" Mother-of-pearl buttons: 4
Size "0" Hooks and eyes: 2
#10-#12 Crewel needle
#20-#22 Embroidery or chenille needle
Fine embroidery thread to match

This would make a wonderful skating ensemble for a French fashion doll. The 12-inch doll is shown wearing the soutache pattern done with 1 mm cotton soutache, while the 18-inch doll's ensemble is done with 2 mm antique wool soutache. Either could be used for the larger pattern. Variations of this type of garment are quite common. In this pattern, the cape extends to both back and front. The coat is sleeveless and bound in silk or wool.

Chemisette: Cut out pieces for chemisette from batiste or silk as follows: one piece 4" x 5" (6" x 6-1/2") for the front, two pieces 4" x 3" (6" x 4-1/2") for the backs, two sleeves, one piece 1" x 6-1/2" (1-1/4" x 10- 3/4") for the waistband, two pieces 1" x 2-1/2" (1" x 3-1/2") for the cuffs. On the bias, cut one neck 1-1/4" x 4" (1-1/4" x 5-5/8").

For the front, fold the fabric in half (2" x 2-1/2") (3" x 3-1/4") to find center front. Stitch three pin tucks 1/16" (1/8"), beginning 1/4" to the left and right of center front. Stitch all six tucks 1/8" (1/4") apart. See front pattern piece for exact location. Then cut out the front. Repeat

with the two back pieces; again refer to the pattern piece for the location of the tucks and the center back folds. Cut out backs. Thread the 2 mm (4 mm) ribbon in the needle and run through the beading or, if using insertion lace, back the lace with ribbon. Stitch three rows of beading on the front and one row on each side of the backs. Refer to the pattern pieces for placement. French seam the shoulder seams. Stitch beading with ribbon across these seams.

Sleeves: Stitch two rows of gathering stitches across the bottom of the sleeves and pull up to fit the cuffs, 2" (2-3/4"). With right sides together, stitch the cuff to the sleeve. Turn the cuff to the wrong side, turn under the seam allowance, and blind stitch. Thread ribbon through the edging lace if it has beading on the top. Otherwise, back the edging lace with ribbon. Trim the cuff with this lace.

Stitch two rows of gathering stitches across the top of the sleeves and gather to fit the armholes. With right sides together, stitch the sleeves into the armholes. Trim the raw edges and overcast these seams. Stitch the sleeve from the bottom of the cuff to the bottom of the chemisette. Trim and overcast.

Turn under the short ends of the waistband 1/4" on each end. With right sides together, stitch the waistband to the bottom of the garment, easing in any fullness. Turn to the wrong side, turn under the seam allowance and blind stitch. The waistband measures 1/4" (5/16") on the right side.

Turn under the short ends of the bias neckband 1/4" at each end. With right sides together, stitch the neckband to the neck edge of the garment. Turn the raw edge to the wrong side, turn under the seam allowance and blind stitch. The neck band measures 1/4" on the right side. Trim the neckband with the lace edging/ribbon the same way as on the cuffs. Close the chemisette with four mother-of-pearl buttons: the first on the neckband, the fourth on the waistband, the other two spaced evenly between them. Stitch worked buttonholes on the other side.

Skirt: Cut one skirt 8" x 25" (11-1/2" x 38-1/2") and one waistband 1" x 5-1/2" (1-1/2" x 9") from the wool. From the cotton cut one skirt for the lining. Find center front and mark with a pin. The *bottom* of the design is 1-3/4" (2-1/2") from the bottom of the skirt without the hem. Following the pattern for the soutache, draw the design on the skirt and extend this pattern to center back. Place the wrong side of the lining against the wrong side of the skirt

Linette is dressed for a skating party in an off-white wool challis ensemble trimmed in black soutache. Her muff and toque are ermine.

and treat as one. With the top edges of the skirt pieces even, shape the skirt as described on page 24 in Chapter 1. With right sides together, stitch the center back seam, leaving open 2-1/2" (3") at the top. Turn under that seam allowance and narrow hem the opening. Turn the bottom edge of the skirt under 1/4" and press. Turn under again 1" (1-1/2") and press again. Blind stitch this hem.

Stitch the soutache design around the bottom of the skirt; stitch in one continuous line, beginning at center back. See page 25 in Chapter 1 for instructions for stitching the soutache.

Pleat the skirt in double box pleats. Measure 3/8" (1/2") on either side of center front, and begin to pin the first double box pleat. First measure two identical pleats 1/2" (1") pointing toward center back. Then fold in two identical pleats pointing toward center front. This forms one double box pleat. There are three-and-a-half double pleats on each half of the skirt top, ending in a double pleat at center back, with a total of seven pleats in the entire skirt. There is 1" (1-1/2") between each pleat. Minor adjustments will be necessary to reach the exact total for the waistline of the doll. For most 12-inch dolls, the skirt

piece will measure about 5" when the pleating is complete. For the 18-inch dolls, it will measure approximately 8" to 8-1/2".

Press in the pleats about one inch down from the top of the skirt. Baste the pleats and remove the pins. Turn to the wrong side 1/4" on each short end of the waistband and press. With right sides together, stitch the waistband to the skirt. Turn the waistband to the wrong side, turn under the raw edge and blind stitch. Press the skirt and waistband. Close the skirt with a size "0" hook and thread loop. The finished length of the skirt measured at center front is 6" (9").

Cape/sleeveless coat: The cape and sleeveless coat are constructed separately and then stitched together with a simple neck facing. Cut one cape, one coat back and two coat fronts; on the bias, cut the neck facing, 3/4" x 4" (3/4" x 7") and two armhole bindings 1" x 4" (1" x 6"), all from wool. Cut one cape, coat back and two coat fronts from lining fabric. Draw the soutache pattern on both the cape and the coat.

Cape: Stitch the two darts on the neck edge and press

toward center back. Stitch the soutache braid as explained on page 25 in Chapter 1. After stitching, press the cape well on the wrong side on a padded ironing board. Stitch the two darts in the neck edge of the lining and press. With right sides together, stitch the lining to the cape from the neck at center front around the entire cape, leaving open at the neck edge. This seam is stitched with a 1/8" (1/4") seam. Turn to the right side and press.

Sleeveless Coat: Stitch shoulder seams and side seams of the coat and press toward center back. Stitch on the soutache and press. Stitch the shoulder seams and side seams of the lining and press toward center back. With right sides together, stitch the coat and the lining together, leaving open at the neck. Turn and press. Pin lining/wool together at the armhole and, with right sides together, stitch the bias binding to the armhole. Trim to even. Turn the binding to the wrong side, turn under the seam allowance and blind stitch. Press. The binding should show 1/8" on the right side.

Beginning at the top front edge, stitch the fringe around the entire cape and coat. Starting at center back, pin the cape to the coat and baste. With right sides together, stitch the bias facing to the cape/coat. Trim to even. Turn the bias fabric to the wrong side, turn under the seam allowance and blind stitch. Press the cape/coat well and close with a hook and thread loop. The finished length of the cape is 4-1/2" (7-3/8") at center front and 5" (8-1/2") at center back.

The chemisette worn with the skating costume is ivory Swiss batiste with tiny antique beading strung with black silk ribbon. Opposite page: Lily's winter ensemble consists of a cardinal red wool skirt and cape/jacket embellished with white wool soutache. Her bonnet and muff are of soft white lamb.

Winter Ensemble with Soutache
from *La Poupée Modèle*, December 1871 - 12-inch Doll

Straight Pieces

Skirt and Skirt Lining.............................8" x 25"
Skirt Waistband ....1" x 5-1/2"
Chemisette Cuffs ....2 (1" x 2-1/2")
Chemisette Waistband........................1" x 6-1/2"

Bias Pieces

Chemisette Neck ....1 1/4" x 4"
Cape/Coat Neck Facing...........................3/4" x 4"
Armhole Binding..................................2 (1" x 4")

12-inch doll

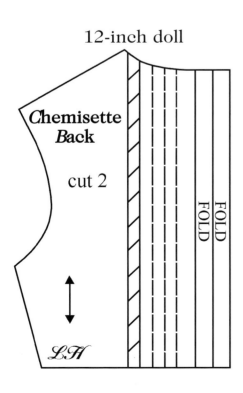

Chemisette Back

cut 2

FOLD
FOLD

LH

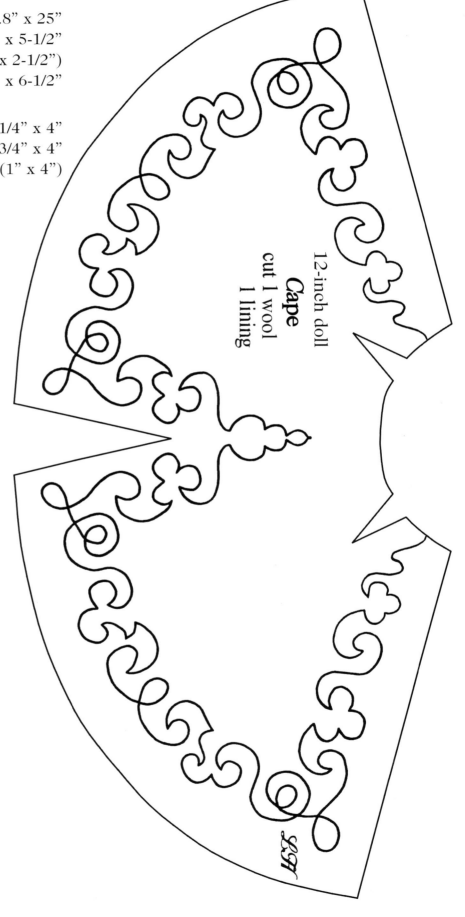

12-inch doll

Cape

cut 1 wool
1 lining

LH

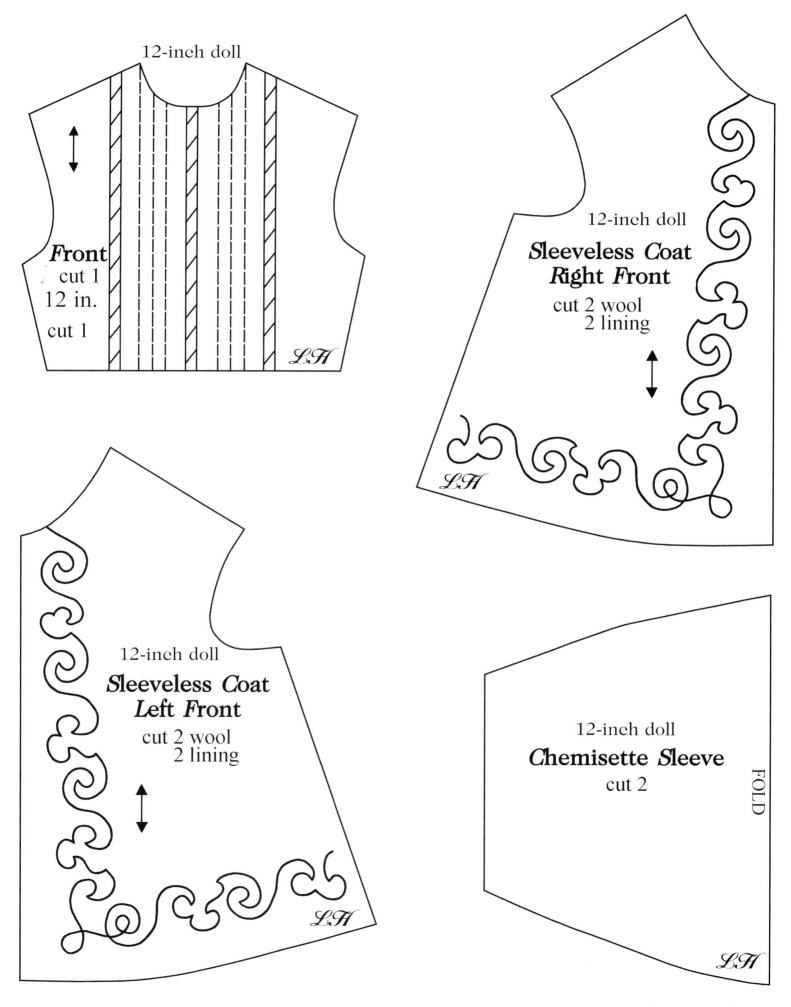

12-inch doll

Front
cut 1
12 in.
cut 1

LH

12-inch doll

**Sleeveless Coat
Right Front**
cut 2 wool
2 lining

LH

12-inch doll

**Sleeveless Coat
Left Front**
cut 2 wool
2 lining

LH

12-inch doll

Chemisette Sleeve
cut 2

FOLD

LH

12-inch doll
**Sleeveless Coat
Back**

cut 1 wool
1 lining

LH

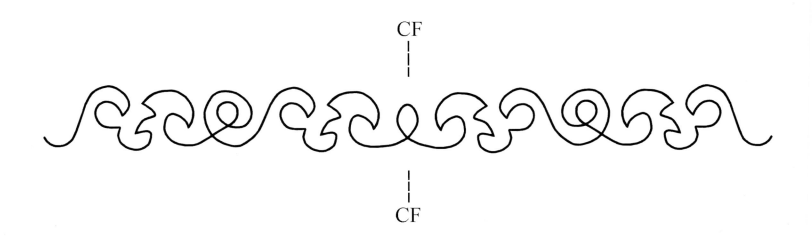

CF

CF

Winter Ensemble with Soutache
from *La Poupée Modèle*, December 1871 - 18-inch Doll

Straight Pieces

Skirt and Skirt Lining ....11-1/2" x 38-1/2"

Skirt Waistband ....1-1/2" x 9"

Chemisette Cuffs ....2 (1" x 3-1/2")

Chemisette Waistband...................1-1/4"x 10-3/4"

Bias Pieces

Chemisette Neck ....1-1/4" x 5-5/8"

Cape/Coat Neck Facing...........................3/4" x 7"

Armhole Binding....................................2 (1" x 6")

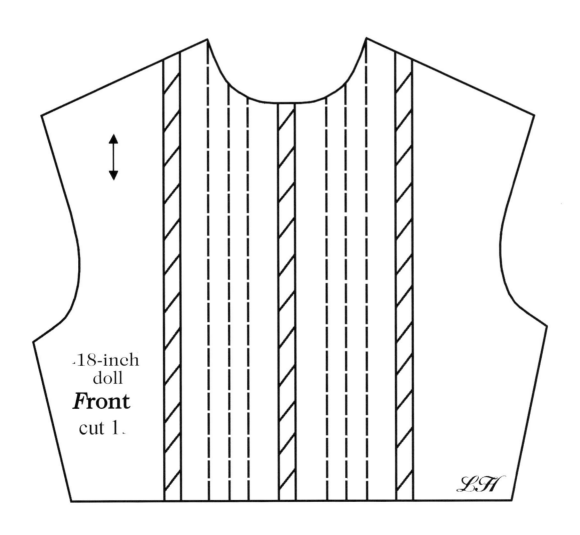

18-inch
doll
Front
cut 1.

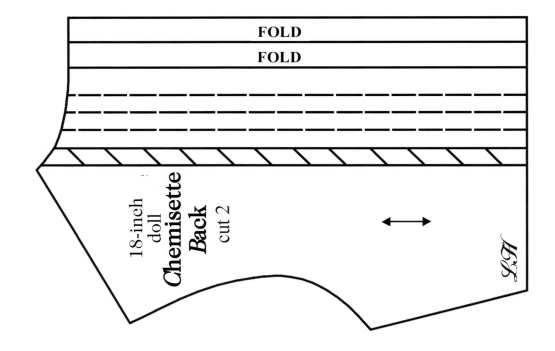

FOLD

FOLD

18-inch
doll
**Chemisette
Back**
cut 2

LH

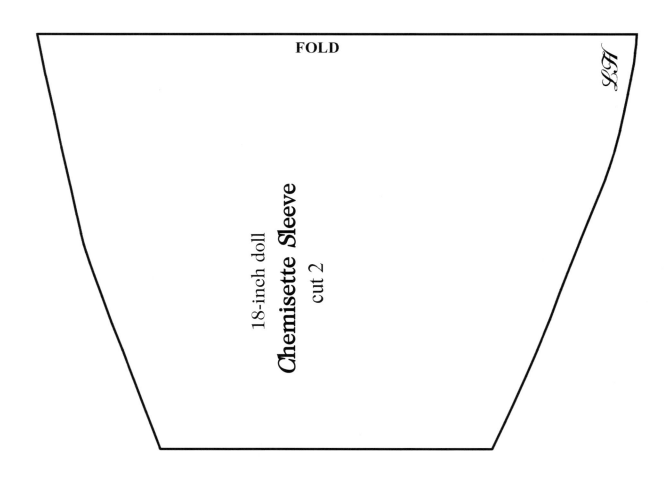

FOLD

LH

18-inch doll
Chemisette Sleeve
cut 2

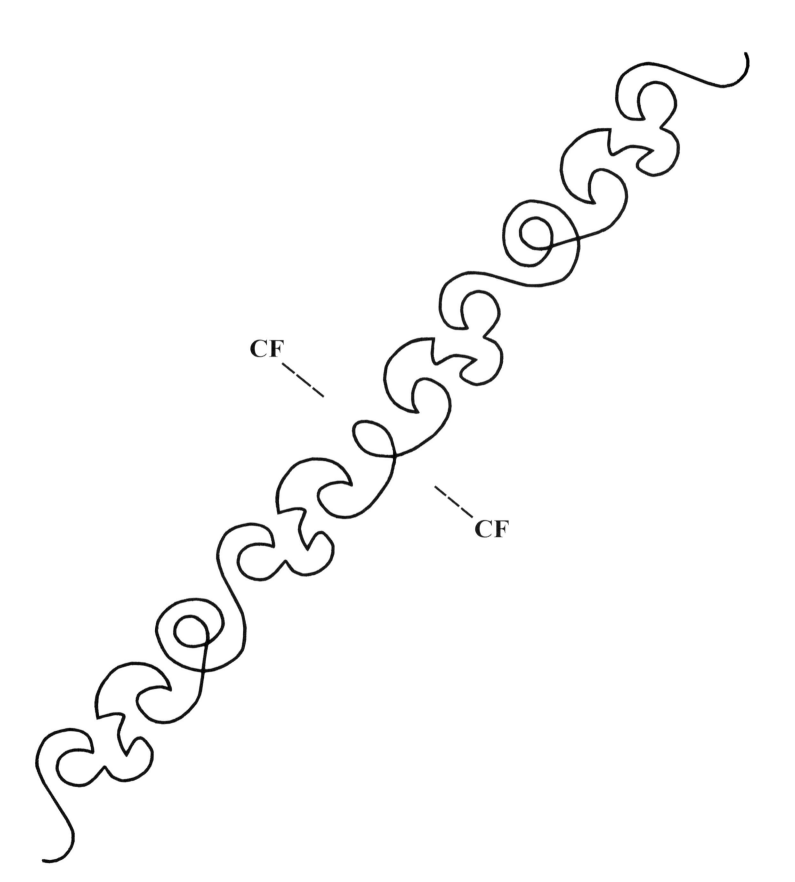

CF

CF

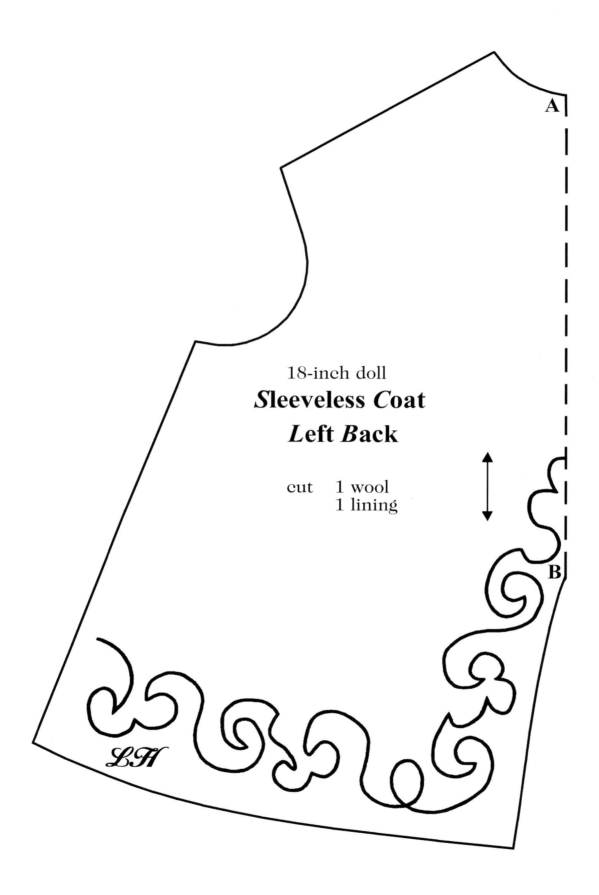

18-inch doll
Sleeveless Coat
Left Back

cut   1 wool
        1 lining

A

B

LH

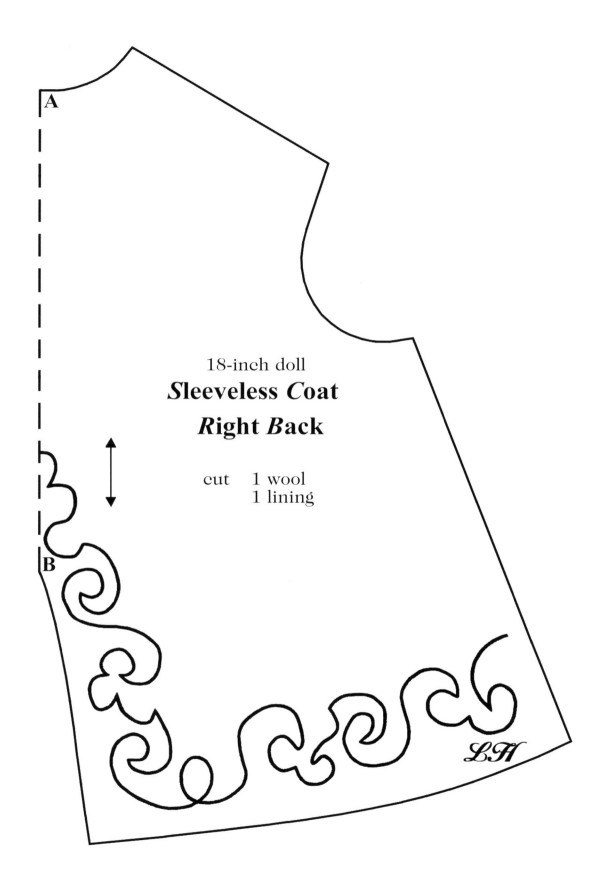

A

18-inch doll
Sleeveless Coat
Right Back

cut   1 wool
       1 lining

B

LH

18-inch doll

Cape-Left

cut   1 wool
       1 lining

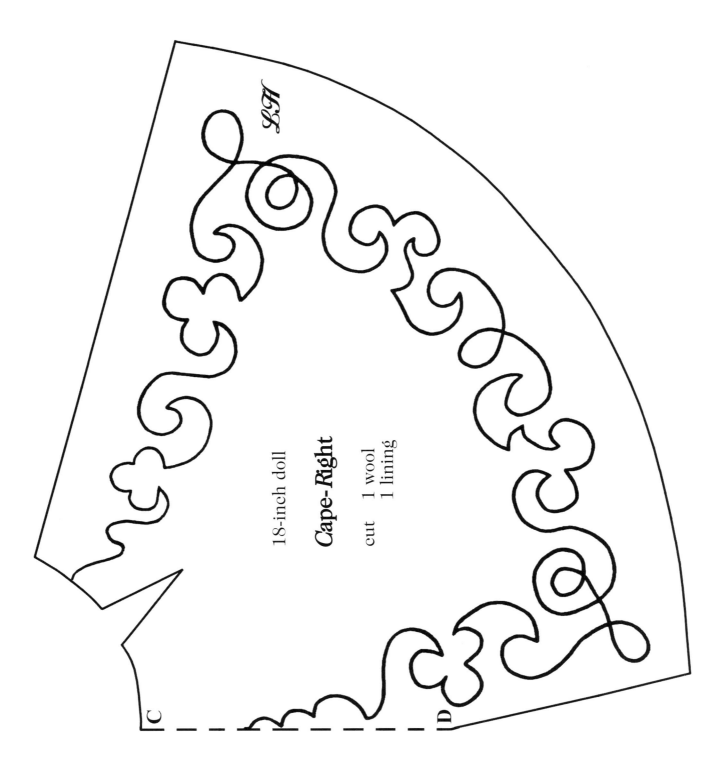

18-inch doll

Cape-*Right*

cut 1 wool
     1 lining

LH

C

D

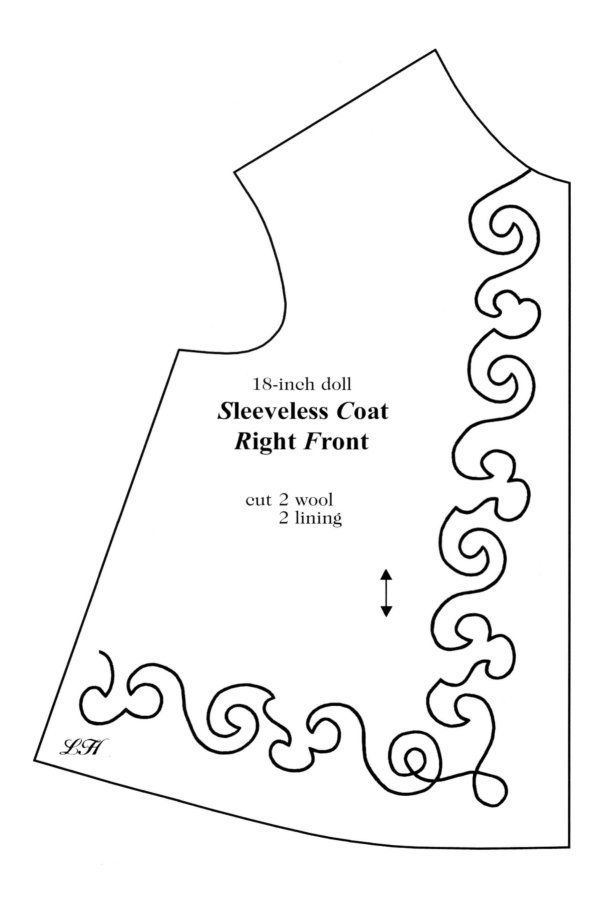

18-inch doll
**Sleeveless Coat
Right Front**

cut 2 wool
2 lining

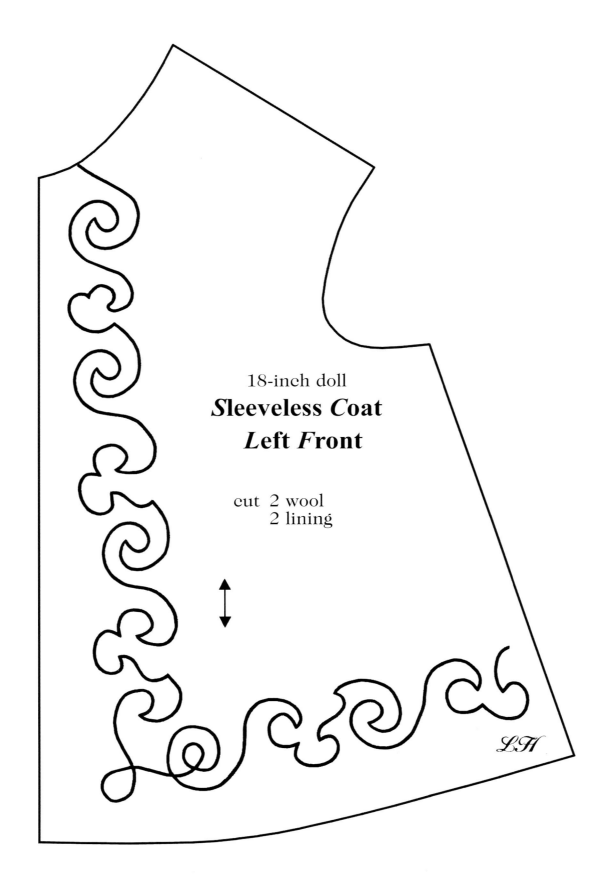

18-inch doll
**Sleeveless Coat
Left Front**

cut 2 wool
2 lining

LH

Capeline: A Fur-Trimmed, Quilted Hood from La Poupée Modèle, February 1866

Materials

Silk taffeta (shown), silk satin (shown), velvet or wool: 9" x 12" (7" x 21")

Fine cotton or silk (shown) lining: 6" x 9" (7" x 12")

Thin batting: 6" x 9" (7" x 12")

Sheer cotton: 6" x 9" (7" x 12")

Lamb (shown), swan's down (shown) or other short-haired fur: 1/2" x 16" (3/4" x 22")

7 mm (1/2") silk ribbon: 24" (1 yard)

#10-#12 Crewel needle and quilting needle

Quilting thread to match

Fine embroidery thread to match

These two samples have been constructed of silk taffeta with lamb trim and silk satin with swan's down. Other equally charming examples could be made from wool with a ruched ribbon trim, or velvet. The close view, opposite page, bottom left, shows how the *capeline* would look with no trim at all, simply bound in a bias silk.

Cut one silk, one batting and one sheer cotton of the brim and back. Trace the quilting pattern on the sheer cotton, as shown on the pattern. Sandwich the three layers together with the silk on top and the cotton on the bottom, and quilt with a quilting needle and thread. You can follow the design from the back side. When all the quilting is finished, stitch the center back seam from "C" to "D." Press open this seam. With wrong sides together, fold in the pleats, as shown on the pattern. With right sides together, stitch the back to the brim matching "D," "A" and two "B's." The pleat at center back is a box pleat. Cut out the lining and stitch the center back seam, fold in the pleats and stitch the back to the brim. Do this in the same way as the quilted piece, but turn the pleats in the opposite direction to match the quilted piece.

With wrong sides together, place and pin the lining to the top. Baste the lining to the top about 1/8" from the edge. Trim all four layers so that they match. Cut bias strips of the main fabric 1" x 18" (1" x 23-1/2"), and piece if necessary. With right sides together, stitch the bias from

center back to center back 1/4" from the raw edge. Turn the other raw edge to the wrong side, turn under the seam allowance and blind stitch. At this point, the hood will look like the close view of the hood. Tie a bow with each loop fi" (3/4") and each streamer 1-1/4" (2-1/4"). Stitch the bow to the center back at the seam line at the bottom of the hood back. Place the hood on the doll, and mark the sides where the ties will go. Cut two pieces of ribbon 7" (9") each for ties and tack on each side. Cut the fur fi" x 16" (3/4" x 22") and stitch or glue it to the binding, beginning and ending at the center back.

The quilted hood for the 12-inch doll is made from ivory silk taffeta and trimmed in lamb fur and ecru cotton grosgrain ribbon.

The pale-gold silk satin hood
has been finished with pale-gold
silk taffeta ribbon and swans
down. Inset: The plain quilted
hood with a simple bias trim is
equally effective.

Capeline: A Fur-Trimmed, Quilted Hood from
La Poupée Modèle, February 1866
12-inch Doll

Bias Piece

Binding...3/4" x 18"

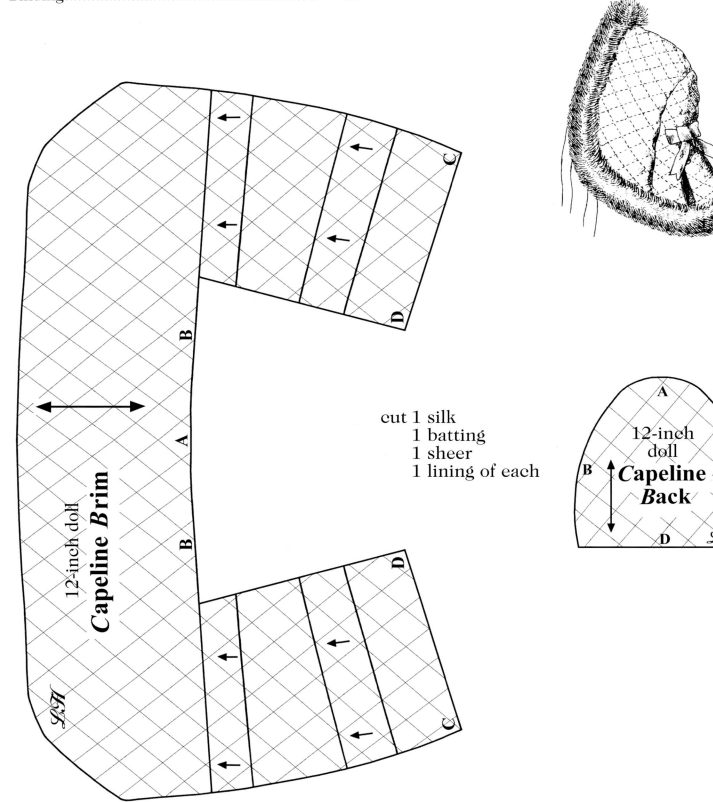

cut 1 silk
     1 batting
     1 sheer
     1 lining of each

12-inch doll

Capeline Brim

12-inch
doll
**Capeline
Back**

Capeline: A Fur-Trimmed, Quilted Hood from
La Poupée Modèle, February 1866
18-inch Doll

Bias Piece

Binding ....1" x 23-1/2"

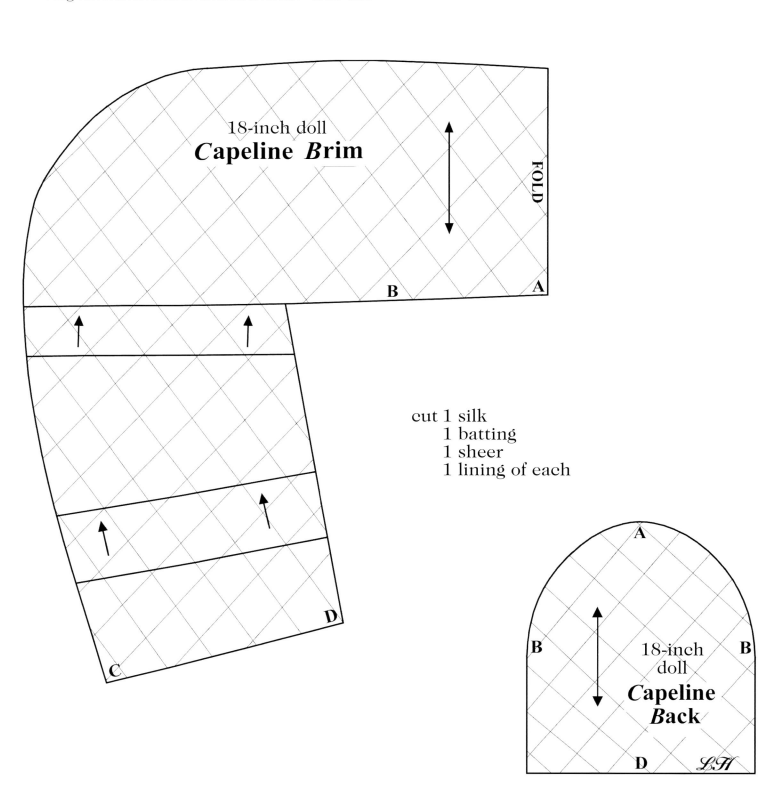

18-inch doll
Capeline *Brim*

FOLD

B   A

cut 1 silk
  1 batting
  1 sheer
  1 lining of each

D

C

A

B   B

18-inch
doll

**Capeline
Back**

D   *LH*

MacFarlane Coat from La Poupée Modèle, *June 1873*

Materials

Lightweight wool (shown): 10" x 45" (22" x 45")

Fine cotton (shown), silk or satin (shown) lining: 10" x 45" (22" x 45")

Twisted silk or cotton cord: 18" (24")

1 mm Cotton soutache: 27" (1 yard)

3 mm-5 mm Beads or buttons: 4

3/16" - 1/4" Buttons: 4 (6)

1/8" Elastic: 3" (4")

3/4" (1-1/4") Silk or cotton fringe: 9" (12")

#10-#12 Crewel needle

#20-#22 Embroidery or chenille needle

Fine embroidery thread to match

This is another version of the coat/cape: a sleeveless long coat with a cape that appears only in the front. A lined hood may be worn, as well, or may rest on the doll's shoulders. See the sketch on page 186 of the back. Both of these samples were made of lightweight wool. The 12-inch doll wears a coat that is lined in cotton, with brass buttons and brown soutache that is accented with brass shoe buttons. The 18-inch doll wears a coat lined in antique green silk satin with matching cording and tassels. The green soutache is highlighted with 3 mm peridot crystals. Antique green glass buttons close the front.

Cut out two coat fronts, two backs, two capes, two pockets and one hood from wool. Cut the same pieces, with the exception of the pockets, from the lining. Draw the soutache design on both the cape and coat pieces. There are four: two rows each of the circular pattern. See page 25 in Chapter 1 for directions for applying the soutache. Stitch it by making a figure 8 of the top and bottom circles, then stitching the circle in between. Add a button or bead at the black dot on the pattern piece. Press the design well before stitching on the bead. With right sides together, stitch the cape. Begin at "A," go across the neck, down the front and across the bottom, stopping at "E." Keep open the side between "A" and "E." Turn and press.

Turn under and press the top of the pockets 3/8" (fi") so they just overlap the first dotted line. Stitch both rows of the casing. Insert the elastic and pull it up so that it measures 1" (1-3/8"). Bind off the elastic. Line up the "A's" on the top front of the coat and cape. Mark the coat just below the bottom of the cape in the middle to position the pockets. Turn the seam allowance of the pockets to the inside and press well. Stitch the pockets to the fronts of the coat.

With right sides together, stitch the back wool coat pieces to the cape pieces, "A" to "E." With right sides together, stitch the two backs of the wool at center back, and the two fronts to the back at the side seam. Press well. With right sides together, stitch the center back seams of the lining. Then stitch the fronts to the back from "A" to "B" and "D" to "C." Press well. With right sides together, stitch the lining to the coat from the top of center front, down the front edge, across the entire bottom edge and up the other front, ending at the neck edge. Turn to the right side and press. Cut two wool arm facings on the bias, 1" x 4-1/2" (1" x 6-1/2"). With right sides together, stitch them to the sleeve openings. Turn the facing to the wrong side, turn under raw edge and blind stitch.

Stitch a worked buttonhole in the wool piece of the hood, as shown on the pattern. Do this is in the wool piece only. With right sides together, stitch the wool hood to the lining, leaving the neck edge open. Turn and press. Stitch two rows of running stitches to form the casing, as shown on the pattern. Insert two pieces of cording 9" (12") each through the casing, coming out at the buttonhole. Fasten on edge of each at the neck opening. Cut the piece of fringe in half. Wrap the fringe tightly around the end of the cording, gluing it in place; this will form the tassels. Gather the neck edge of the hood to fit the neck edge of the coat. With right sides together, stitch the hood to the coat, with the hood on top and matching the "G's" at center back. Cut a piece of lining fabric on the bias for the neck facing, 1" x 5-1/2" (1" x 6-1/2"). With right sides together, stitch the facing to the coat/hood. Trim and press facing to the wrong side. Turn under the raw edge and blind stitch.

Stitch four (five) buttons on the left side of the front, beginning at the neck and every 1-3/8" down. Stitch worked buttonholes on the right side to match. Pull up the hood cording to fit the doll's head. Tie the cord in a bow.

Lily is attired for a winter's day in a black wool coat/cape lined in green antique silk satin. Her beautiful feather muff is by Sylvia Mac Neil.

MacFarlane Coat from *La Poupée Modèle*, June 1873 - 12-inch Doll

Bias Pieces
Neck Facing ....1" x 5-1/2"
Armhole Facing ....2 (1" x 4-1/2")

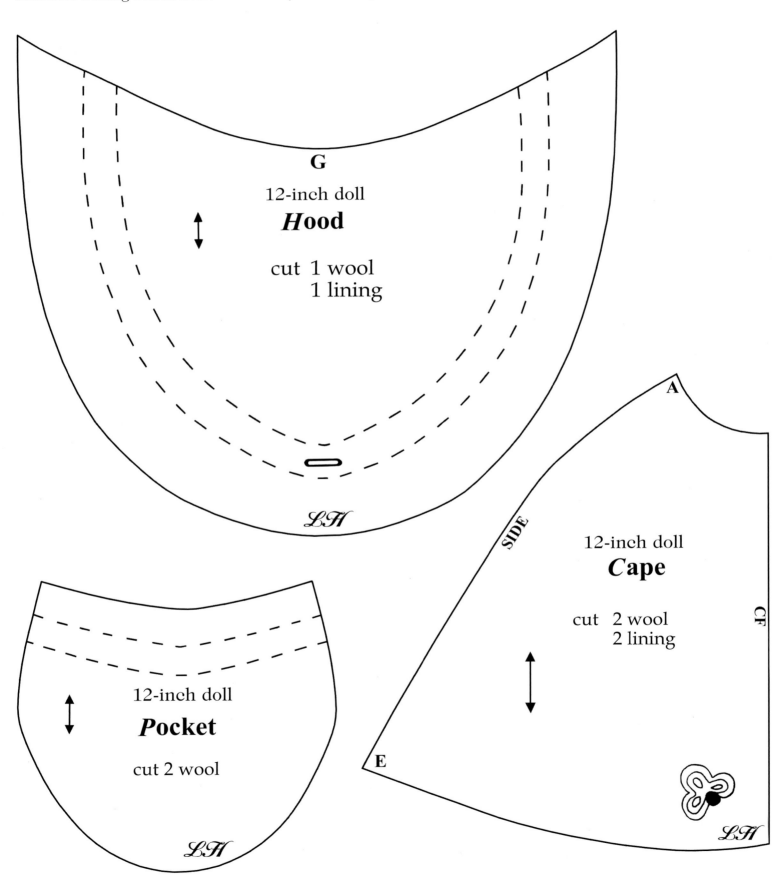

G

12-inch doll
Hood

cut 1 wool
    1 lining

LH

A

SIDE

12-inch doll
Cape

cut 2 wool
    2 lining

CF

E

12-inch doll
Pocket

cut 2 wool

LH

LH

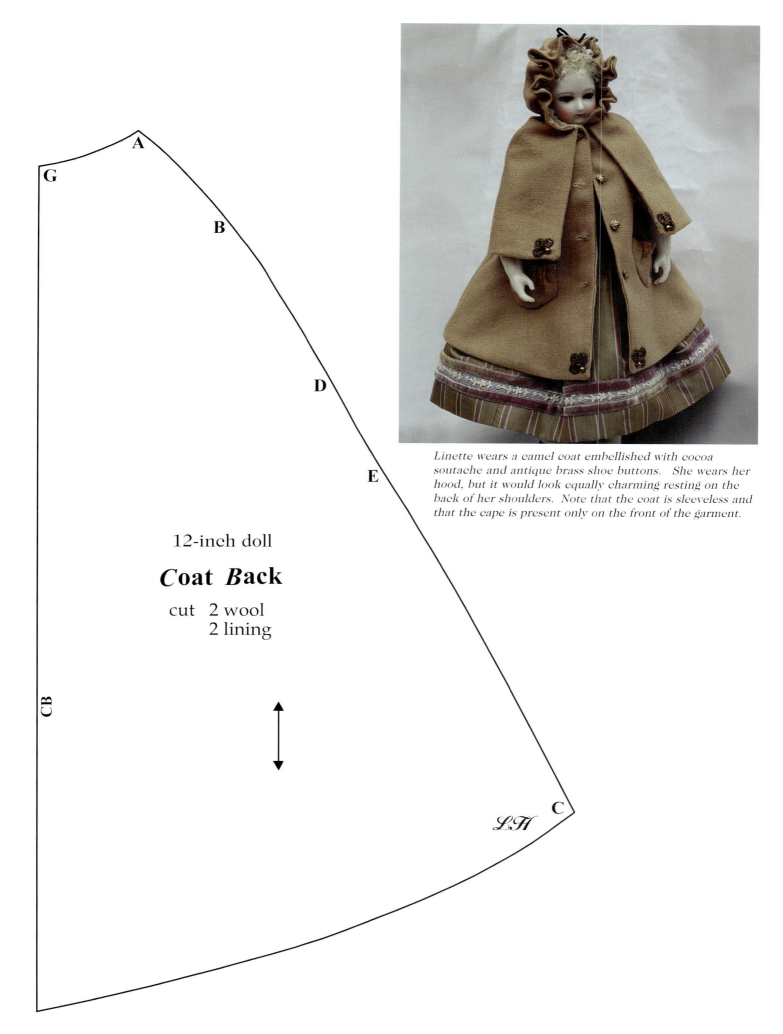

G

A

B

D

E

C

L H

CB

12-inch doll

Coat Back

cut 2 wool
      2 lining

Linette wears a camel coat embellished with cocoa soutache and antique brass shoe buttons. She wears her hood, but it would look equally charming resting on the back of her shoulders. Note that the coat is sleeveless and that the cape is present only on the front of the garment.

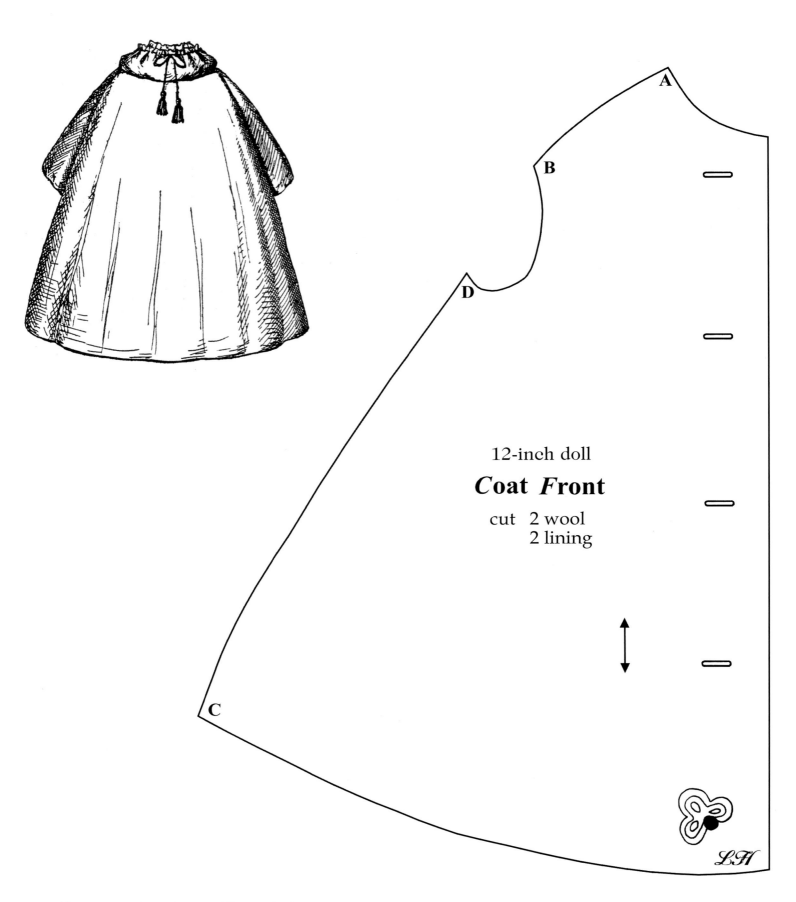

12-inch doll

Coat Front

cut 2 wool
     2 lining

MacFarlane Coat from *La Poupée Modèle*, June 1873 - 18-inch Doll

Bias Pieces

Neck Facing ....1" x 6-1/2"
Armhole Facing ....2 (1" x 6-1/2")

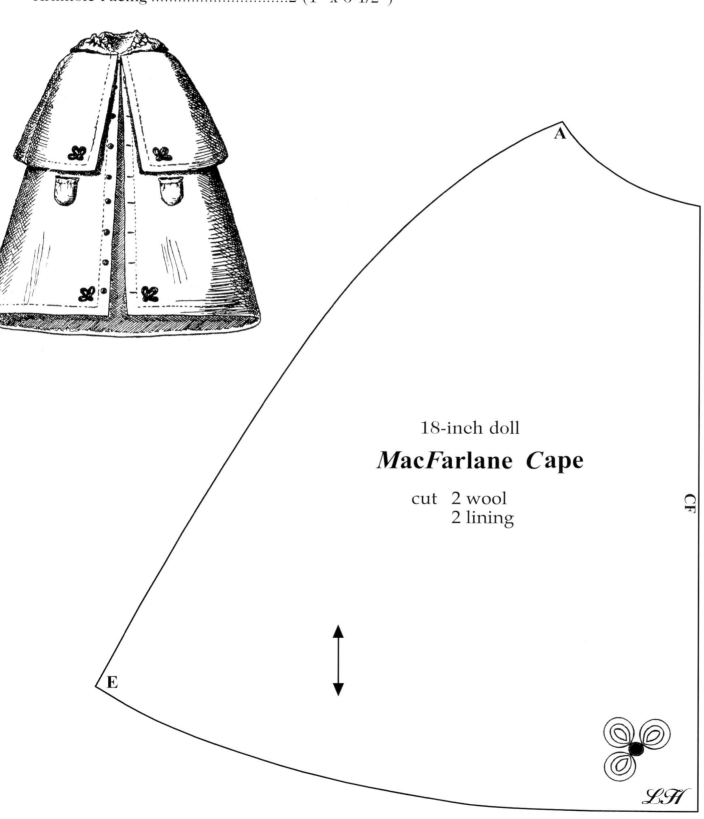

A

18-inch doll

MacFarlane Cape

cut   2 wool
      2 lining

CF

E

LH

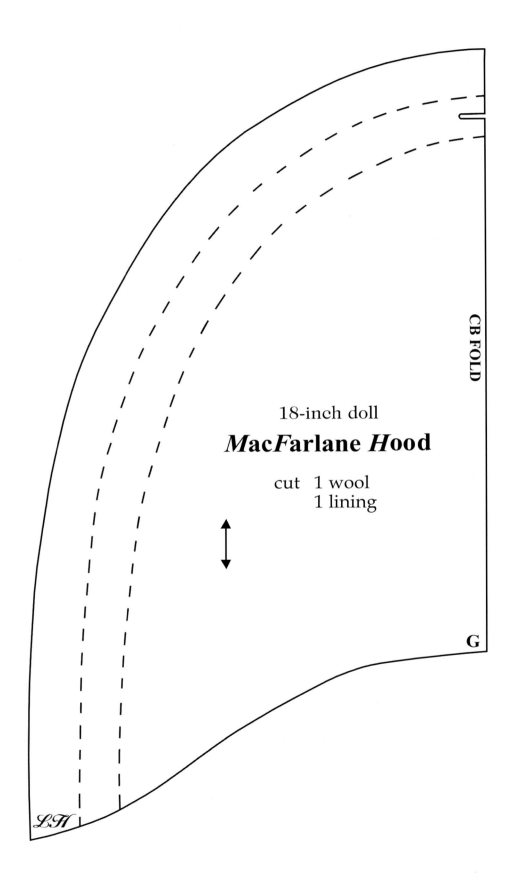

18-inch doll

MacFarlane *Hood*

cut 1 wool
1 lining

CB FOLD

G

ℒℋ

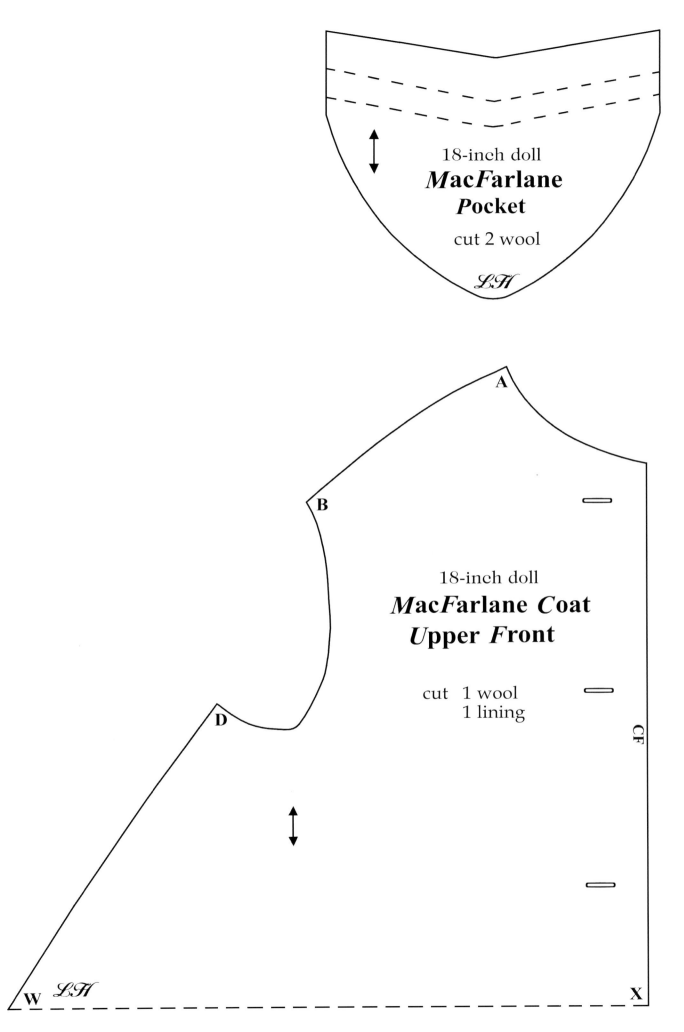

18-inch doll
MacFarlane Pocket

cut 2 wool

LH

A

B

18-inch doll
MacFarlane Coat Upper Front

cut   1 wool
     1 lining

CF

D

W   *LH*

X

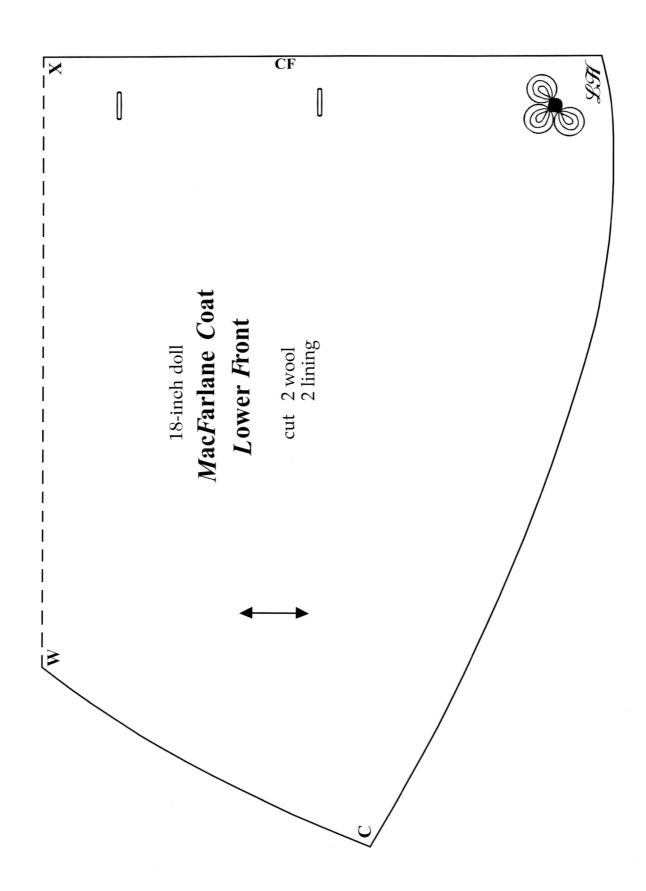

X

CF

W

C

18-inch doll

MacFarlane Coat
Lower Front

cut 2 wool
2 lining

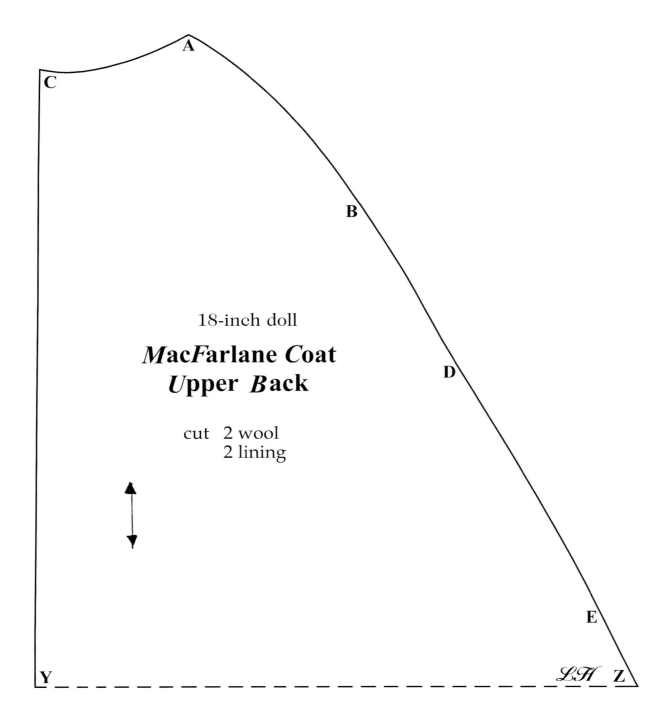

C

A

B

18-inch doll

MacFarlane Coat
Upper Back

cut 2 wool
       2 lining

D

E

Y

LH Z

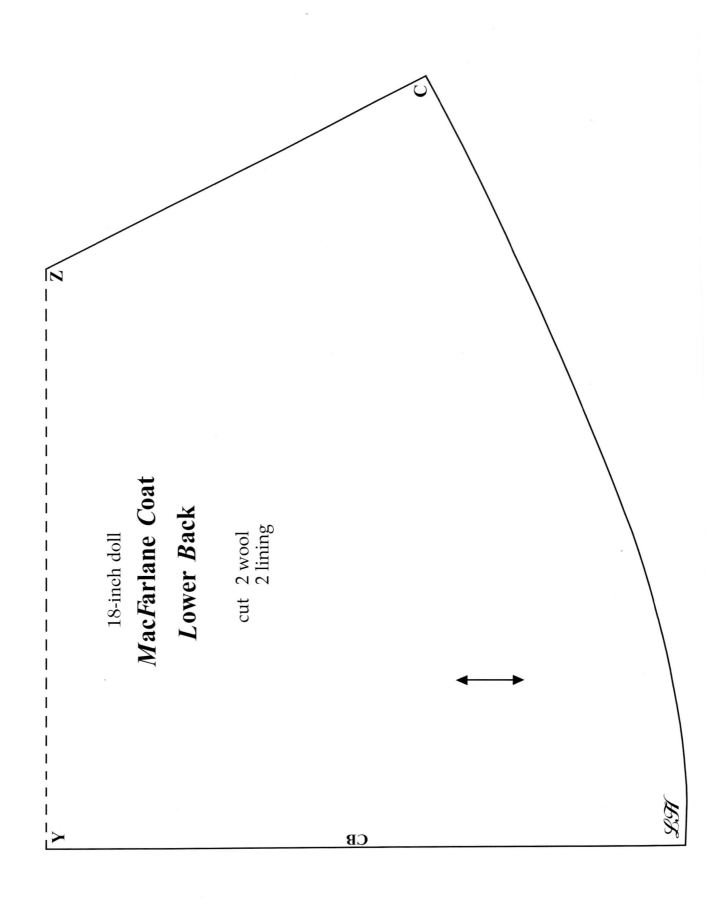

18-inch doll

MacFarlane Coat

Lower Back

cut 2 wool
2 lining

Evening Cape from La Poupée Modèle, March 1865

Materials

Lightweight wool (shown), silk taffeta (shown) or satin: 15" x 21" (22" x 36")

Silk taffeta (shown) or other silk lining: 15" x 21" (22" x 36")

1 mm (2 mm) Cotton soutache: 8-1/2 yards (13 yards)

1/8" Grosgrain or silk satin ribbon: 56" (80")

3/4" (1") Silk or cotton fringe: 48" (67")

1/8"- 3/8" Decorative trim for inside: 38" (57")

1/8" Twisted cord: 14" (19")

#10-#12 Crewel needle

#20-#22 Embroidery or chenille needle

Fine embroidery thread to match

Size "0" Hook and eye: 1

Capes were very popular for outerwear during this period. This is a dressier cape to wear over an evening gown. The 12-inch pattern is sewn in wool challis; the 18-inch pattern is antique silk taffeta. To make the 18-inch pattern, photocopy the 12-inch pattern at 145 percent. Although 2 mm antique wool soutache was used for the larger model, 1 mm would be equally effective. This same cape pattern may be used to enhance a daytime ensemble and would be particularly effective with the dresses on pages 84, 99, 107 and 128 in Chapter 3. To adapt the cape for wear with daytime ensembles, shorten the cape so that it measures 4-3/4" (6-1/4") in the front and 5"(7-1/2") in the back. Use the same fabric and trim as the dress. If you don't use fringe, lengthen the cape fi" (3/4") overall.

Cut out the three paper patterns for the cape and tape together. Cut two pieces of the main fabric and two of the lining. Stitch the darts of the lining, pressing toward center back. With right sides together, stitch the center back seam of the lining. Press and lay aside.

Stitch the darts of the outside fabric, pressing toward center back. Stitch the center back seam and press to one side. Trace a single line for placement of the grosgrain ribbon from center back to center back, then stitch the ribbon from center back to center back. Trace the soutache design on the cape, again beginning at center back, and stitch the soutache from center back to center back. See page 25 in Chapter 1 for directions for the soutache. Stitch first above the grosgrain line, then below, then above, repeating until the first round is completed, ending at center back. Steam press the entire cape well before beginning the second round. Stitch the second round, and press again. With right sides of the cape and lining together, stitch around the entire cape, leaving open two to three inches at the bottom edge to turn. Trim this seam, turn to the right side, blind stitch the opening closed, and press again. Stitch a row of fringe across the bottom edge, turning under the raw edges at each end. On the inside of the cape, stitch over the edge of the lining with the decorative trim for the inside. Centering it, stitch a 14" (19") twisted cord along the neck edge. Knot each end of the cord. Stitch or glue the remaining fringe to make two tassels at the ends of the cord. Begin by placing the heading of the fringe against the knot at the end of the cord. Wrap around and around, stitching or gluing as you go, using about 5" of fringe for each tassel.

The evening cape for 18-inch Lily is fashioned from green antique shot-silk taffeta. It is trimmed in antique wool soutache, gold grosgrain ribbon and ivory wool fringe.

Linette's 12-inch evening cape is made from lavender wool challis lined in ivory silk taffeta, complemented by ivory and ecru embellishments. The closure at the neck is a hook-and-thread eye with cording and tassels.

Evening Cape from *La Poupée Modèle*, March 1865 - 12-inch Doll

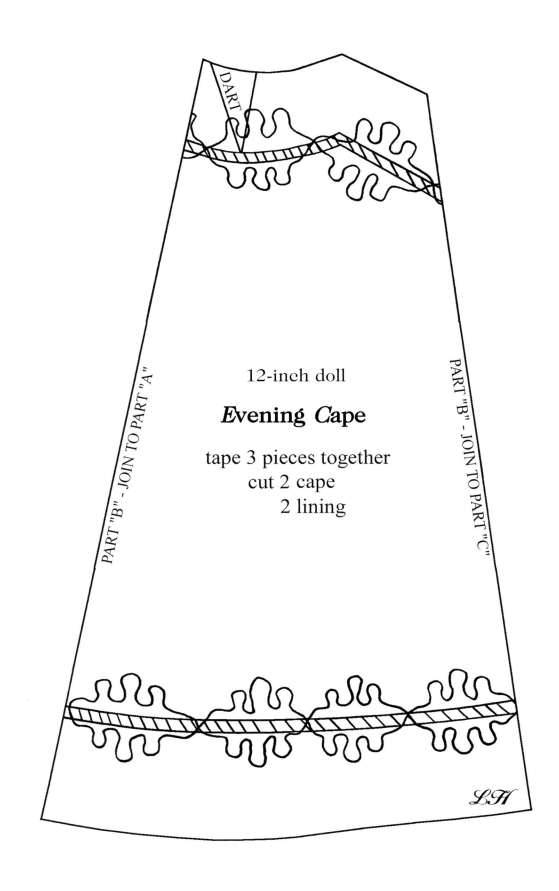

DART

PART "B" - JOIN TO PART "A"

PART "B" - JOIN TO PART "C"

12-inch doll

Evening Cape

tape 3 pieces together
cut 2 cape
2 lining

LH

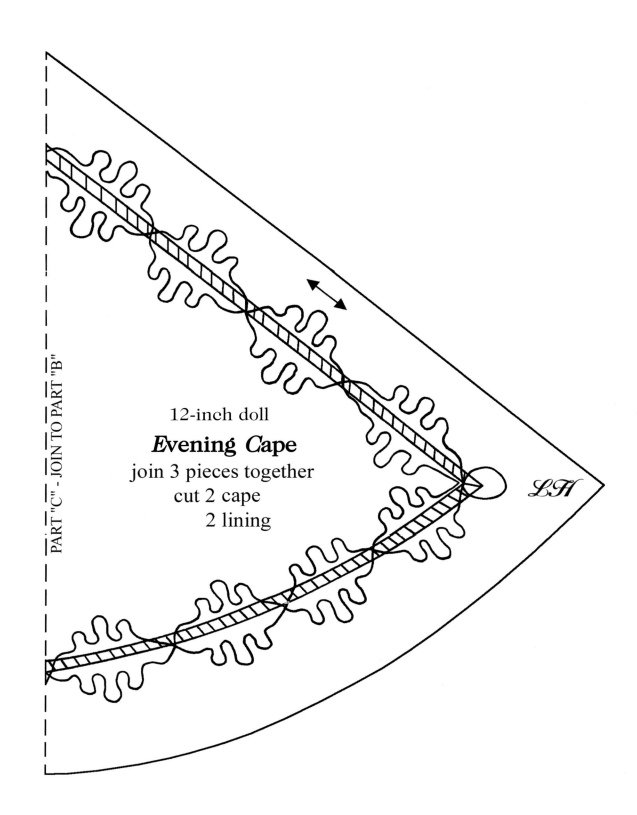

PART "C" - JOIN TO PART "B"

12-inch doll
Evening Cape
join 3 pieces together
cut 2 cape
2 lining

LH

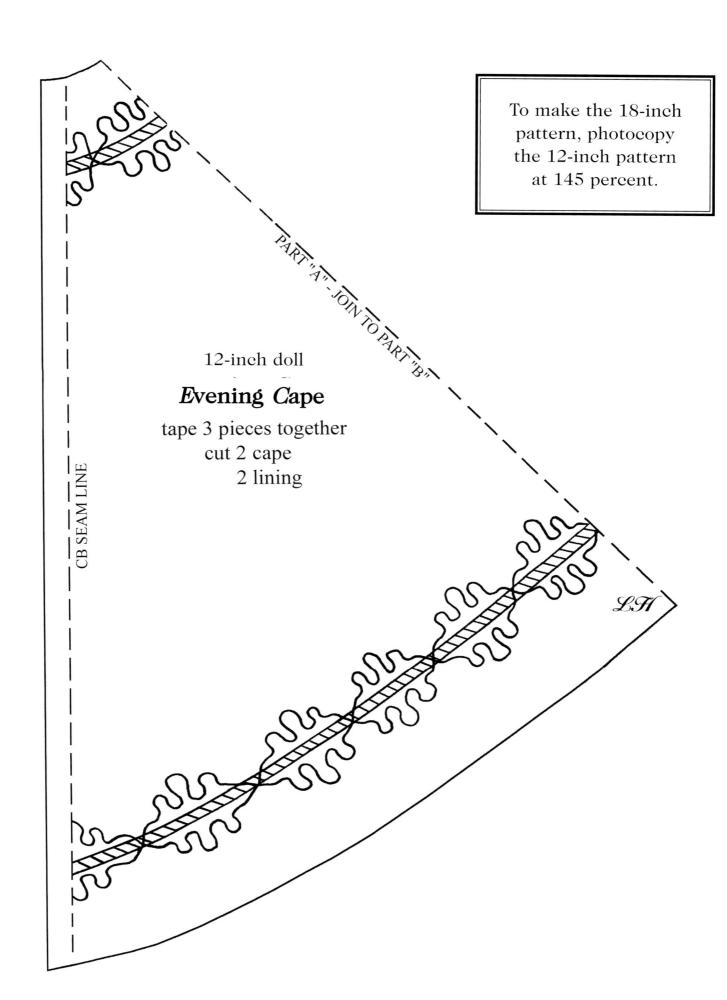

To make the 18-inch
pattern, photocopy
the 12-inch pattern
at 145 percent.

PART "A" - JOIN TO PART "B"

12-inch doll

Evening Cape

tape 3 pieces together
cut 2 cape
2 lining

CB SEAM LINE

LH

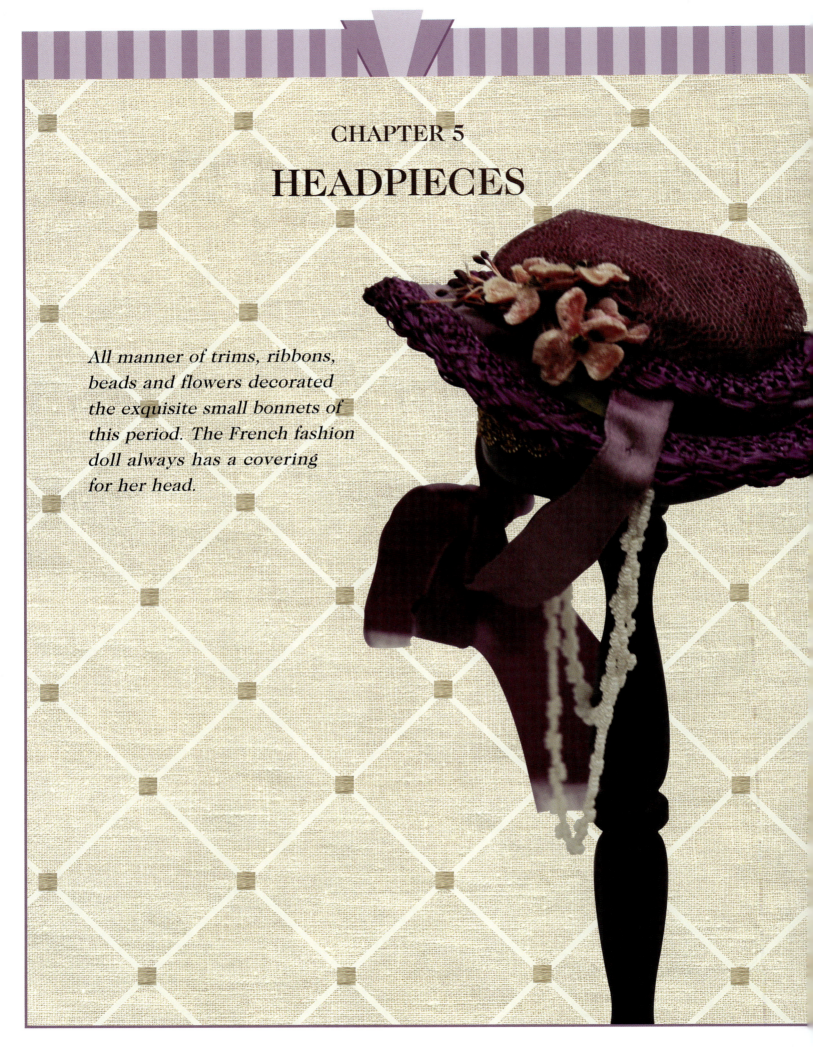

CHAPTER 5
HEADPIECES

All manner of trims, ribbons, beads and flowers decorated the exquisite small bonnets of this period. The French fashion doll always has a covering for her head.

Crown
cut 1 buckram

**DO NOT CUT
OUT CIRCLE**
LH

12-inch doll
Bonnet
cut 1 Bonnet
1 lining

LH

Chapeau Auvergnate
from La Poupée Modèle, December 1870

Materials

Silk taffeta (shown), other silks, lightweight wool:
    4" x 6" (5" x 8")
Swiss cotton tulle (shown) or silk netting: 4" x 6"
    (5" x 8")
Silk taffeta (shown) or fine cotton for lining:
    1-1/2" x 6" (2" x 8")
Lightweight buckram: 3" x 5" (4" x 6")
6 mm Silk satin ribbon: 21" (27")
3/8" (1/2") Lace edging: 12" (15")
20-22 Gauge cotton-covered wire: 7" (9")
Trimmings: Flowers, stamens, leaves (shown),
    feathers (shown)
#10-#12 Crewel needle
Matching fine embroidery thread

This is a very basic bonnet that can be interpreted in many ways. The samples are shown in red silk taffeta, with trimmings of flowers on one and red and black feathers on the other. You could also use ruchings of silk or silk satin ribbon around the crown.

Bonnet: Cut one crown (with spokes) and one brim from buckram. Cut out the twelve spokes as shown on the pattern. Cut one fabric brim and one crown of both silk and netting.

With a whip stitch, sew the cotton-covered wire to the outside of the buckram brim. Overlap and wrap a small amount at the end. With wrong sides together, and the net on top, baste the net and silk of the fabric brim together at the outside and inside of the circle edges. Fold this fabric brim around the buckram brim. The insides will line up with each other. Pin each quarter at back, front and each side. Stitch around the inside circle, stitching all three layers together. Then stitch around the outside circle of the net and silk, gathering as you go so that the outside edge of the buckram is covered and your stitching is on the inside of the bonnet. This gathered side will be the underside of the brim.

With wrong sides together, baste the net and silk of the fabric crown together at the outside edge. Center this piece over the buckram, as indicated by the dotted line on the buckram crown pattern. Stitch the fabric to the buck-ram piece along the outside edge. Place this piece over a circular object, such as a pill container, and push down, giving it a couple of shots of steam from an iron, which will give it a slightly rounded shape. Then place the crown on top of the brim, centering it. Push the tips of the spokes to the wrong side and stitch around this circle.

Lining: Take the silk lining 1-1/2" x 6" (2" x 8") and, with right sides together, seam the short ends. Turn to the right side and press. Fold on the long side so that the piece measures 3/4" x 5-1/2"(1" x 7-1/2"). Stitch a gathering stitch along the folded long edge of the silk, pull up tight, and bind off. Fold raw edges to the wrong side and stitch the lining to the inside of the bonnet. Distribute any extra full-ness evenly around the outside edge.

Bend the front brim up as shown on the sketch on page 202. Cut the lace in half, 6" (7-1/2") and gather by pulling the thread in the heading to fit the front brim. Stitch both pieces of this lace to the raised part of the brim, one slightly lower than the other. Make a bow with 1-1/4" (1-1/2") streamers and stitch it in place at the center back of the bonnet. Cut the remainder of the ribbon in half, and stitch it to each side of the bonnet just in back of the brim. Glue or stitch flowers and leaves, or feathers, onto the raw edge of the bonnet, between the crown and the brim, from one side of the bow to the other. You may tie the silk satin ribbon under the doll's chin in a bow.

The bonnet for the 18-inch doll features dyed red and black feathers. Opposite page: The silk and tulle bonnet for the 12-inch doll is trimmed with Valenciennes lace with leaves and red flowers.

Chapeau Auvergnate
from *La Poupée Modèle*, December 1870
12-inch Doll

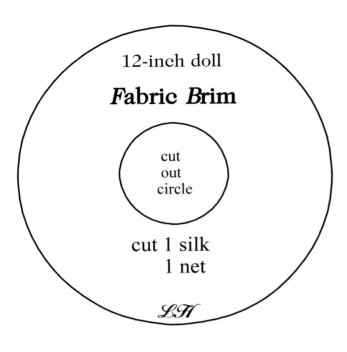

12-inch doll

Fabric Brim

cut
out
circle

cut 1 silk
1 net

LH

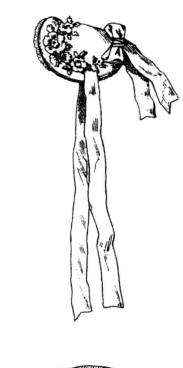

12-inch doll
**Fabric
Bonnet Crown**
cut 1 silk
1 net

LH

12-inch doll

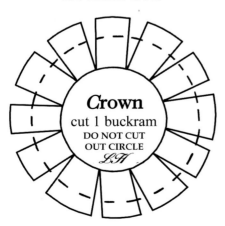

Crown
cut 1 buckram
DO NOT CUT
OUT CIRCLE
LH

Bonnet Brim

12-inch doll

cut
out
circle

LH

cut 1 buckram

Chapeau Auvergnate
from *La Poupée Modèle*, December 1870
18-inch Doll

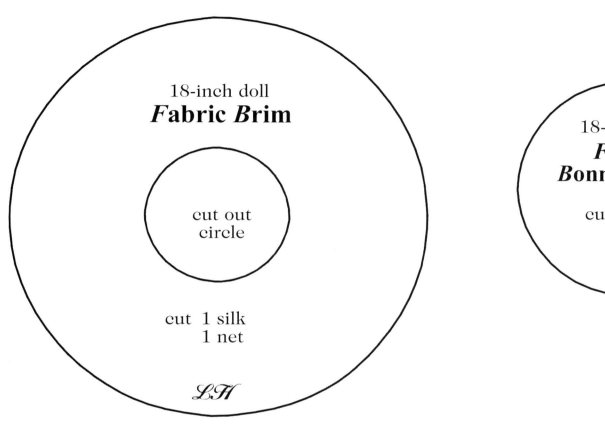

18-inch doll
Fabric Brim

cut out circle

cut 1 silk
1 net

LH

18-inch doll
Fabric Bonnet Crown

cut 1 silk
1 net

LH

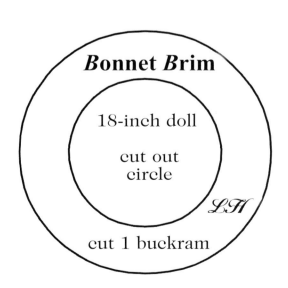

Bonnet Brim

18-inch doll

cut out circle

LH

cut 1 buckram

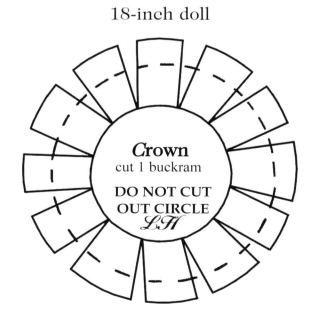

18-inch doll

Crown
cut 1 buckram

DO NOT CUT OUT CIRCLE
LH

Chapeau Fanchon
from La Poupée Modèle, *April 1865*

Materials

Lightweight buckram for base: 3" x 5" (3-1/2" x 6")

Cotton velvet (shown), silk: 3" x 5" OR 1/4" straw, 2 yards + 1/4" velvet ribbon, 9" (shown)

Silk for lining: 3" x 5" (3-1/2" x 6-1/2")

1/2" Edging lace: 9" (12")

3/8" Edging lace: 8" (14")

1/8" Decorative trim: 12" (16")

Several flowers, stamens, leaves

7 mm (12 mm) silk ribbon for ties: 12" (18")

20-22 Gauge cotton covered wire: 12" (16")

Size 10-12 Crewel needle, size 13 beading needle

Matching fine embroidery thread

If covering with pearls as shown: approximately 40 (50)

Flirtation ribbons: 10", 4 mm velvet ribbon (14", 4 mm velvet ribbon)

6-8 Pearls or crystal beads 3-5 mm; 2 tiny crystal beads

This is another very popular bonnet from this period. It was frequently made either with straw or fabric, usually silk or velvet. The bonnet for the 12-inch doll is cotton velvet embellished with 2 mm pearls, while the bonnet for the 18-inch doll is made from antique straw. The flirtation ribbons trailing the back of each bonnet were designated to be worn by young unmarried ladies and were abandoned once a woman was married. Although the materials for both bonnets are similar, the order in which they are applied to the bonnet is different, so the instructions are presented separately. Patterns are also presented for making the 18-inch bonnet from fabric. Another version of this bonnet is seen on the 12-inch doll on page 109 in Chapter 3.

12-inch bonnet from fabric: Cut out the bonnet form of lightweight buckram. With a whipping stitch, apply the cotton-covered wire to the outside edge of the form, overlapping and wrapping a little at the end. Cut out silk and lining pieces from the bonnet pattern; cut them on the bias. Stitch the top fabric around the buckram form, covering the top side of the bonnet with about 1/4" on the wrong side. The stitching is done with a whip stitch from the wrong side; take care not to have the stitches show through to the right side. With a beading needle and thread, stitch the 2 mm pearls to the bonnet, scattering them evenly over the top. Gather the fi" lace to fit the back of the bonnet by pulling the heading thread. Stitch to the back. Gather the 3/8" edging lace to fit the front half of the bonnet by pulling the heading thread, and stitch to the front. Fold the seam allowance of the lining to the wrong side and stitch to the under side of the bonnet with a whipping stitch, so that the threads do not show on the right side. Stitch or glue the decorative trim over the edge of the lining. Cut two pieces of 7 mm silk ribbon, 6" each, and fasten to each side of the bonnet. When the bonnet is complete, these can either hang down on the doll's shoulders or be tied under the chin.

Flirtation ribbons (for both sizes): Cut two pieces of velvet ribbon 2-1/2" and 3-1/4" (4" and 5") each. Fold one end in a point and, using a beading needle and thread, stitch the beads as follows: Alternate pearls and crystals and finish with tiny crystal bead. Then go back through the larger beads only and secure the thread at the "v" at the bottom of the ribbon. Stitch this to the "v" at the center back of the bonnet. Using the rest of the velvet ribbon, tie a bow and stitch it over the hanging ribbons.

Then stitch or glue flowers and leaves at the center front of the bonnet, just under the front edge. See the drawing of the bonnet on page 207, or the photos on the opposite page and page 206, for placement. Bend the sides of bonnet down to fit the head.

18-inch bonnet from straw: Cut out the bonnet form from lightweight buckram. With a whipping stitch, apply the cotton-covered wire to the outside edge of the form, overlapping and wrapping a little at the end. Turning under short ends and folding in half lengthwise, stitch the 4 mm velvet ribbon across the front curved edge of the bonnet form. Half of the ribbon is on the top and half is on the wrong side. Starting at the front edge, just below the velvet ribbon, glue strips of straw over the entire bonnet. Unravel a small amount at the cut edge of the straw. Identify and pull one of the two cotton threads to curve the straw. Each row of straw overlaps the previous one by less than 1/8". Wrap the raw edges of the straw around the ends at each side of each row. Work all the way to the back of the bonnet so that the entire top surface is covered.

This Fanchon bonnet for the 12-inch doll is made from antique velvet and lace.

Gather the 1/2" lace to fit the back of the bonnet by pulling the heading thread, and stitch or glue it to the back of the bonnet. Gather the 3/8" edging lace to fit the front half of the bonnet by pulling the heading thread, and stitch or glue it to the front edge. Cut the silk lining on the bias from the bonnet pattern. Fold the 1/4" seam allowance to the wrong side and stitch to the underside of the bonnet. Stitch or glue the decorative trim over the edge of the lining. Cut two pieces of 12 mm ribbon 9" each and fasten to each side of the bonnet. When the bonnet is complete, these can either hang down on her shoulders or be tied under her chin. The flirtation ribbons and flowers are constructed by the same method as on the bonnet for the 12-inch doll.

The antique straw version of the bonnet is for the 18-inch doll.

Chapeau Fanchon
from *La Poupée Modèle*, April 1865
12-inch Doll

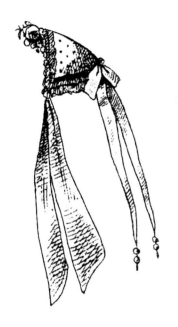

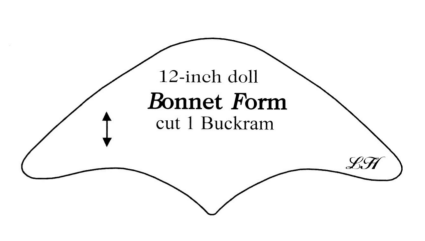

12-inch doll
Bonnet Form
cut 1 Buckram

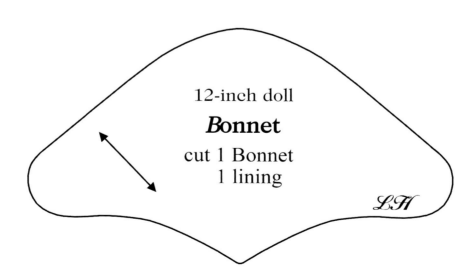

12-inch doll
Bonnet
cut 1 Bonnet
1 lining

Chapeau Fanchon
from *La Poupée Modèle*, April 1865
18-inch Doll

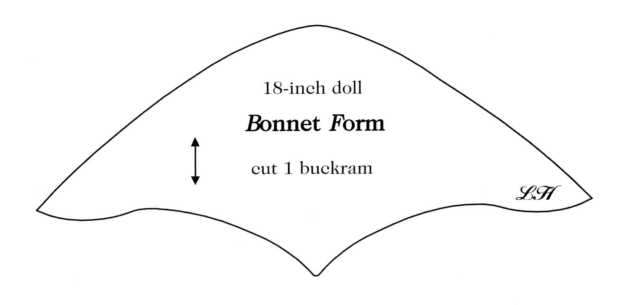

18-inch doll

Bonnet Form

cut 1 buckram

LH

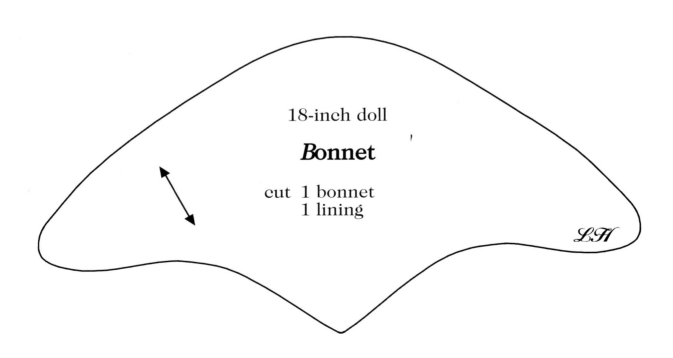

18-inch doll

Bonnet

cut 1 bonnet
1 lining

LH

Fur Muff from *La Poupée Modèle, January 1869* and Fur Toque

Materials

Fur (ermine, lamb shown): 5" x 7" (6" x 8")
Silk taffeta (shown), other silk or cotton batiste for lining: 5" x 7" (6" x 8")
Lightweight buckram: 1-1/2" x 4" (2" x 6")
Thin batting: 1-1/2" x 4" (2" x 6")
Optional cording for muff: 15" (18")
Several pieces of decorative trim
#10-#12 Crewel needle
Matching fine embroidery thread
Glue

The muff pattern is from *La Poupée Modèle* and the fur toque is a copy of an antique. The set is made from ermine for the 12-inch doll and from lamb for the 18-inch doll. Any type of short-haired fur could be used; the set would also be attractive in silk or cotton velvet, or velour. The muff may be hand held, or a twisted silk cording may be added to hang around the doll's neck. The trims on the two examples are ermine tails, antique silk balls and antique tassels. The drawing from *La Poupée Modèle* shows a simple muff with two-colored fur. The choice is yours.

Muff: Cut one muff body, 2" x 4-1/8" (2-5/8" x 6") from fur. Cut one muff lining, 2" x 4-1/8" (2" x 6"). Cut one muff buckram 1-3/8" x 4"(2" x 5-3/4") and one muff batting 1-3/8" x 4"(2" x 5-3/4") from lightweight buckram and thin batting 1-1/2" x 4" (2" x 6"). Make a sandwich of the fur, buckram and batting, centering the buckram and batting on the fur. Fold in and crease the fur 3/16" on each long end. With right sides together, stitch or glue the sandwiched fur with 1/4" seam on the short ends. With right sides together, seam the short ends of the lining. Turn to the right side. Turn under the seam allowance of the lining and whip stitch to the edge of the fur. 1/8" of fur should show on the wrong side. Turn the muff to the right side. If you want the muff to hang from the doll's neck, insert the cording through the muff. Adjust the length so that the muff sits at the waist. Tie a knot in the cord. The knot should rest inside the muff. Often the muffs were perfectly plain, but this 18-inch doll's muff has two hanging ornaments composed of a pearl, bead cap and silk ball attached to the body of the muff, and two antique tassels attached to each side at the lower edge. The 12-inch doll's muff has an ermine tail attached to the body and two silk balls attached to the outer edges on each side. Ribbon bows would also be appropriate.

Toque: Cut one bonnet top and one bonnet side 3/4" x 6-1/2" (1" x 7-3/4") of both fur and lining. The seam allowance for both the fur and the lining is 1/8". When stitching fur to fur, use an overcast or whipping stitch. Stitch the short ends of the sides. With right sides together, stitch the side to the top of the bonnet. Repeat with the lining. Turn under the lower raw edge of the side 1/4" and, if you are using fur, glue to the side. If using fabric, blind stitch it to the side of the toque.

Turn the raw edge of the bonnet lining to the wrong side, and press well. With wrong sides together, stitch the lining to the fur. The 12-inch doll's toque is trimmed with an ermine tail; the 18-inch doll's is trimmed with three of the same silk ball/bead combination as the muff.

The toque and muff for the 18-inch doll are lamb fur trimmed with antique beads and tassels. The muff box was made by Sylvia Mac Neil.

The fur toque and muff for the 12-inch doll are made from ermine and trimmed with ermine tails.

Fur Muff from *La Poupée Modèle*, January 1869 and Fur Toque - 12-inch Doll

Straight Pieces

Bonnet Side ....3/4" x 6-1/2"
Bonnet Side Lining............................3/4" x 6-1/2"
Muff Body...2" x 4-1/8"
Muff Buckram ....1-3/8" x 4"
Muff Batting ....1-3/8" x 4"
Muff Lining ....2" x 4-1/8"

12-inch doll

Bonnet Top

cut 1 fur
1 lining

LH

Fur Muff from *La Poupée Modèle*, January 1869 and Fur Toque - 18-inch Doll

Straight Pieces

Bonnet Side ....1" x 7-3/4"
Bonnet Side Lining............................1" x 7-3/4"
Muff Body...2-5/8"" x 6"
Muff Buckram ....2" x 5-3/4"
Muff Batting ....2" x 5-3/4"
Muff Lining...2" x 6"

18-inch doll

Bonnet Top

cut 1 fur
1 lining

LH

Chapeau Pamela from La Poupée Modèle, April 1866

Note the two-strand "necklaces" of beads that hang from the front side of the bonnet. During this era women did not wear much jewelry, but made up for this with the embellishments on their bonnets. The bonnets for both the 18-inch and 12-inch dolls are decorated with pearls. The sequence of beads shown in *La Poupée Modèle* is used for the 18-inch doll's bonnet. This beading is shown on page 214. The 12-inch doll's bonnet has two simple strands of pearls.

Cut one buckram bonnet brim. Overlap the buckram at the "x" markings and stitch this narrow end together. With a whipping stitch sew the cotton-covered wire to the inside and outside edges of the buckram circle.

Add 1/4" around the entire outside edge of the bonnet brim pattern, and cut out two silk pieces. With right sides together, stitch the short seam marked "x" to form two circles. With right sides together, stitch the inner circle, turn to the right side and press. Place the silk fabric to encase the buckram circle. Turn under the 1/4" seam allowance, and stitch on the outer edge to encase the whole piece. Stitch the straw on the top and under sides of the outer edge of the circle. Stitch each side on the inner edge, then stitch all layers of the outer edge together with a whip stitch.

Cut two pieces of tulle for bonnet crown. Place one on top of the other and stitch around the outside edge to gather to fit the inner edge of the bonnet. Stitch this circle to the right side of the bonnet. Cut two 7" (9") pieces

of ribbon and stitch them on either side of the bonnet on top of the edge of tulle. These ribbons tie under the doll's chin. Stitch the second row of straw over the raw edge of the tulle and ribbon. Unravel the cut ends of the straw and select the two cotton threads. Pull the thread on the outer and inner edges of the straw to fit this circle. On this same edge, inside the bonnet, stitch the 1/8" (1/4") decorative trim to finish this edge. Decorate the left front side of the bonnet with a few small flowers and stamens.

Beading: Two beaded strands are attached just in front of the ribbons on the side of the bonnet; the shorter one is 4" (7") and the longer is 7" (10"). These can be made of any type of seed bead. Begin by threading the #13 beading needle and attaching the thread just in front of the ribbon. String beads until you reach the desired lengths. Fasten on the other side. When the bonnet is completed, bend the bonnet on each side to fit the doll's head. It comes to a rounded point at center front and center back. Tie the bow under the doll's chin.

This green bonnet for the 12-inch doll features a simple pearl "necklace" trim.

This Pamela bonnet is modeled by the 18-inch antique Huret. Note the beading trim on the pattern on page 214.

Chapeau Pamela
from *La Poupée Modèle*, April 1866
12-inch Doll

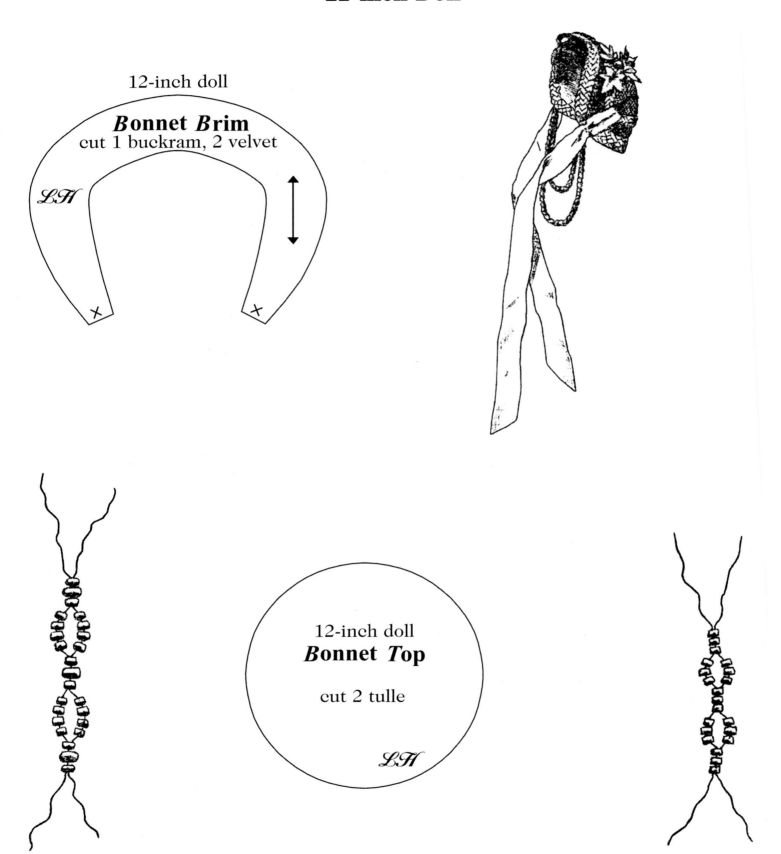

12-inch doll

Bonnet Brim
cut 1 buckram, 2 velvet

LH

×   ×

12-inch doll
Bonnet Top

cut 2 tulle

LH

Chapeau Pamela
from *La Poupée Modèle*, April 1866
18-inch Doll

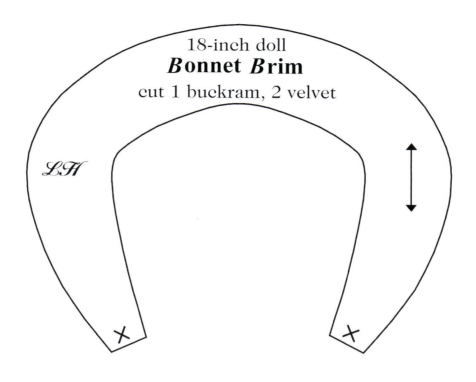

18-inch doll
Bonnet Brim

cut 1 buckram, 2 velvet

LH

X   X

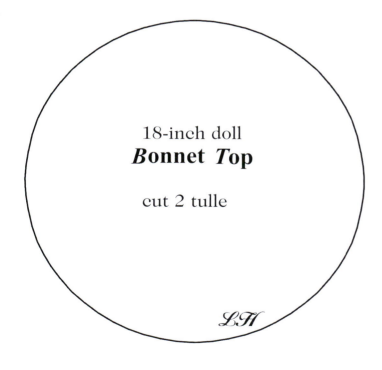

18-inch doll
Bonnet Top

cut 2 tulle

LH

This Pamela bonnet for the 18-inch doll is made from all antique straw, tulle, ribbon and flowers.

CHAPTER 6
ACCESSORIES

From underpinnings to dressing gowns, a multitude of accessories is required to properly complete the French fashion doll's wardrobe.

2-inch
doll
tocking

cut 2

LH

FOLD

A

B

A

12-inch doll
***Empire Hoop
Front***

cut 1

A

CF FOLD

LH

Apron from *La Poupée Modèle, April 1874*

Materials

Cotton broadcloth (shown) or linen (shown):
   9" x 27" (12" x 36")
Cotton batiste: 7" x 6" (10" x 8")
1 mm cotton soutache: 4-1/2 yards (6-1/2 yards)
Stranded embroidery floss: 1 yard
Fine embroidery thread to match
Size "0" (1) Hooks and eyes: 2
#10-#12 Crewel needle
#18-#20 Embroidery needle

Many types of aprons were shown in *La Poupée Modèle* over the years. Some were tailored and plain, worn over the dresses for daily tasks, and others were of fine silk. This one was made of cotton or linen, worn to avoid soiling Lily's dress in the kitchen or garden and, on the advice of Mlle Péronne, was either ecru, grey or some other subtle color. The soutache is stitched in a serpentine pattern and can be done either free hand, or by drawing on the design as shown on each pattern piece. The embroidery is stitched with one strand in a color to match the soutache. Only the collars and sleeves are lined. This A-line garment was made to be worn over the doll's very full skirts.

Spray starch both fabrics first. Cut one front, two backs, two sleeves, two pockets, two back collars and one front collar from apron fabric. Cut two sleeves, one front collar and two back collars from lining fabric. French seam the shoulder seams and side seams. Press both toward the center back. Narrow hem the center back openings and bottom edge. Roll and whip the entire neck edge.

Draw on the serpentine soutache pattern as shown on the pattern pieces or stitch one free-handed. See page 25 in Chapter 1 for directions for applying the soutache. Stitch the higher band across the bottom first. Note that on the samples this can be from 1/2" to 1" from the finished bottom edge. Then stitch from the neck edge at center back, down the back, across the bottom edge and up the other side to the neck. The soutache rests just inside the narrow hem.

Sleeves: With right sides together, stitch the lining to the sleeve, leaving open at the armhole. Turn and press. Draw and stitch the soutache pattern as shown on the sleeve

pattern. The open sides of the sleeve line up with the shoulder seam. Trim and overcast these seams.

Pockets: Draw on the embroidery pattern and stitch with one strand of embroidery thread. Note that the pattern piece for the pocket shows the pattern on the *wrong* side. Turn the flap down and draw and stitch on the right side. The stitches used are the stem for both the 12-inch and 18-inch patterns: granitos (12-inch pattern) and satin (18-inch pattern). See pages 22 and 23 in Chapter 1 for instructions for these stitches. Turn under the seam allowance of the pockets 1/8" and press. Stitch the soutache on the flap, then bring it through to the right side of the pocket using the larger needle.

Pin the pocket to the apron front, as shown on the pattern. When stitching the soutache pattern to the pocket, stitch it also to the apron. Finish the pocket with one or two tacking stitches to hold down the flap.

Collars: There are three collars: one for the front and two for the back. Draw on the embroidery designs and stitch them in the same manner as you did the pockets. With right sides together, stitch the apron fabric to the lining of all three collars. Leave open about one inch on each piece. Turn to the right side, turn under the raw edges and blind stitch this opening. Outline all three pieces with soutache, as shown on the pattern pieces. Tack the collars to the neck edge in two or three places for each piece. First tack the back pieces, then the front, with the front piece over-lapping the back pieces. Close the apron with two hooks and thread eyes, one at the neck edge, the second 1/2" (3/4") down. The apron measures 5-1/2" (8") at center front.

Lily wears her apron constructed from antique ecru linen and trimmed in ivory soutache and embroidery over her winter skirt. Opposite page: Linette's neutral grey apron is brightened by a simplified purple embroidery.

Apron from *La Poupée Modèle*, April 1874 - 12-inch Doll

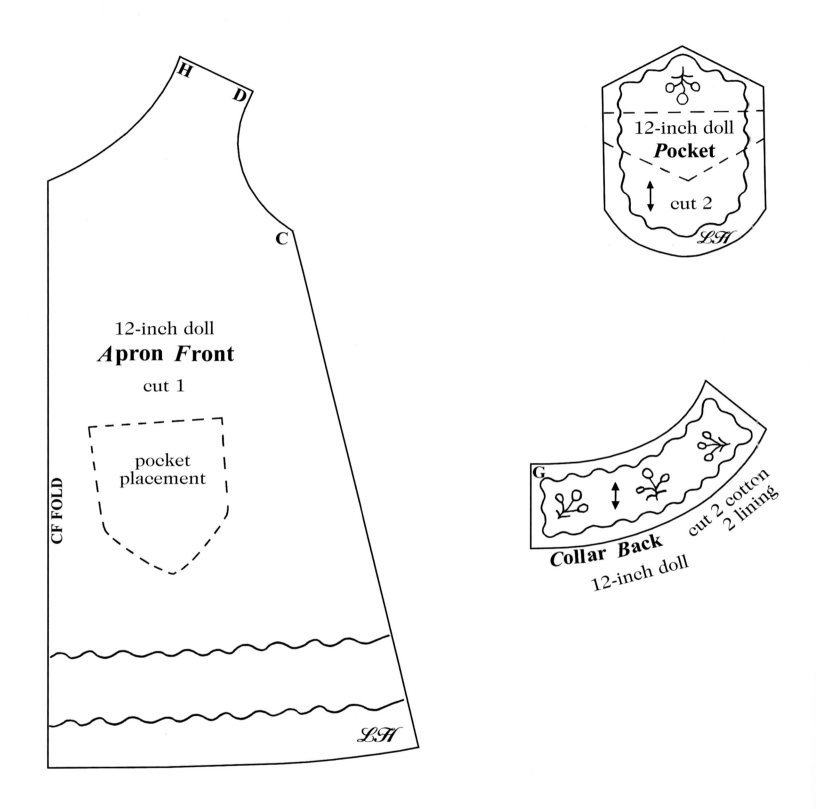

12-inch doll
Pocket
cut 2

12-inch doll
Apron Front
cut 1

pocket
placement

CF FOLD

G

Collar Back
cut 2 cotton
2 lining
12-inch doll

12-inch doll **Sleeve**
cut 2 cotton, 2 lining

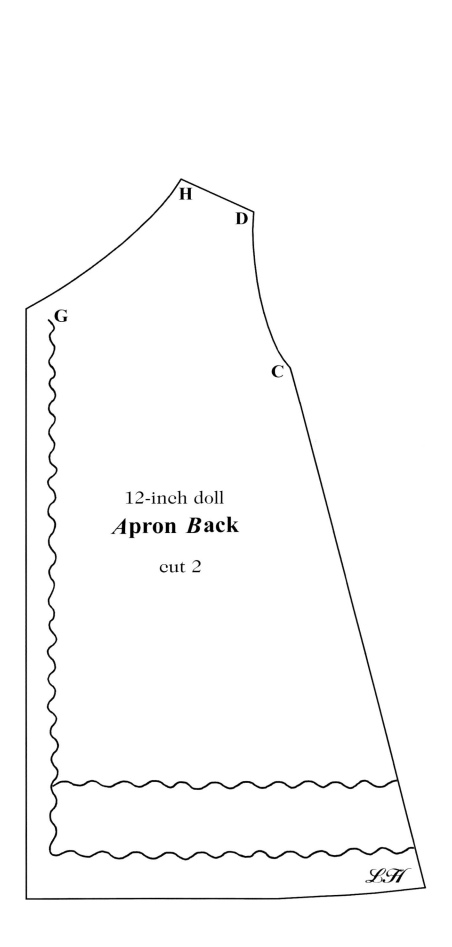

12-inch doll
Apron Back

cut 2

G

H   D

C

LH

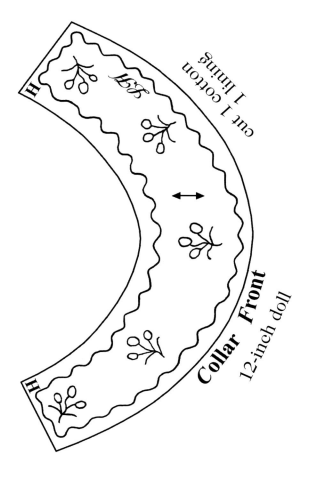

Collar Front
12-inch doll

cut 1 cotton
1 lining

H

H

LH

Apron from *La Poupée Modèle*, April 1874 - 18-inch Doll

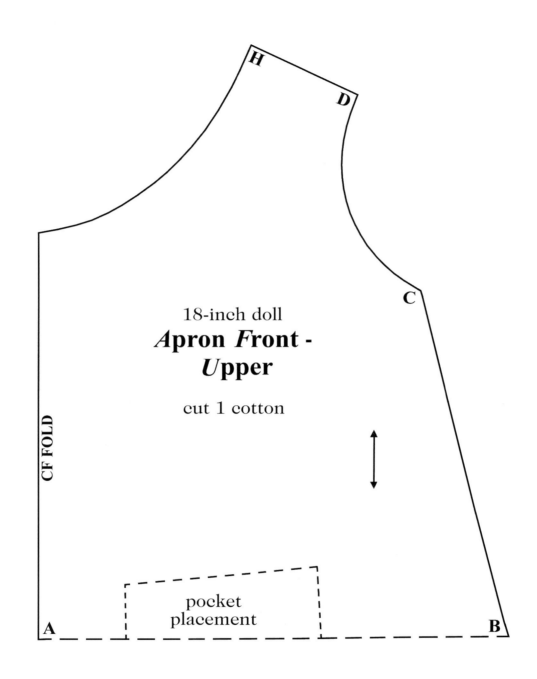

H

D

C

CF FOLD

18-inch doll
Apron Front - Upper

cut 1 cotton

pocket
placement

A

B

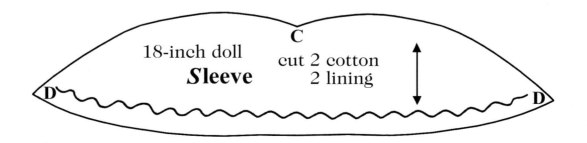

C

18-inch doll
Sleeve

cut 2 cotton
2 lining

D

D

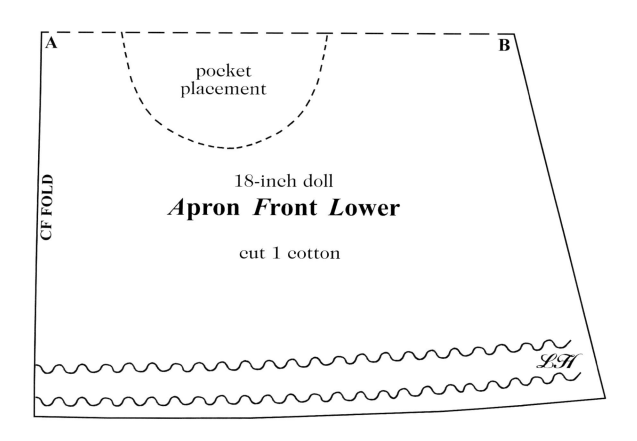

A

B

CF FOLD

pocket
placement

18-inch doll
Apron *Front Lower*

cut 1 cotton

LH

Apron from *La Poupée Modèle*, April 1874 - 18-inch Doll

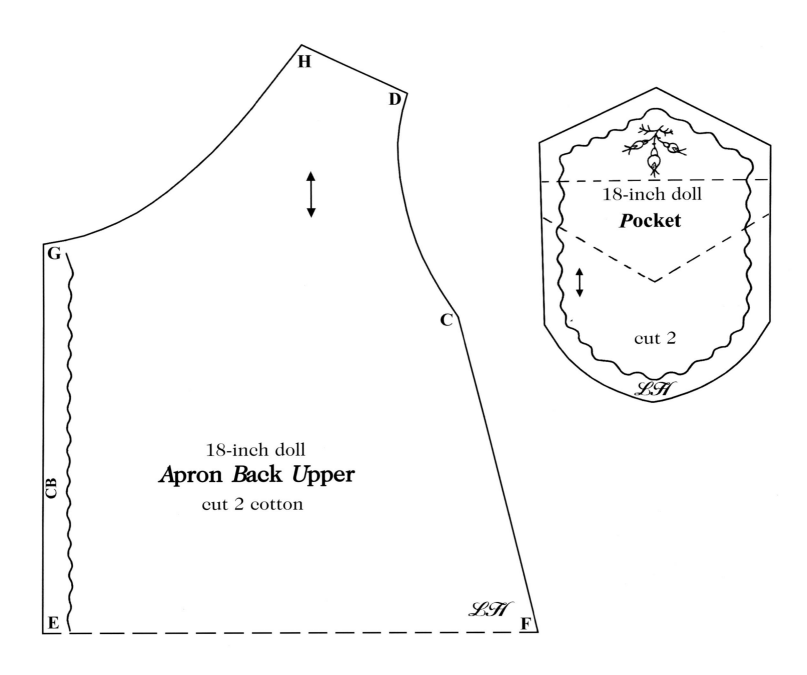

H

D

G

CB

18-inch doll
Apron Back Upper

cut 2 cotton

C

E   *LH*   F

18-inch doll
Pocket

cut 2

LH

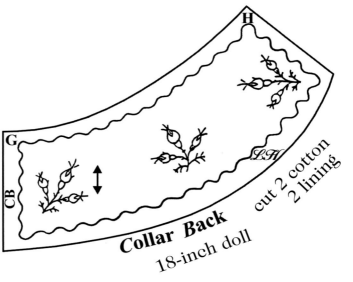

H

G

CB

LH

Collar Back
18-inch doll

cut 2 cotton
2 lining

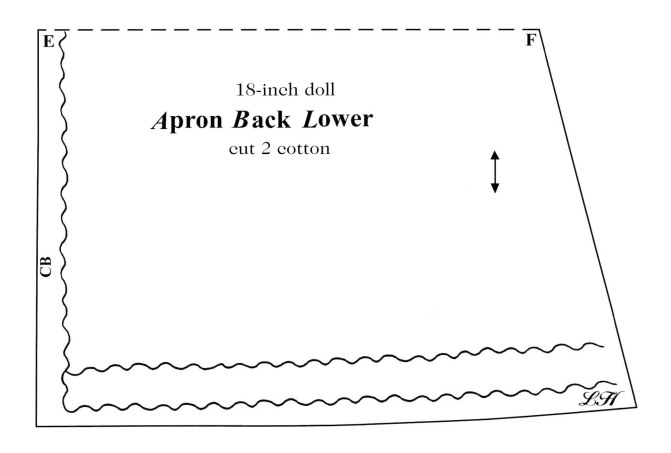

E   F

18-inch doll
Apron Back Lower
cut 2 cotton

CB

LH

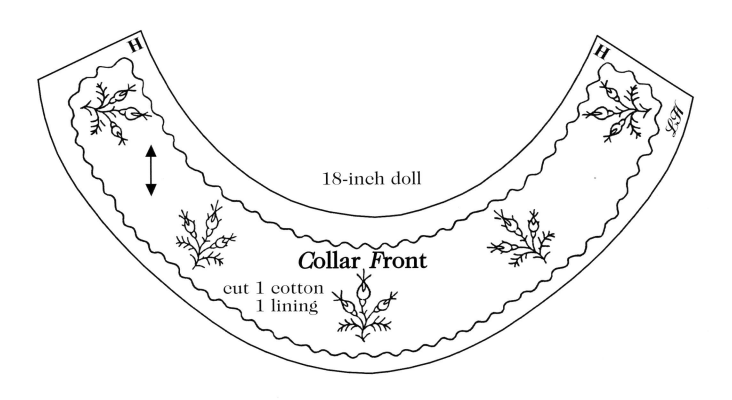

H   H

18-inch doll

Collar Front

cut 1 cotton
1 lining

LH

Boned Corset
from La Poupée Modèle, *November 1871*

Materials

Cotton sateen (shown) or cotton twill: 4" x 8"
   (5" x 13")
Boning (see below): 10-1/2" (17-1/2")
6 mm Silk satin ribbon to match fabric: 14" (20")
6 mm Blue (shown) or red (shown) silk satin
   ribbon: 14" (20")
Stranded blue or red embroidery floss: 1-1/4 yards
   (2 yards)
1/8" Cotton twill tape: 16" (24")
1/8" Brass eyelets (optional, see directions): 5 (7)
Fine embroidery thread to match
#10-#12 Crewel needle

Of all the garments from *La Poupée Modèle* that have survived the years, the corset is the one most often seen. It was made from cream or ivory fabric, with either blue or red trim. An example of each is shown here. Boning material is available in 3 mm width, but an easy alternative is to cut the pieces 3 mm in width by the necessary length from plastic milk or soft drink bottles. The ends should be rounded to avoid piercing the fabric.

The seam allowance for the corset is 1/8" and is included in the pattern. Spray starch the fabric before beginning to work. Cut one front, two backs and two gussets. You may wish to seal all edges of the fabric to keep them from fraying. With right sides together, stitch the gussets to the front piece. Stretch the gusset as you stitch to make the pieces match. Press this seam down. With right sides together, stitch the backs to the front. Press these seams towards the back. Turn under center backs 1/4" and press to a sharp edge. Using a back stitch, as explained on page 21 in Chapter 1, stitch the "v"s at the top of the front, as shown on the pattern. Stitch a back stitch down the gusset seams at bottom front and side seams; this will hold the seams in place. The five casings are made with silk satin ribbon to match the fabric. Attach them to the wrong side of the corset and, using the back stitch, stitch in place with the colored embroidery thread. The stitching must be done on the very edge of the ribbon.

Cut five bones a skimpy 2-1/4" (3-1/2"). The five bones

of the corset are located at center front, on each side of center front and inside the eyelets on the back. It is very important that the bones be a little short of the length of the corset to keep them from poking through the fabric. When the bones are in place, stitch the fan pattern of five stitches at the top and bottom of the corset, as shown on the pattern. Stitch the slanting parallel lines on the back of the corset, as shown on the pattern and in the photograph. Work 5 (7) eyelets in the back of the corset, using an eyelet applicator and brass eyelets or a buttonhole stitch. See directions for the buttonhole stitch on page 23 in Chapter 1. Bind the upper and lower edges of the corset in silk satin 6 mm ribbon that matches the embroidery floss. You may either press the ribbon in half lengthwise and secure both edges at one time, or use a running stitch on the front, turn to the wrong side, and blind stitch the back. Lace the eyelets with 1/8" twill tape.

Lily's 18-inch corset is made of antique twill and stitched in the most classic color, red.

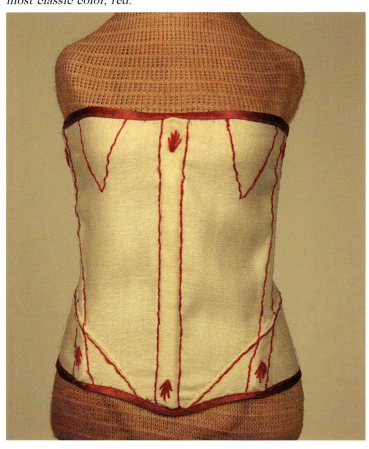

Linette's 12-inch corset is cotton sateen, stitched in blue.

Boned Corset
from *La Poupée Modèle*, November 1871
12-inch Doll

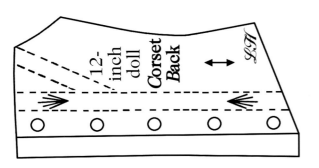

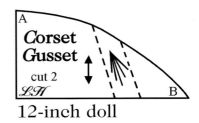

12-inch doll

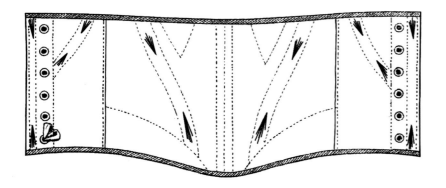

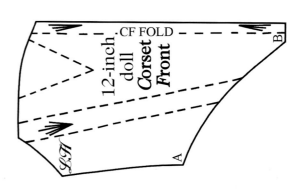

Boned Corset
from *La Poupée Modèle*, November 1871
18-inch Doll

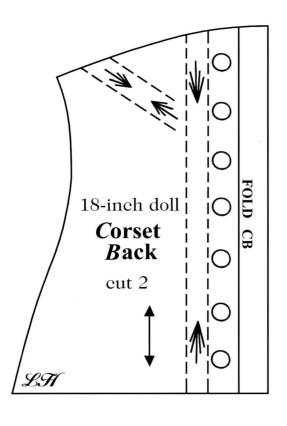

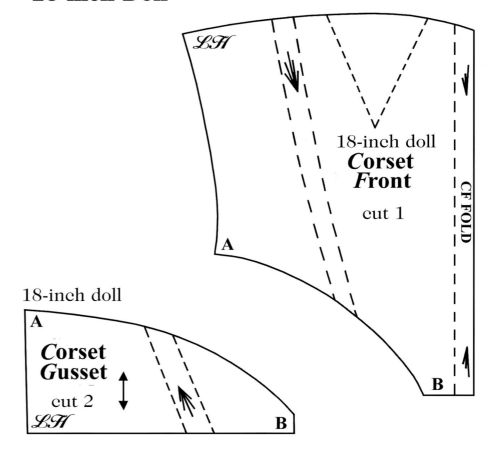

Caged Hoop

Materials

3/8" (1/2") Woven cotton twill tape: 1 yard
   (1-1/2 yards)
Size 18-gauge cotton-covered hat wire: 1-1/4 yards
   (55")
Metal connectors: 3
Fine embroidery thread to match
Size "0" (1) Hook and eye: 1
White and instant glue (see below)
#10-#12 Crewel needle

The caged hoop was the first type of hoop to be worn by French fashion dolls. This one wired garment replaced the many full crinolines that came before. It was worn under the full gathered skirts of the period and was soon replaced by the Empire hoop, which came into fashion once skirts evolved to have the fullness moving toward to the back, and an A-line front panel without gathers. Wire connectors, small tubes into which you can insert and glue the hat wire, are available on the market. If you cannot find any, you may use adhesive tape as a substitute. Please note that on the samples the wire was first soaked in coffee so it would match the ecru tape. The connectors were painted antique gold, as most of the antique hoops had brass connectors.

Cut three pieces of wire: top: 12" (13"), middle: 13-1/2" (18") and bottom: 15" (24"). Cut six pieces of cotton twill tape: one piece 5-1/2" (8-1/2") for the waistband and five pieces, each 6" (9"). Turn under short ends of the waistband 1/4" on each end and blind stitch.

If using connectors: Unravel 1/8" from each end of the three wires. Place a couple of dots of white glue on the wire and a dot of instant glue in one hole of the connector. Insert the wire into the connector and let dry completely. Repeat with the other two wires. Form the three wires into circles and insert the other ends of the wires into the connectors in the same manner.

If using tape: Using a double thread, stitch the two ends of each wire together with several stitches, wrapping the thread around the wire as you go. When this is stable, cover the wire where it is joined with a few dots of white glue. Let this set up for a minute or two, then wrap twice with a

heavy tape. You may then paint the tape to match the wire.

Attach the five pieces of woven tape 1/8" (1/4") up from the bottom of the waistband tape. Stitch them on the wrong side and space them evenly. The first one is about 1/4" (1/2") from center back, and each of the others is about 1" (1-3/4") apart. Repeat with the three circles of wire, stitching the tape around the wire. The connectors (tape) should be at center back. Measure carefully so that the hoop hangs evenly. The finished length of the hoop is 5" (8"). Close the waistband with a hook and eye.

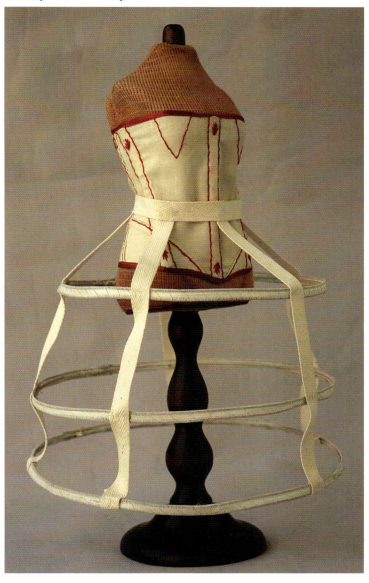

Lily's 18-inch caged hoop is constructed of antique wired crinoline tape and twill tape.

Linette's 12-inch caged hoop is made from 18-gauge covered wire, twill tape and gold painted metal connectors.

Empire Hoop from La Poupée Modéle, *April 1867*

Materials

Cotton broadcloth (shown) or linen (shown):
   9" x 22" (12" x 36")

Swiss cotton batiste for wire casings: 4" x 54"
   (8" x 40")

18 or 20 gauge cotton-covered hat wire: 56" (75")

1" (1-1/2") Swiss cotton embroidered edging:
   3/4 yard (48")

3/16" Mother-of-pearl buttons: 2

Fine embroidery thread to match

#10-#12 Crewel needle

During the late 1860s, skirts begin to change in shape. As the 1870s approached, the silhouette changed from a full gathered or pleated skirt to a four- or five-piece gored skirt. This new skirt had a flat A-line front, with side and back pieces that were gathered or pleated, pushing all the fullness to the back and creating a bustle effect for the skirt. This *Cage Empire* was designed to be worn under these skirts.

Cut out the body of the hoop from cotton broadcloth or linen: one front on fold, two backs, a front waistband, 1" x 2-3/4" (1" x 4-1/2"), a back waistband, 1" x 3-1/2" (1" x 5-1/2"), and four front/side opening pieces, 5/8" x 2-3/4" (5/8" x 4").

To prepare the cotton batiste cases that will contain the wire, you will need approximately 52" for the entire garment. Iron the batiste, spraying it first with spray starch. You may work with the entire 54" piece, or cut it in half to make it easier to manage. Fold the bottom edge up 1/8" and press to a sharp edge. Fold up again 3/8" and press to a sharp edge. Trim this fabric so that you have one long piece of batiste 54" or two 27" pieces that are 3/8" in width with 1/8" turned under at each long edge for the 12-inch pattern. For the 18-inch pattern you need two pieces 3/8" x 40".

French seam the entire center back seam. French seam the side seams, leaving open above "B." Beginning at the center back, using a running stitch, sew the batiste strips to the wrong side of the skirt on both the top and bottom edges. Then stitch the three bustle pieces that are shown on the pattern at the top of the skirt. Note that the bottom curved strips meet at center back and the top strip is one continuous piece.

Cut two pieces of hat wire 18" (26") each and insert them into the two casings at the bottom of the skirt. It is much easier if you coat the ends of the wire with a little white glue to keep them from fraying. Overlap each piece 1/4" at center back, bind with thread and cut off excess. Cut two pieces of wire 6" (7-1/2") each and insert in the lower bustle casings. They will meet at center back. Trim the edges of the wire so that the wire falls 3/16" from the side seam. (You will bind these edges.) Insert the remaining 4" (6-1/2") of wire into the top casing, again trimming the edges so that you can bind the openings.

Bind the side openings as follows: turn under the short bottom edge 1/4" and press. With right sides together, stitch one strip to the opening. Turn the strip to the wrong side, turn under the seam allowance of the raw edge and blind stitch. Repeat with the other three strips. After the four strips have been stitched, stay stitch across the bottom of the openings to stabilize.

Waistbands: With right sides together, stitch the back waistband to the back of the skirt, easing in any fullness if necessary. Turn the raw edge to the wrong side, turn under the seam allowance and blind stitch. Repeat with the front waistband. Close the skirt with two buttons and thread loops, placing the buttons on the back waistband.

Fold the embroidered edging strip 1/4" to the *right* side and press. French seam the short ends. Stitch two rows of running stitches, and gather to fit the bottom of the skirt. Stitch on the wrong side, beginning at center back so the 1/4" (3/8") of the embroidered edging extends beyond the bottom of the skirt. The finished length of the skirt measured from center front is 7" (9-7/8").

Linette's 12-inch cotton broadcloth Cage Empire *is trimmed with antique Swiss embroidery.*

Empire Hoop from *La Poupée Modéle*, April 1867 - 12-inch Doll

Straight Pieces

Waistband: Front ....1" x 2-3/4"
Waistband: Back ....1" x 3-1/2"
Front/Side openings.....................4 (5/8" x 2-3/4")

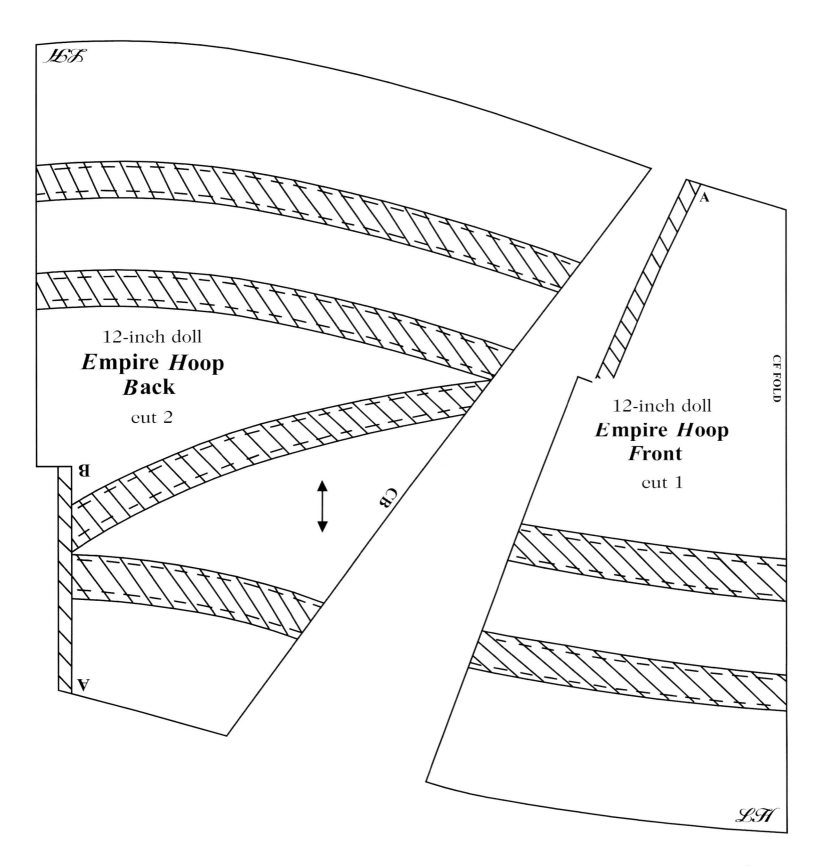

12-inch doll
Empire Hoop Back
cut 2

12-inch doll
Empire Hoop Front
cut 1

Empire Hoop from *La Poupée Modéle*, April 1867 - 18-inch Doll

Straight Pieces

Waistband: Front ....1" x 4-1/2"
Waistband: Back ....1" x 5-1/2"
Front/Side openings ....4 (5/8" x 4")

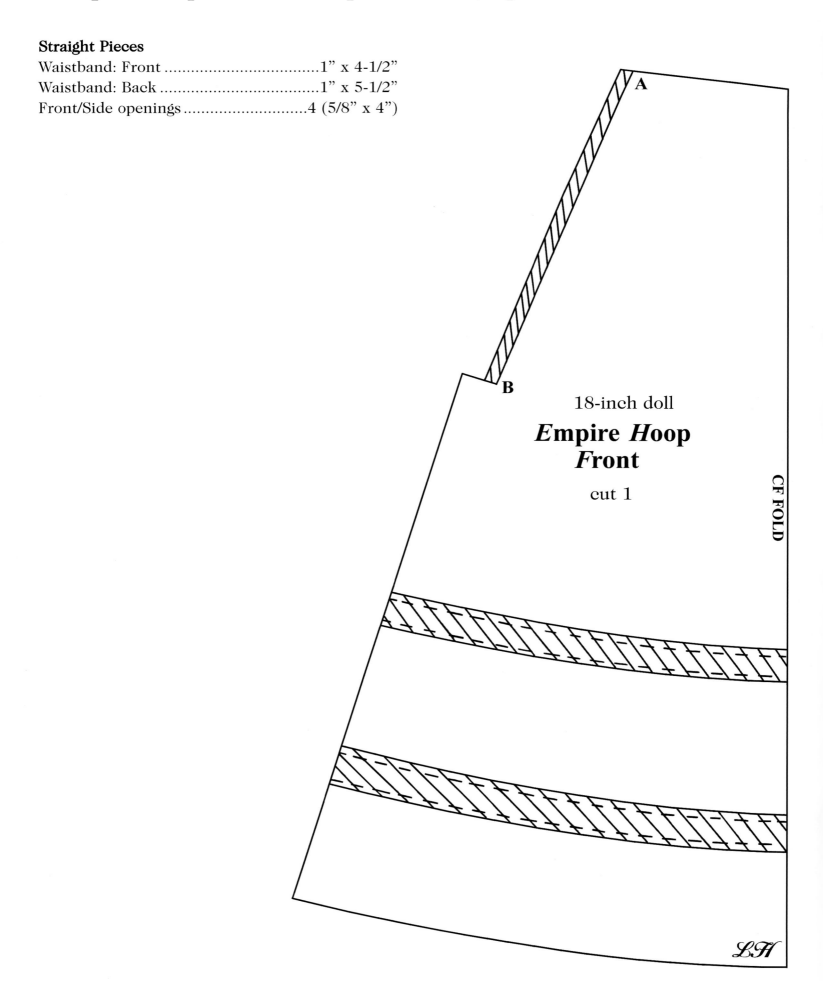

18-inch doll

Empire Hoop Front

cut 1

CF FOLD

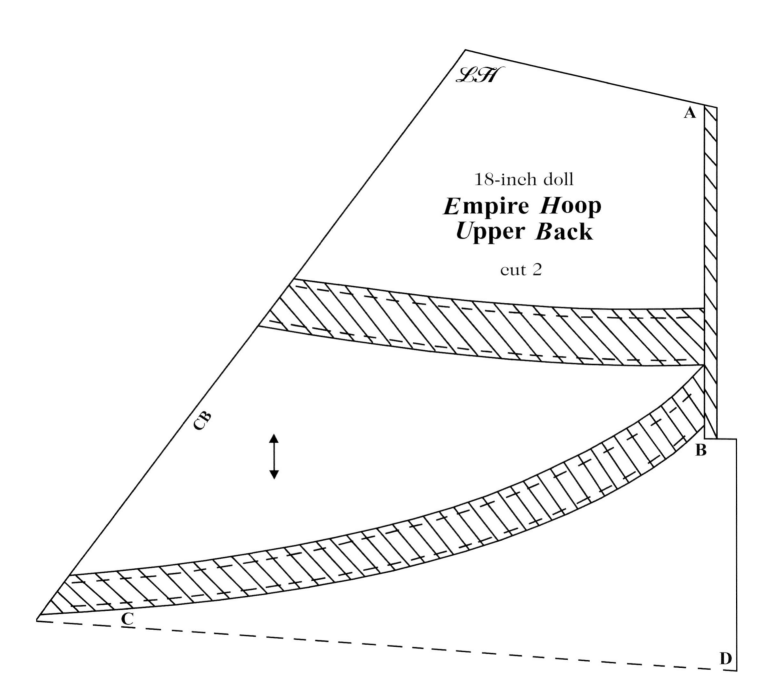

LH

A

18-inch doll
**Empire Hoop
Upper Back**

cut 2

CB

B

C

D

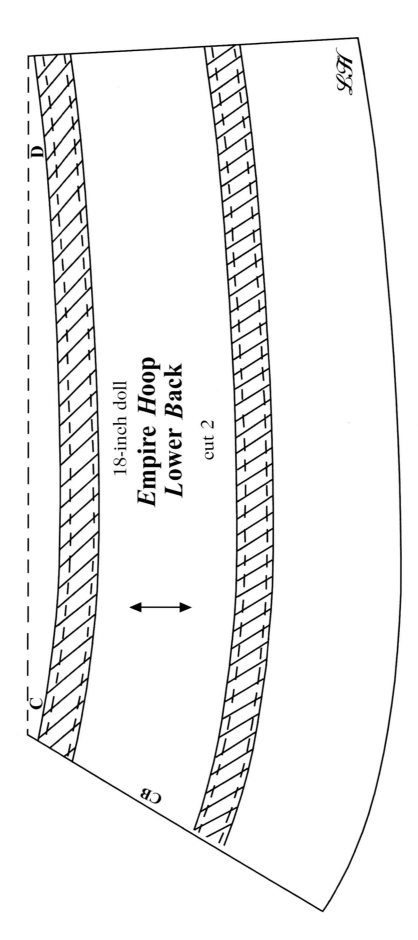

18-inch doll
Empire Hoop
Lower Back

cut 2

D

C

CB

LH

Stockings from La Poupée Modéle, *February, 1872*

Materials

Knit cotton (shown) or silk (shown): 6" x 12"
    (7" x 14")
Stranded embroidery thread, cotton or silk:
    1/2 yard
Fine embroidery thread to match
#10-#12 Crewel needle

The measurements for the material listed above will make one pair of each of the two patterns. There are many types of knit fabric that you can use, but those with a horizontal stretch seem to fit the doll the best. The embroidery pattern shown on the pattern page, from *La Poupée Modéle,* is optional, but was shown frequently on the doll stockings and is very attractive. The other pattern is one that I have used for all types and sizes of dolls. It is determined by three measurements: the circumference of the leg just below the knee, the circumference of the leg at the ankle, and the length from the toe to just below the knee. Then 1/8" is added to each side for seam allowance, and 1/4" is added to the top edge for the hem.

Pattern from *La Poupée Modéle*: If you are using fabric with a one-way stretch, use this for the horizontal placement and remove 1/8" from the width of the stocking. Cut two of the stocking pattern on the fold, and two sole patterns. With right sides together, backstitch from the top of the stocking to "B." Overcast this seam. Pin the sole to the stocking, matching "A's" and "B's." Stitch and overcast this seam. Turn the top edge to the wrong side 1/4". Blind stitch with ease. Turn to the right side and press.

Embroidery (optional): The embroidery design can be stitched on just the outside of the stocking or on both sides if you wish. Trace the "clock" design on the fabric with a #1 pencil. Stitch using tiny straight stitches and one strand of embroidery floss. This can be done with a contrasting color, tone on tone, or matching thread; all of these have been used on the antique stockings.

Alternate pattern: As above, if you are using fabric with a one-way stretch, use this for the horizontal placement and remove 1/8" from the width of the stocking. Cut two of the stocking pattern on the fold. With right sides together, back stitch from the top of the stocking to the toe. Without cutting the thread, overcast this seam from the toe to the top of the stocking. Turn the top of the stocking 1/4" to the wrong side and blind stitch with ease. Turn to the right side and press.

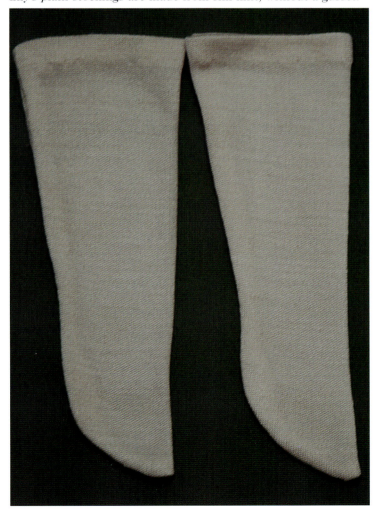

Lily's plain stockings are made from silk knit, without a gusset.

Stockings from *La Poupée Modéle*
February 1872 - 12-inch Doll

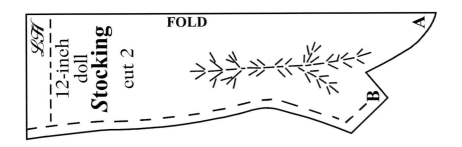

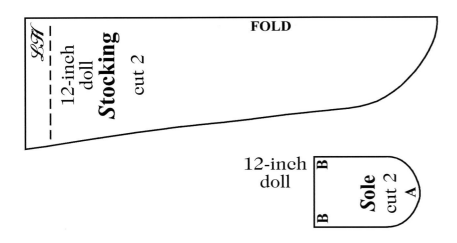

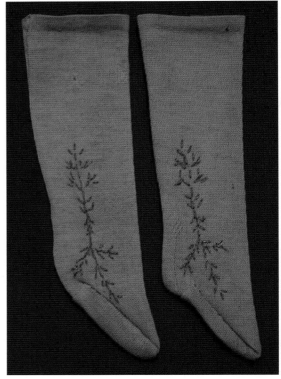

Lily's dress stockings are from the pattern in La Poupée Modéle *and feature delicate embroidery on the sides.*

Stockings from *La Poupée Modéle*
February 1872 - 18-inch Doll

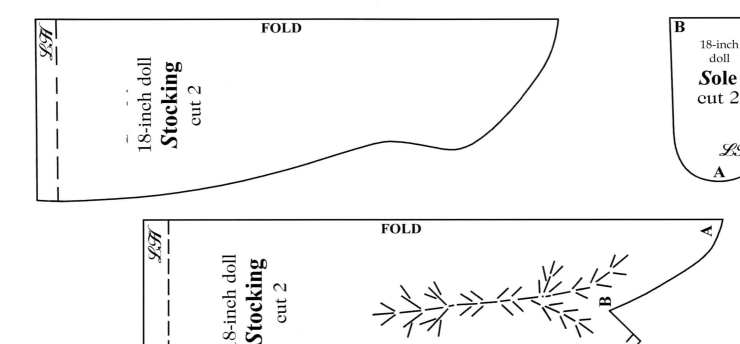

Demi-trained Dressing Gown
from La Poupée Modèle, *April 1872*

Materials

Fine wool: 12" x 38" (18" x 56" or 36" x 36")
Silk taffeta (shown), broadcloth or cotton batiste
    lining: 18" x 38" (18" x 56" or 36" x 36")
1 mm Soutache: 8 yards (12 yards)
1/8" - 3/16" Braid: 2-1/2 yards (4 yards)
Fine embroidery threads to match
Size "0" (1) Hooks and eyes: 4 (5)
#10-#12 Crewel needle

The rather formal dressing gown was an important addition to the French fashion doll's wardrobe. It was not only worn in the lady's dressing room, but also could be her attire at the breakfast table. Although we see examples in cotton and silk, this particular one was made of fine wool trimmed in silk, cotton or wool braid and cotton soutache. The two samples are each made a little differently. The gown for the 18-inch doll features two rows of braid trimming the long seam of the sleeves; there is no soutache or braid on the left opening of the gown. The gown for the 12-inch doll shows only one row of braid on each sleeve and the soutache stitching is on both the left and right front, with the braid on the right side only. The pictures show 18-inch Lily and 12-inch Linette wearing their dressing gowns over a basic set of underpinnings, including hoops.

Cut two fronts, one back, two sides, two upper sleeves, two lower sleeves and one cape from the fine wool. Cut the same pieces from the lining fabric, adding the bias neck facing, 3/4" x 4-1/4" (3/4" x 6"). Assemble the gown and lining separately.

Stitch the wool pieces. With right sides together, stitch shoulder seams and press toward the back. Stitch the side seams to the back, matching notches, and press toward the back. Stitch the side seams to the front, matching notches, and press toward the back. Repeat with the lining fabric. With right sides together, stitch the long seams of both upper and lower wool and lining pieces of the sleeves, then press to one side.

Trace the loop soutache design on the cape, both sleeves and the body of the gown. The cape pattern shows the exact placement. Use the main soutache pattern for the sleeves and the body of the garment. Note that the soutache appears on both sides of the long seam of each sleeve. The lower line of the soutache pattern should be placed 1/2" from the outer edge of the three pieces. See page 25 in Chapter 1 for soutache instructions.

When the soutache is complete, apply the braid. Stitch the braid on just below the soutache on all the pieces; outline the long seam of each sleeve with it and then stitch it across the bottom edge.

Press well both the body of the wool and the lining. With

Linette wears her 12-inch demi-trained gown of fine ivory wool trimmed in serpentine-stitched dark-green soutache, with a matching embroidered edging.

Lily's 18-inch dressing gown is constructed of antique green wool with black soutache and black embroidered edging.

right sides together, stitch from the neck edge of center front, down the front, across the bottom and up the other front to the neck. Turn and press. Baste around the sleeve openings, and trim if necessary. Baste the two fabrics together at the neck edge.

With right sides together, stitch across the bottom of the sleeve/lining. Open up and press. With right sides together, fold again, wool to wool, and lining to lining, and stitch. Turn the wool to the right side over the lining and press. Baste the top of the sleeves, lining and wool together. Trim if necessary. With right sides together, stitch the lining to the cape, leaving open at the neck edge. Turn, press, and baste the neck edge.

With right sides together, stitch the sleeves into the armholes, easing if necessary. The long seam of each sleeve should line up with the shoulder seam. Trim the sleeve seam and overcast. Pin the cape to the gown and baste. With the right side of the neck facing against the right side of the cape, and short ends pressed 1/4" to the wrong side, stitch the facing to the cape/neck. Trim to 1/8". Turn the facing and seam to the wrong side, turn under the raw edge and blind stitch. Finish the gown with 4 (5) hooks and thread eyes. The top hook is at the neck, and the others are 1-1/4" (1-1/2") apart. The finished length of the gown at center front is 10" (14-1/2").

This close view shows the finished sleeve and cape; note the placement of the trims.

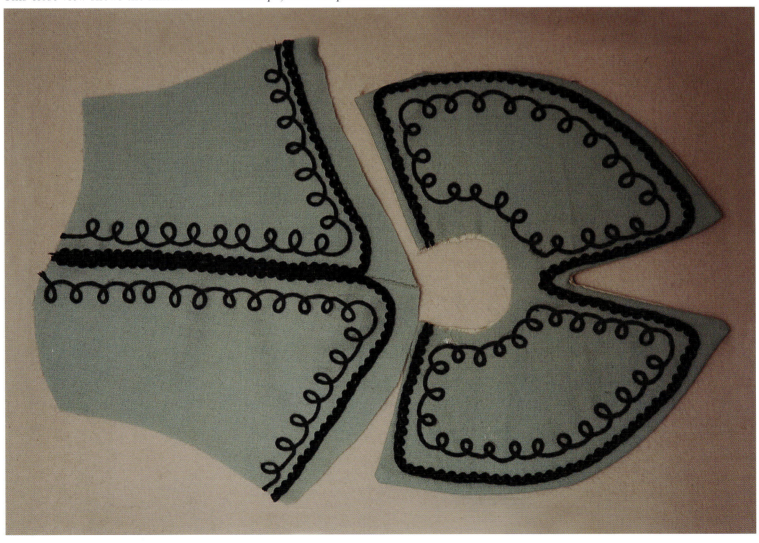

Demi-trained Dressing Gown
from *La Poupée Modèle*, April 1872 - 12-inch Doll

Bias Piece
Neck Facing ....3/4" x 4-1/4"

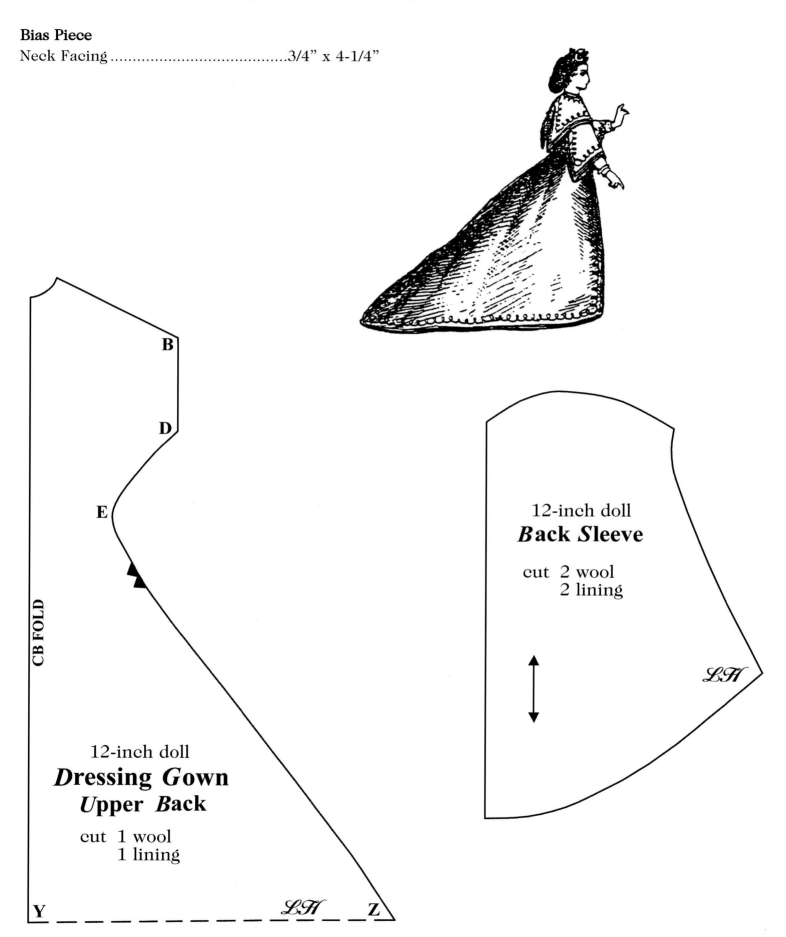

B

D

E

CB FOLD

12-inch doll
Dressing Gown
Upper Back

cut 1 wool
1 lining

Y *LH* Z

12-inch doll
Back Sleeve

cut 2 wool
2 lining

LH

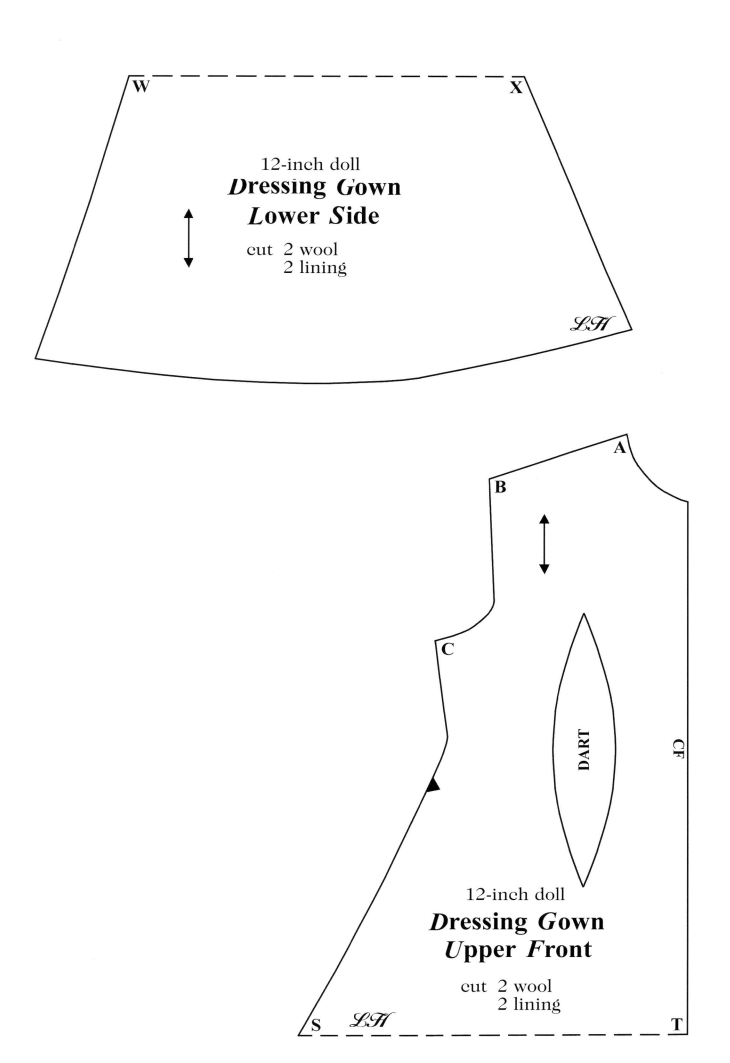

W

X

12-inch doll
**Dressing Gown
Lower Side**

cut 2 wool
2 lining

LH

A

B

C

DART

CF

12-inch doll
**Dressing Gown
Upper Front**

cut 2 wool
2 lining

S *LH*

T

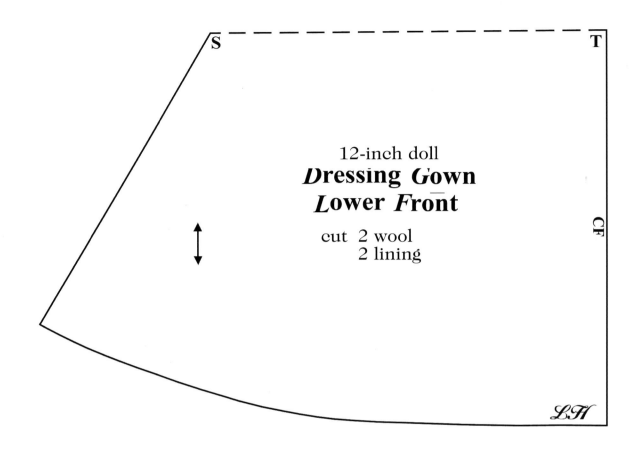

S   T

12-inch doll
**Dressing Gown
Lower Front**

cut 2 wool
2 lining

CF

LH

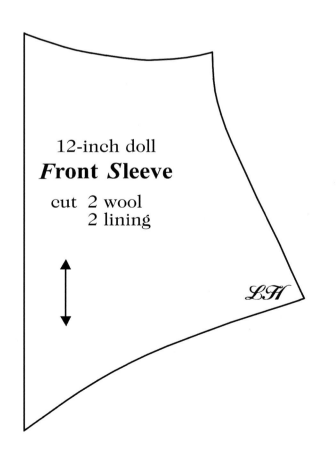

12-inch doll
Front Sleeve

cut 2 wool
2 lining

LH

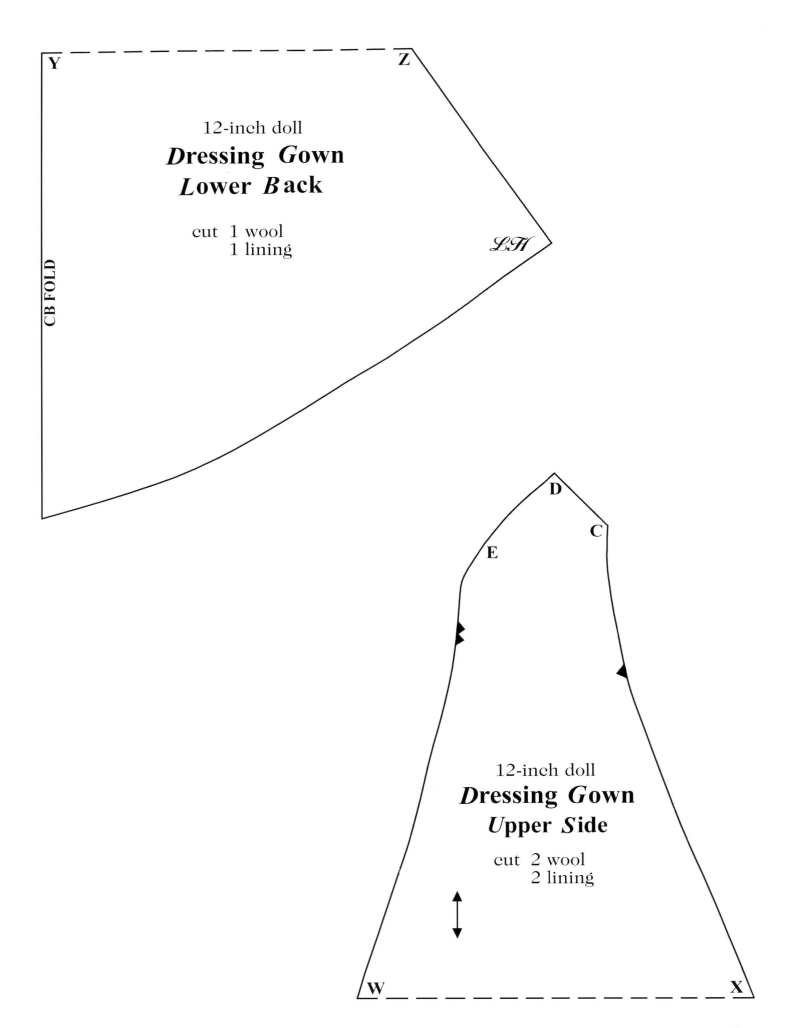

Y   Z

12-inch doll
**Dressing Gown
Lower Back**

cut 1 wool
1 lining

CB FOLD

LH

D

C

E

12-inch doll
**Dressing Gown
Upper Side**

cut 2 wool
2 lining

W   X

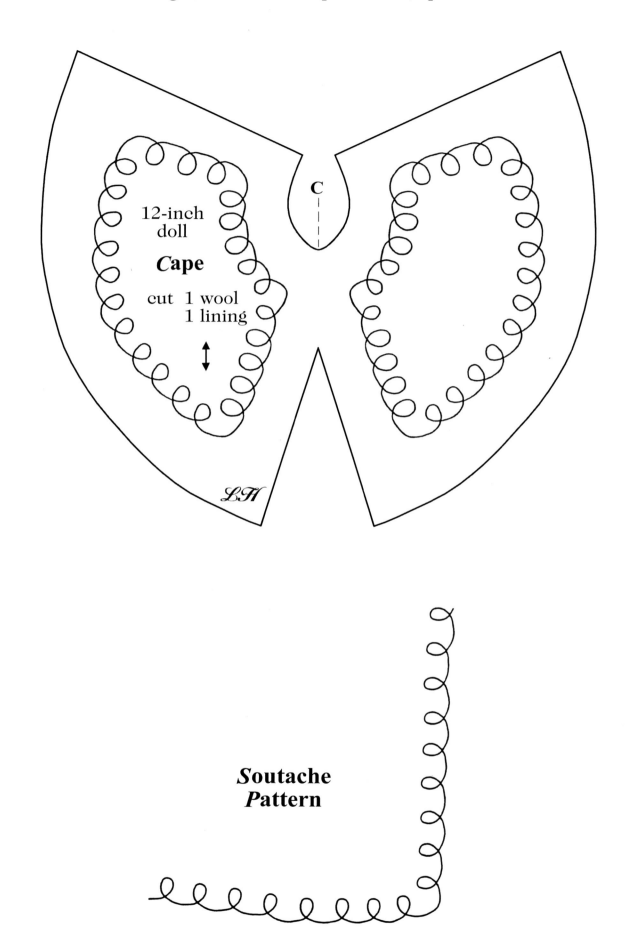

12-inch
doll

Cape

cut 1 wool
1 lining

C

LH

**Soutache
Pattern**

Demi-trained Dressing Gown
from *La Poupée Modèle*, April 1872 - 18-inch Doll

Bias Piece
Neck Facing ....3/4" x 6"

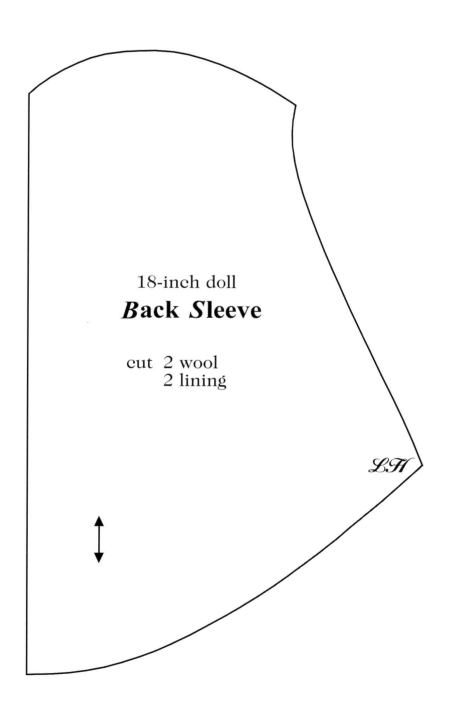

18-inch doll
Back Sleeve

cut 2 wool
2 lining

LH

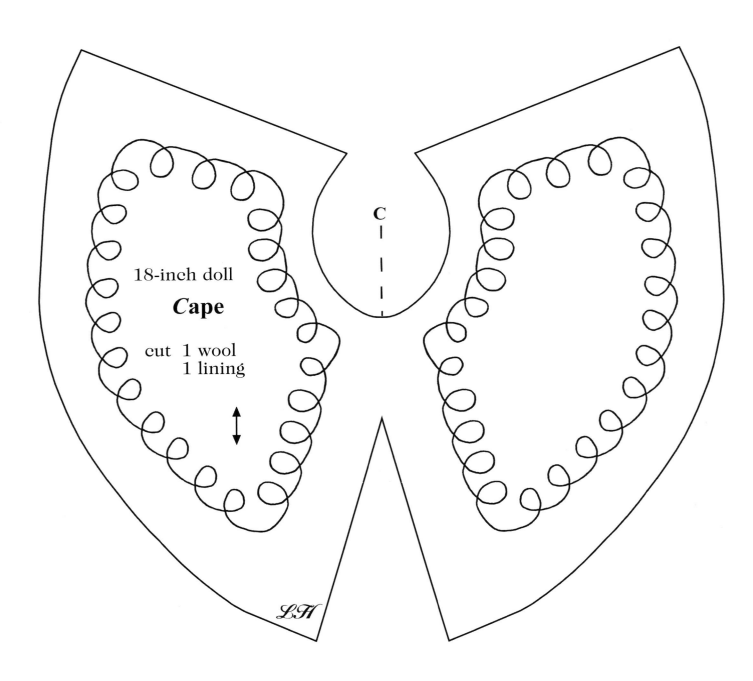

18-inch doll

Cape

cut 1 wool
1 lining

C

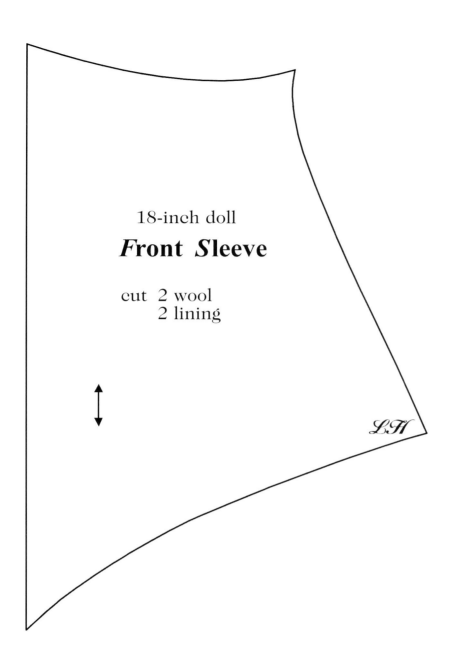

18-inch doll
Front Sleeve

cut 2 wool
2 lining

LH

**Soutache
Pattern**

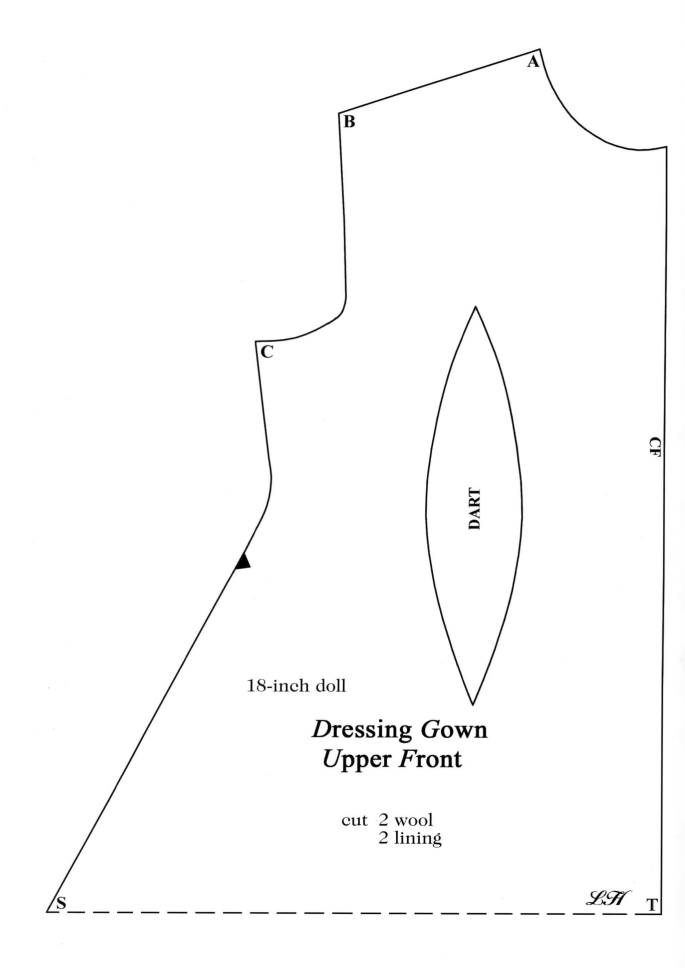

A

B

C

CF

DART

18-inch doll

Dressing Gown
Upper Front

cut 2 wool
2 lining

S

LH

T

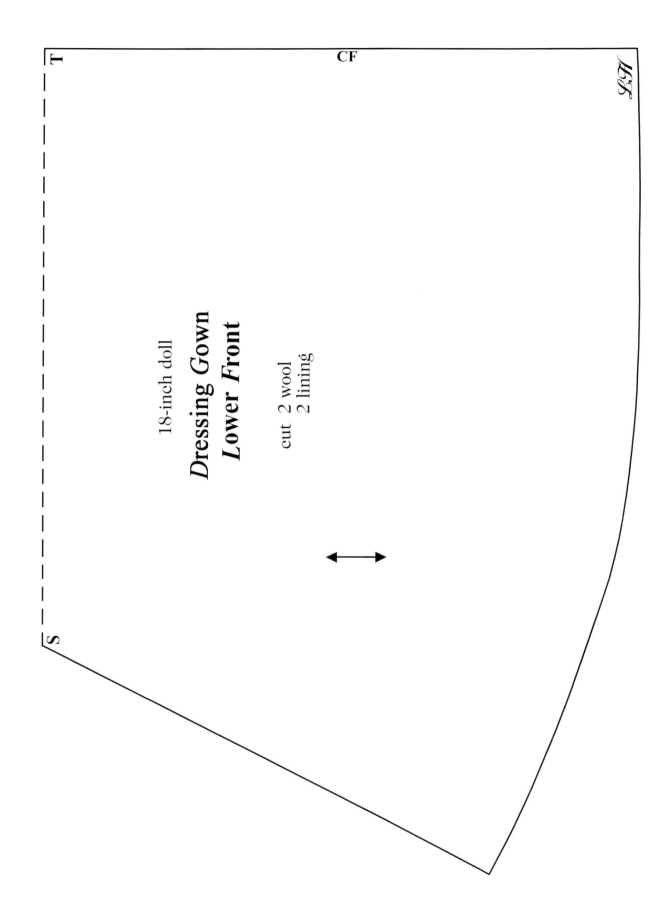

T

CF

𝓛𝓗

S

18-inch doll

Dressing Gown
Lower Front

cut 2 wool
2 lining

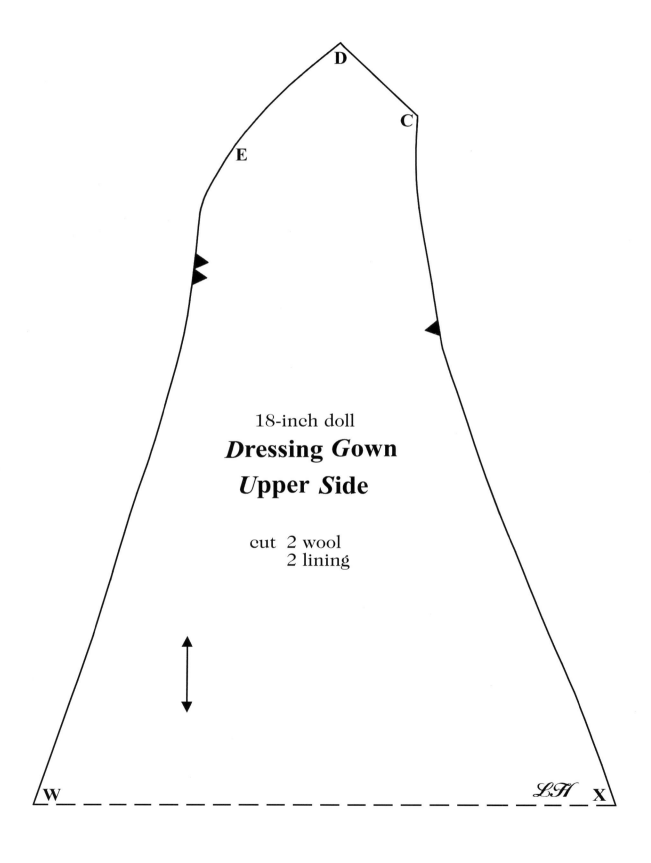

18-inch doll

Dressing *Gown*

Upper *Side*

cut 2 wool
     2 lining

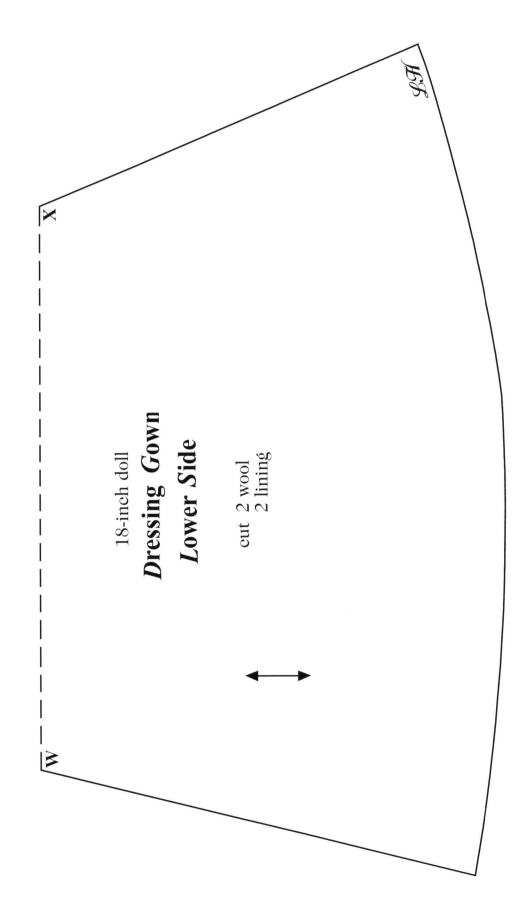

X

W

18-inch doll
Dressing Gown
Lower Side

cut 2 wool
2 lining

LSH

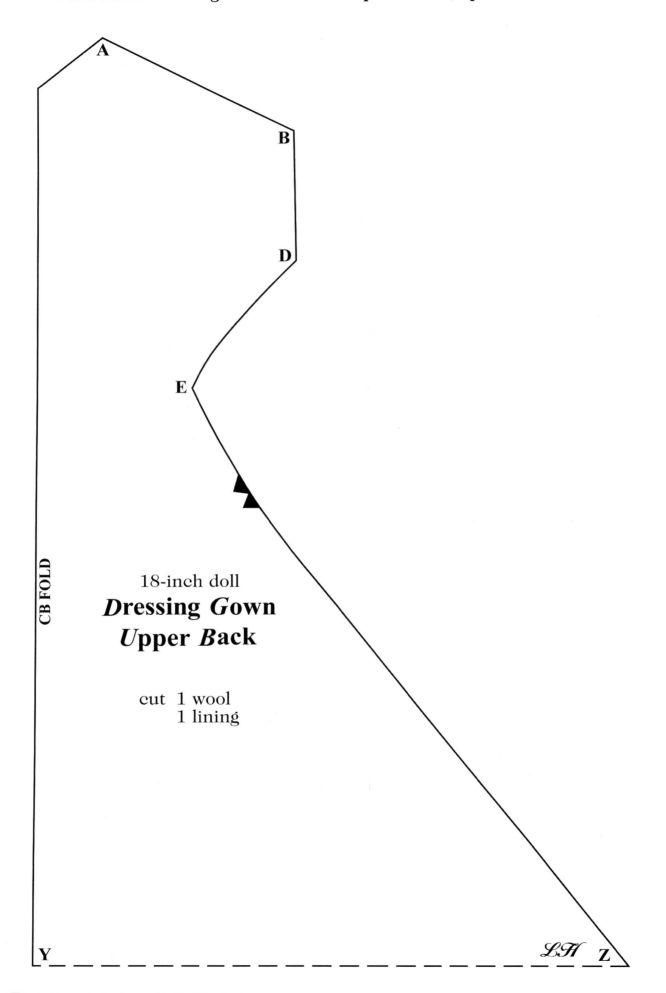

A

B

D

E

CB FOLD

18-inch doll
Dressing Gown
Upper Back

cut 1 wool
1 lining

Y

LH Z

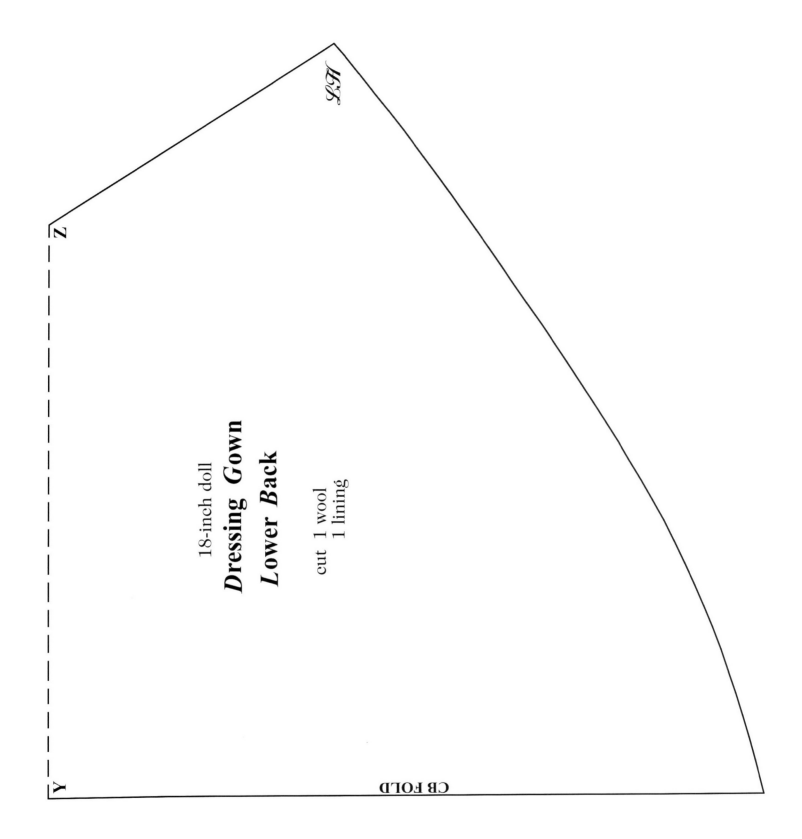

Z

Y

𝓛𝓗

CB FOLD

18-inch doll
Dressing Gown
Lower Back

cut 1 wool
1 lining

BIBLIOGRAPHY

Arnold, Janet. *Patterns of Fashion 2, 1860 – 1940.* London: MacMillan, 1975.

Bucknell, Peter A. and Margot Hamilton Hill. *The Evolution of Fashion, 1066 – 1930.* London: B. T. Batsford, 1987.

Coleman, Dorothy S., Elizabeth A., and Evelyn J. *The Collector's Book of Doll Clothes, 1700 – 1929.* New York: Crown Publishers, 1975.

Colton, Virginia, ed. *Reader's Digest Complete Guide to Needlework.* New York: Reader's Digest Association, 1979.

Cunnington, Phillis and Cecil Willet. *The History of Underclothes.* New York: Dover Publications, Inc., 1992.

Gardiner, Sue, ed. *A - Z of Embroidery Stitches, 1.* Kent Town, South Australia: Country Bumpkin Publications, 1997.

_____. *A - Z of Embroidery Stitches, 2.* Kent Town, South Austalia: Country Bumpkin Publications, 2007.

Mac Neil, Sylvia. *The Paris Collection.* Cumberland, MD: Hobby House Press, 1992.

Seeley, Mildred and Colleen. *Study of the Fashion Dolls of France.* Revised Edition. Livonia, MI: Scott Publications, 1995.

Tarnowska, Marie, *Fashion Dolls.* Cumberland, MD: Hobby House Press, Inc., 1986.

Theimer, François. *La Poupée Modèle, First Period, 1863 – 1873.* Paris: Polichinelle Publishing, 1993.

_____. *Encyclopedia Polichinette, Volume 6.* Grantsville, MD: Hobby House Press, 1997.

Theimer, François and Danielle. *The Encyclopedia of French Dolls, Volume I.* Annapolis, MD: Gold Horse Publishing, 2003.

_____. *The Encyclopedia of French Dolls, Volume II.* Annapolis, MD: Gold Horse Publishing, 2006.

_____. *The Huret Book: The Parisian Dolls, Volume 1.* Paris: Polichinelle Publishing, 2008.

_____. *The Panorama of Parisienne Dolls: Parisienne Dolls, Volume 2.* Paris: Polichinelle Publishing, 2009.

Theriault, Florence. *The Trousseau of Blondinette Davranches,* Annapolis, MD: Gold Horse Publishing, 1994.

Thieme, Otto Charles et al. *With Grace and Favor, Victorian & Edwardian Fashion in America.* Cincinnati, Ohio: Cincinnati Art Museum, 1993.

La Poupée Modèle, Journal des Petite Filles, 1864 – 1865. Paris: Bureau du Journal des Demoiselles, 1865.

La Poupée Modèle, Journal des Petites Filles, 1873 – 1874. Paris: Bureau du Journal des Demoiselles, 1874.

RESOURCES

Doll Artisan Guild International, Inc.
P. O. Box 1113
Oneonta, NY 13820
Phone: (607) 432-4977
Email: Info@dollartisanguild.org
Website: www.dollartisanguild.org
Mold for 18-inch Leontine, (Rohmer) mold #DAG87

Louise Hedrick
LH Studio
Elm Grove, WI 53122
Email: lh.studio@att.net
Fabrics, trims, laces and patterns

Ursula Laepple
Sanmaro-Atelier
Bergwaldstr. 28, D-75391
Gechingen/Germany
Email: Sanmaro-Atelier@t-online.de
Phone: +49-7056-966942
Fax: +49-7056-966943
Fabrics, laces and trims (catalog emailed free of charge; catalog with samples upon request)

Pam Lembo
Cat's Paw Accessories
336 Candle Lake Rd.
Brookfield, CT 06804
Phone: (203) 775-4717
Website: www.catspawonline.com
Specializes in accessories for French fashion dolls

Alice Leverett
Alice Leverett Originals
8201 Shady Grove Rd.
Jacksonville, FL 32256
(904) 928-0427
Email: alice@justalice.com
Website: www.justalice.com
Ultimate Fashion dolls, accessories, patterns

Janice Naibert
Phone: (301) 774-9252
Email: janicenaibert@comcast.net
Ebay:
http://stores.shop.ebay.com/Janice-Naiberts-Store
Fine reproduction French fashion and other fabrics, silk fringe, 1 mm soutache and other fine trims

New York Doll Products Co., Inc.
107 Main St.
Otego, NY 13825
Email:
info@newyorkdollproducts.com
Website:
www.newyorkdollproducts.com
Molds, composition bodies, porcelain slip, china paints

Imp. DUPUY. Paris

Journal des petites filles.

La Poup